ALEXA WEST GUIDES

The Solo Girl's Travel Guide, Puerto Vallarta, Mexico with Sayulita and Riviera Nayarit

ISBN: 9798549445772

The Solo Girl's Travel Guide updates this guidebook year-round as businesses grow, change, and even sometimes, close. If you notice a change we should know about, please let us know at hello@thesologirlstravelguide.com so we can update our guide for future travelers!

STOCK OUR BOOK

Want to stock our book in your shop, store or platform? Send us an message at hello@thesologirlstravelguide.com

TRAVEL WITH INTEGRITY

It feels good to support the people and places in this book.

We are about to introduce you to good people, good places and good businesses that deserve your time.

the SOLO GIRL'S TRAVEL GUIDE

PUERTO VALLARTA

——— MEXICO ———

WITH SAYULITA & RIVIERA NAYARIT

ALEXA WEST GUIDES

WHAT READERS ARE SAYING...

"Stick with me here... I *know* that this is a travel guide for Puerto Vallarta. But what the title and description don't tell you is that it's essentially a bible for HOW to travel... which goes far beyond just the MX details. The book starts with 'The Golden Rule of Mindful Travel' and continues that theme throughout- encouraging you to minimize your footprint on the earth and use your (hard-earned) travel dollars to support the local economy. Essentially this is a 2 for 1... you get allll the scoop on PV and the insider info that Alex and Emy have expertly sourced PLUS you get their best-kept secrets on how to travel in a way that makes the world a better place. Do yourself a favor and buy this NOW!!"

-Kat

"This book is wonderful. The way it's written, the information and tools and advise like QR codes and links to important recourses like insurance companies are invaluable. However what I love most about this book is the author.

Alexa West does not just write books, she creates community through her work. Just check out her FB groups and jump into a world of supportive amazing women around the world....Girls in Bali, Girls in Global, Girls in Puerto Vallarta. All places to find information about the area, meet new friends and learn. This is not a book. It's a small piece of a massive movement to empower women to take charge of their power to explore the world and grow to be their best selves. I am a huge fan and look forward to seeing more of the world through her eyes!"

-Gaby

"I have been visiting the Puerto Vallarta area for over 15 years. I like to explore blindly on my own, rather than getting touristic recommendations from an author who is usually older than me and in a different stage of their life. This book is the NOT THAT. It is everything I didn't know I needed for an area that I thought I knew everything about.

There are so many great secrets in this book! The best street tacos, the least touristy beaches, which neighborhoods to stay in vs live in, which bus lines to take, and which is the most fun Airbnb experience.

I never found use in the past, in buying an entire book on one area when i could just go on different blogs and do my own research- but this book combines all that research into one place so that you dont have to do it yourself. It includes QR code links, maps, pictures, and lists that you can reference as you go... without wasting time mapping and planning it all yourself when you should be enjoying your vacation. The details are so important too- like which side of the recommended hotel to stay on, where to get covid tests, which bus line to take, how much a taxi costs to different areas. I appreciate these tips.

This isnt a short little online blog with excessive selfies and minimal actual travel info... this is everything you need to know in a visually appealing, light weight, easy to read book that will fit in your purse. I love it and would recommend it to all my friends. I have finally found another travelers opinions that are so like my own, that I would trust her recommended itinerary to plan my whole vacation. Coming from a solo traveler who likes to plan and be in control of everythings- thats a big deal. I have personally found so many more areas to explore after reading this book... I cant wait to go back!! Love love love it!!!!!!"

-Sunny Anne

EVERY GIRL SHOULD TRAVEL SOLO AT LEAST ONCE IN HER LIFE.

You don't need a boyfriend, a travel partner or anyone's approval to travel the world. And you don't need a massive bank account or an entire summer off work.

All you need is that wanderlust in your blood and a good guidebook in your hands.

If you've doubted yourself for one moment, remember this:

Millions of girls travel across the globe all by themselves every damn day and you can, too.

You are just as capable, just as smart, and just as brave as the rest of us. You don't need permission- this is your life.

Listen to your gut, follow your heart and remember that the best adventures start with the simple decision to go.

"IF YOU WANT TO LIVE A LIFE YOU'VE NEVER LIVED, YOU HAVE TO DO THINGS YOU'VE NEVER DONE."

Look for this sticker
when you travel!

THESOLOGIRLSTRAVELGUIDE.COM

RECOMMENDED BY

the
Solo Girl's
Travel Guide

FOLLOW US ON
INSTAGRAM & FACEBOOK

@SOLOGIRLSTRAVELGUIDE

I was here! And I love it for you!

PS. DON-T FORGET TO TAKE
A PICTURE AND TAG ME!

The 7 Travel Commandments

BY THE SOLO GIRL'S TRAVEL GUIDE

01 SLOW TRAVEL

Count experiences, not passport stamps.

02 BE A TRAVELER, NOT A TOURIST.

Don't go through your trip (and life) on the shallow end. Dive deep. Put your phone down. Be present.

03 TRAVEL ECO

Bring your own water bottle, canvas bag, and reusable straw to help you avoid single-use plastics.

04 MIND YOUR IMPACT

Leave every place better than you found it. Take a piece of trash from the beach and be kind to people you meet.

05 VOTE WITH YOUR DOLLAR

When possible, choose to support local businesses, eat locally sourced food, join tour companies that operate ethically (aka don't work with animals, respect the environment, benefit their local communities) and/or businesses that just treat their staff really really well.

06 TRUST YOUR GUT

Listen to that little voice inside you. When something doesn't feel right, back away. When something feels good, lean. Your intuition will lead you to beautiful places, unforgettable moments, and new lifelong friends.

07 CARRY YOUR POSITIVITY

Ever had a crappy day and then a stranger smiles at you and flips your entire mood? Travel can be hard, but your positivity will be your secret weapon. Happy vibes are contagious. Even when we don't speak the local language, a smile or a random act of kindness tips the universal scale in the right direction for you and the people you meet along your journey.

It feels good to support the people and places in this book.
We are about to introduce you to good people, good places and good
businesses that deserve your time.

CHANGING THE WAY -
AND THE WHY
WE TRAVEL THE WORLD

Hi. I'm Alexa

I'm not here to get rich or reach 1 million followers on Instagram.

I'm here because I want to change the way we travel as women.

I want to help you find yourself.

I want to fling you to the other side of the world, out of your comfort zone (but still safe, I got you), and help you get so totally lost that you find yourself.

And I do that by connecting you to the most beautiful places, the kindest people, the most challenging opportunities, and the most rewarding experiences.

Do you know what kind of woman this will create?
A happy woman who shines so bright that everyone she comes in contact with is illuminated too.

I'm here to turn your light up, girl.

I'm here to help you connect you to the experiences that will change you.
...and get the best Instagram photos, too, of course.

To glow up on your travels, remember Travel Karma.

Travel to give and you will get.

The Solo Girls Travel Guide

Ditch the touristy travel guides that feel like they were written for your nerdy cousin who wears socks with sandals. **This is #1 Travel Guidebook Series for Women (and couples).**

Plan your dream Mexico trip in **a short amount of time** on **any budget** - all while avoiding the scams, creeps and tourist traps...and skip ahead to the beaches and adventures that are worth your time (and money).

This comprehensive travel planner takes you on a tour around Banderas Bay and Riviera Nayarit to the must-see towns and villages

BE A TRAVELER, NOT A TOURIST

This book is written by two travel experts from America and Mexico. And together, you get the most comprehensive Mexico travel planner on the market.

In this guide you will find spas and luxury resorts, but you'll also find rich Mexican culture and traditions that most travelers would never be able to access on their own. With Alexa's explorer blood and Emilia's Mexican roots, The Solo Girl's Travel Guide Mexico Series is the golden ticket to experiencing Mexico in a way that hasn't yet been done. We are on a mission to reinvent Mexico for you.

What This Guide is Not...
✕ An overwhelming collection of tourist destinations
✕ A 15-hour read that feels like homework
✕ A book written by some dude who doesn't understand what it's like to travel as a woman.

Speaking of men, since the success of The Solo Girl's Travel Guide, I've had many guys ask me, "Yeah, but why a girl's guide?"
Um, because us women constantly have to ask ourselves questions like....

➤ Are there drugs in my drink?
➤ Is that dark alley filled with serial killers?
➤ Am I going to be kidnapped and sold to the highest bidder?

The answer is usually NO, but for us girls, "usually" doesn't cut it. In order to be wild and carefree, we've got to feel 100% safe. And you've never found a travel guide to take your safety into consideration... so, here we are.

Go into your vacation knowing you're being given the **BEST, the SAFEST, and the TOTALLY WORTH it spots.** Let your hair down and tell your mom not to worry. I've got you.

So, as we get into this guide – I want to make a few promises to you:

✦ I won't bullshit you and tell you a beach is awesome if it's not.
✦ I will tell you what spots are worth your time - and what spots to skip.
✦ And I will make planning this vacation so easy and so fun!!!

Your bags may not be packed, but your vacation officially starts now.

Oh, and once you've bought this book...we're officially friends. I'm here if you need me. Just write me on Instagram ➤ @SoloGirlsTravelGuide.

TABLE OF CONTENTS

About the authors

ALEXA WEST

Hi, I'm Alexa.

Back in 2010, I was a broke-ass Seattle girl who had just graduated from college and had about $200 to my name. I was faced with two choices: get a job, a husband, and have 3 babies plus a mortgage…or sell everything I owned, travel the world and disappoint my parents.

Obviously, I made the right choice.

For the past 10 years, I've been traveling the world solo. I've played every travel role from being the young volunteer and broke backpacker to flying to exotic islands to review new luxury hotels and give breath to struggling tourism industries.

Now I spend my days as an explorer on a mission to change the way that women travel the world. I want to show you places you've never seen and unlock hidden doors you never knew existed in places you may have been before. I want to create a path for you where you feel safe while diving deeper into cultures and countries beyond your own – whether for a week, a year, or a lifetime. And that's what I'm doing.

As the creator of The Solo Girl's Travel Guide, I can write whatever the hell I want. I want to write about things that matter and adventures that change you. So, follow in my footsteps and let's do this together.

xoxo, alexa

@__helloemilia

EMILIA IGARTUA

Have you ever felt stuck and stagnant, like there's got to be more to life?

It was 2019 and I was feeling juuuust like that. So I decided to travel far away from my routine, alone. I bought a ticket to Bali, along with a certain travel guide that changed my life: The Solo Girl's Travel Guide to Bali.

I spent 1.5 months exploring the island, following my travel guide, visiting temples, exploring the depths of the ocean, and making new friends...but most of all, getting to know myself. My solo trip was an IV drip for my very dehydrated soul. It brought me back to life and unlocked a whole new world of possibilities I never knew existed. The trip was a success.

And just when my 1-month exploration was ending, when I was supposed to return home...the pandemic happened. I got stuck in Bali indefinitely and thank goodness I did, because serendipity brought me to Alexa. She quickly became my soul sister and partner in crime, and now we are writing an entire Mexico guidebook series together.

These days, Alexa and I spend our days creating books and spaces for badass girls who want to step out of their comfort zones and live a life of wander and wonder.

Oh and did I mention that I'm Mexican? Like, born and raised in Mexico. I know, I know, my English is amazing – I get that a lot. So just know that The Solo Girl's Travel Guide's Mexico series is filled with my local girl knowledge, tips, friends, beaches and adventures that no gringo would ever know about...

So follow this guide, and follow your gut.
You'll find nothing but magic ahead.

con amor, emilia

Don't forget your playlist!

FLIGHTS.,

AIRPORTS,

WALKING AROUND TOWN...

TRAVEL IS A LITTLE BIT MORE MAGICAL

WHEN GOOD MUSIC IS INVOLVED.

SEE A GIRL TRAVELING W ITH THIS GEAR?
SAY HI.

SHE'S YOUR SISTER IN THE

Solo Girl's Travel Club

CARRY THIS GEAR
AS AN INVITATION TO FRIENDSHIP

COLLECT YOUR GEAR HERE:

OR AT THESOLOGIRLSTRAVELGUIDE.COM

BANDERAS BAY

INTRODUCTION TO

BANDERAS BAY

WHERE PUERTO VALLARTA LIVES

welcome to
Banderas Bay

Banderas Bay, or Bahia de Banderas en espanōl, is a misunderstood slice of Mexico located on the west coast with a coastline that stretches for 41 miles starting in the south at Boca de Tomatlan up north near San Pancho. Inside Banderas Bay, you'll find the popular Puerto Vallarta located in the state of Jalisco and the other emerging towns located in the next state up called Nayarit. To keep things simple, we often refer to those whole area as Banderas Bay.

All along the coast, you'll find hidden coves, huge resorts, hip beach towns, small Mexican neighborhoods (where the best food hides) and scattered islands. With so much cultural and geographical diversity (plus iconic surf spots), there's a vibe for everyone no matter your adventure craving!

Banderas Bay hosts millions of visitors a year and is a hub for international expats that come to stay for its high quality of living, chill vibes, exciting food scene, and generally sunny weather.

But it's not all about beach hopping and surfing! Banderas Bay is home to an impressive collection of underwater life including humpback whales, giant manta rays, dolphins and a wide range of game fish making it an oceanic-wonder...plus some insanely good food.

In this book, we're covering one of Mexico's most famous travel destinations: Puerto Vallarta (duh). But we are here to debunk the idea that Puerto Vallarta is too "touristy". Because I say, things stop being touristy once you stop traveling like a tourist. So don't count Puerto Vallarta out just yet! And also...don't get stuck in Puerto Vallarta. The smaller towns up north, as you are about to find out, are absolutely worth you time.

Banderas Bay

WITH THE HELP
OF AN ACTUAL MAP

7

6

5

4 **3**

TOWNS TO KNOW

2

- Pacific Ocean

1 PUERTO VALLARTA

2 NUEVO VALLARTA

3 BUCERIAS

4 LA CRUZ DE HUANACAXTLE

5 PUNTA MITA

6 SAYULITA

7 SAN PANCHO

Towns to Explore...

PUERTO VALLARTA

The most misunderstood town in Mexico! Puerto Vallarta, part of the Jalisco province, is so much more than all-inclusive resorts and bachelorette parties (although, they're pretty great for those if you ask me). Puerto Vallarta is the biggest city in the bay and home to the airport. Here you'll find big resorts and an abundance of touristy activities like parasailing and pirate ship cruises, but you'll also find hidden waterfalls and quiet beaches...if you know where to look. Puerto Vallarta is broken down into neighborhoods and zones which we will detail in the Puerto Vallarta chapter.

JUST SOUTH PUERTO VALLARTA

Conchas Chinas, Mismaloya and Boca de Tomatlan are three expat areas that are worth a visit if you want to explore off the beaten path or unpack your bags and stay a while as an expat. You'll hear these three spots mentioned often in the sections where we talk about beach and waterfall adventures.

NUEVO VALLARTA

Expats and families have settled into Nuevo Vallarta and brought the comforts of home with them. Think gated communities, golf courses, couples with kids, and nights out for Italian food and drinks. If you're looking to settle in Mexico, come have a look at Nuevo Vallarta.

BUCERIAS

A small residential town with 5 miles of sandy beach and some cute restaurants, Bucerias is quite comfortable for long-term living, but not as exciting for visiting on vacation, in our humble (yet super cool) opinion. Unless! Kite surfing is your thing. Bucerías has a decent kite surfing scene.

LA CRUZ DE HUANACAXTLE

La Cruz for short, this little fishermen's town is known for its high-end marina, around which life revolves. La Cruz is all about sailing, sunsets and seafood with some of the best views of the entire bay and even whale watching in the winter! However, that being said - unless you're a pirate with a ship that needs to dock or a digital nomad looking to work by the beach, La Cruz might not meet your getaway needs. #UltraQuiteLife

PUNTA MITA

What has been referred to as a "micro destination", Punta Mita is a tiny little town that once you're there...you're there. The beach and the town are navigable by foot and take no effort at all to restaurant hop. This little town may be small, but it's gastronomy scene is big. Hang out at the main beach or treat yourself to the best beaches in the bay by staying at The St. Regis and Four Seasons Punta de Mita.

SAYULITA

Sayulita used to be a quiet fishing village but now, it's a hot spot for digital nomads and hippie surf chicks. It's extremely safe, walkable, and full of cafes, markets and cocktail bars where barefoot expats spend their days surfing, meeting with friends, working at a cafe, and just living the beachy expat life.

SAN PANCHO

What Sayulita was 10 years ago: a bohemian surf spot full of expats. But San Pancho is about so much more than surfboards and sunsets. It is a truly unique spot with a lively local life and a thriving art scene. If you're traveling to "disconnect to connect"...San Pancho is where you need to head.

So how do you create your itinerary without coming up with a serious case of FOMO (aka fear of missing out)?

In the beginning of each chapter, I'll help you identify which town is right for you and how long I recommend you stay. You can also hop to page 264 where I've created a few itineraries which you can follow.

Alexa's Top 10's
FOR BANDERAS BAY

TOP 10 HOTELS & RESORTS

01 Four Seasons, *Punta Mita*

PHOTO / FOUR SEASONS

02 PAL.MAR Hotel Tropical, *San Pancho*

03 Hotel Agua de Luna, *San Pancho*

04 Villa Lala Boutique Hotel, *Boca de Tomatlan*

05 Grand Velas All-Inclusive, *Nuevo Vallarta*

06 Xinalani Retreat, *Quimixto*

07 AzulPitaya, *Sayulita*

08 Hotel Ysuri, *Sayulita*

09 Las Alamandas, *2.5 hours south from Puerto Vallarta*

10 Hilton Hacienda All-Inclusive, *Puerto Vallarta*

TOP 10 MUST-DO EXPERIENCES

01 Whale Watching, all over

02 Boat Tour with Chica Loca Boat Tours or Ally Cat Sailing, all over

03 Taco Tour & Tequila Tasting with @VallartaLocalFoodTours

04 Spa Day at MedSpa, Puerto Vallarta

05 Zip Line with Canopy River, Puerto Vallarta

06 Hike to Yelapa Waterfall, Puerto Vallarta

07 Horseback up to Quimixto Waterfall, Puerto Vallarta

08 Hike from Boca de Tomatlan to Las Animas, Puerto Vallarta

09 Surf Lesson in Sayulita or San Pancho

10 Attend a Drag Show, Puerto Vallarta

TOP 10 BEACHES

01 Four Seasons, *Punta Mita*

02 Litibú Beach, *North Punta Mita*

03 Playa Los Muertos, *Sayulita*

04 Las Animas, *Puerto Vallarta*

05 Marietas Island, *Puerto Vallarta*

06 Destiladeras, *La Cruz de Huanacaxtle*

07 Yelapa Beach, *Puerto Vallarta*

08 Playa La Lancha, *Punta Mita*

09 Playa Mal Paso, *Sayulita*

10 Punta Monterrey, *Las Lomas (near to San Pancho)*

WE MADE IT EASY TO KEEP TRACK OF YOUR BUCKET LIST WITH THIS JOURNAL.

the
Banderas Bay Survival Guide

FAST FACTS:

LANGUAGE: Spanish

POPULATION: 127.6 million

TOTAL AREA: 761, 610 square miles

CURRENCY: Mexican Peso

TIME ZONE: Central Daylight Time (GMT -5)

RELIGION: Roman Catholic

THE FOOD

There's so much more to discover beyond tacos and enchiladas! From moles (mole-lays) to (tluh-yoo-duhs), each region in Mexico has its own unique way of doing Mexican food. In fact, Mexico's gastronomy world is so vast and complex that it has been declared a "Masterpiece of the Oral and Intangible Heritage of Humanity".

Translation: Mexican food is a treasure to be studied, preserved, and adored. Mexican cuisine is about way more than food: it's about history, cultural practices, traditions, spirituality and rituals - all embedded into daily life. Food is going to be a huge part of your Mexico journey, so buckle (or maybe unbuckle) up.

THE RELIGION

Quick history lesson: Mexico, prior to the European arrival, was populated by advanced ancient civilizations like the Mayans and the Aztecs (think pyramids and hieroglyphics). These civilizations developed complex cultures, systems and even polytheist religions where they worshipped deities related to nature and other intangible concepts like destiny and fortune.

But then the Spanish came and ruined all that cool stuff. The Spanish conquered the area, building churches on top of pyramids and temples, and replacing the many ancient gods with Jesus Christ and the Holy Trinity. Today, Mexico as we know it is a Roman Catholic country (rather than the mystical one it could have been). However, same as it happened with culture and population, beliefs evolved and swirled around into one big melting pot of rituals, traditions and beliefs.

In Mexico, you'll find the most devoted Catholics. But you will also find empty churches in southern rural towns where natives sacrifice chickens following pre-Hispanic rituals. served and is still very much alive especially in religion.

In the area of Banderas Bay, however, the predominant ancient civilization were the Huicholes (also known as Wixarika) and some indigenous groups are still around. Their culture has been beautifully preserved and is still very much alive especially in religion.

WHAT ARE THESE?

You'll see these diamond shaped crafts all around, which are woven by fathers for their newborn children. They're called *Ojos de Dios* or *s'kuli.*

These Huichol amulets are for power and protection, and represent the eye of the God Kauyumari (represented as a blue deer) through which he sees the world. You'll find them in all sizes and color combinations.

And even though they carry a spiritual meaning, they're the perfect souvenir to take home. A little extra magic protection can't hurt.

PHOTOS /
EMILIA IGARTUA

THE PEOPLE

Mexican people have two reputations. 1. Being warm and friendly towards friends and strangers. And 2. Being hot-blooded telenovela stars who run on jealousy and passion. The first is true and the second is about 30% true depending on who you're dealing with and what the relationship is between you.

But in order to impossibly generalize an extremely diverse population who come from different cultures, the most fair statement is to say that Mexican people love to play and joke around. Mexican people are pretty easy going in life and with time; don't be surprised when you learn that punctuality is not a big deal here.

Mexico, especially in the coastal places, seems to live to its own rhythm and time. In general, Mexicans will make you feel very welcome and will integrate you easily into their communities. And you may even end up as part of *"la familia"* (the family).

THE CRIME

Puerto Vallarta has been rated the safest destination in Mexico. In fact, with such low crime rates, you're safer here than in most cities in the USA. Crimes that do occur are in the form of petty theft such as pickpockets and bag snatchers. Use common sense and a couple extra safety tips that we cover on page 281, and you'll be just fine.

THE VOLTAGE

Mexico's voltage is 127 Volts / 60 Hz frequency, same as in the USA and Canada. So don't worry, you won't need to be hauling around any chunky adapters! However, depending on where you're staying, you might find Type A plugs (you know, those that only have the two flat thingys). So, if your charger / cord is Type B (two flat contact pins plus a third cylindrical one...) make sure to bring those ones so you can plug in anywhere.

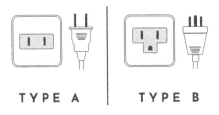

TYPE A | TYPE B

DO YOU HAVE ANY SPECIFIC QUESTIONS ABOUT MEXICO?

As your designated local guide, I'm always happy to respond to any doubts about my country. Shoot me your questions via DM...or just come say hi.

 Scan the code or find me at @__helloemilia

How about the weather?

WHEN TO VISIT...

If you have vacation time to use, use it! Any time of year is good to travel to Puerto Vallarta & the Banderas Bay as long as you plan your activities accordingly.

So, here's what you need to know.

Weather can vary depending on where in Mexico you are. The Banderas Bay area has mostly tropical weather as it's surrounded by rainforest! Sometimes it's rainy and cool, and other times it's hot and humid.

SPRING: Most people consider spring to be the best time to visit Banderas Bay because the weather is nice and skies are clear with little rain! It's hot enough for a bathing suit but not so hot that you're melting. That being said, however...more travelers flock to Banderas during this time.

SUMMER: Less tourists, more heat. You will be sticky. Your dress will cling to your body. You will get caught in late afternoon rainstorms. You need a pool, air-conditioning and lots of frozen margaritas!

FALL: I prefer to visit PVR in this moderate-temperature season that offers sun, rain, and fabulous prices! This is the shoulder season I was talking about! But hey, keep an eye out as prices begin to rise by the end of November!

WINTER: Welcome to high season! Less rain and more comfortable temperatures, but more tourists and higher flight & room prices. Winter in Mexico attracts Snowbirds, aka people who seek to escape the cold weather at home and trade it in for Mexican sun!

—

"Official" Best Time to Visit: October – June

Alexa's Vote on the Best Time to Visit: Spring (April, May, June) & Late Fall (October, November)

WHY?

High Season (December – April) is the busiest time of the year to visit Puerto Vallarta. Travelers are trading their winters for Mexico's beach weather.

Low Season (July-September) is when fewer people visit, mostly due to hot and sticky weather, and so you get quieter and less crowded beaches.

The key, then, to hitting the sweet spot is to come between High Season and Low Season otherwise known as "Shoulder Season". The weather is nice. Flights and hotels are cheaper. And there are less people to share the beach with!

Best Time For Diving & Snorkeling	November through May
Busiest Time To Visit	July through September; and Easter week (avoid the crowds!)
High Season (The Most Tourists)	December through April
Low Season (The Least Tourist)	July through September
Hottest Weather	July through September
Wettest Weather	July through September (susceptible to hurricanes)
Hottest Month	July
The Most Humid Month	August

Visas for Mexico

Start with a tourist visa.

W H A T : A tourist visa allows you to stay in Mexico for 6 months as a tourist.

H O W : You just show up. No need to prepare a single document and it's free.

T I P : When you arrive in Mexico, you will fill out a declaration card that you will hand to immigration at the airport. Have the address of your hotel ready to write on your declaration card as proof that you're a tourist. Also, as long as you've read this book and have an idea of what fun things you want to do in Mexico, you'll be granted entry into Mexico easy-peasy.

hey!

WANT TO TRAVEL WITH US?
CHECK OUT GO BABY GLOW TOURS.

What to Pack
for Banderas Bay

First, don't stress. As long as you have your passport, bank card and a decent backpack, you're ready for Mexico. Anything you need or forget at home can be found here. There's Walmart, Costco, and malls in the area - many showcasing colorful and traditional summer clothing from a multitude of local, independently owned shops. And just wait until you check out the open air markets!

So, no matter what you do or don't pack - you'll be just fine.

But let's take this opportunity to get organized now so you don't have to spend your vacation hunting for things you forgot.

As you know, I've been traveling for over a decade. I've got this packing thing down and here is what I recommend to my girlfriends traveling to PVR.

◇ PASSPORT WITH AT LEAST 6 MONTHS VALIDITY

Some countries enforce it and some countries don't- but to play it safe, you need to have at least 6 months validity on your passport. For example, if it's January 1st, 2019, and your passport expires before June 1st, 2019, they might not let you in the country and you'll have to return home immediately.

◇ TRAVEL INSURANCE

Yes, you do need it.

Everything from minor bouts of food poisoning to helicopter medevac off a mountain, a standard travel insurance policy is a non-negotiable in my (literal) book.

 World Nomads which offers full-coverage plans for extremely reasonable prices.

Safetywing is also a really affordable option, especially if you're traveling long term.

◇ THE PERFECT BACKPACK OR SUITCASE

Mexico is covered in cobblestone streets and beaches. You really don't want to be pulling a rolling suitcase behind you. You want a bag you can carry. I prefer no wheels.

◇ *The Bag I Recommend...The Osprey Farpoint 40 Litre Backpack*

 It's been over 5 years that I've been using this bag. I love it so much that I just bought the exact same model again to use for another 5 years.

◇ WALKING SHOES

Bring 3 pairs of shoes...

> ➤ 1 Pair of Flip Flops or Slides
> ➤ 1 Pair of Cute Walking Sandals
> ➤ 1 Pair of Hiking / Running Shoes

◇ OB TAMPONS OR A MENSTRUAL CUP

You're going to be in a bathing suit on the beach and out on the water! And if you've never used a menstrual cup, they are a game changer. Save money every month, go 12 hours with no leaks & swim with no drips.

◇ QUICK DRY TOWEL

Hostel girls! Hostels usually don't provide towels so it's nice to bring a travel towel of your own. Not a total necessity, but a quick dry (usually some kind of microfiber) towel is nice to have- especially during rainy season when the heat isn't there to dry things quickly. Plus, it can double as your beach towel!

◇ TROPICAL WEATHER MAKE-UP

 Humidity is no joke. Most foundations get super greasy and eyeshadows crease like it's their job. My makeup bag is pure perfection when it comes to long-lasting, humid, tropical weather products. Scan this code to check out my travel makeup collection.

◇ EMERGENCY MONEY SOURCE / $100 CASH US

Have a secret stash of cash and a backup credit card in case you get in a sticky situation. Keep this emergency money source separate from your other cards and cash so that if you lose your wallet, you won't lose the secret stash, too.

◇ BANK CARDS

Travel with two cards – either 2 debit cards or 1 debit + 1 credit. In the case that your bank flags one card with fraudulent activity and disables it, you'll want to have a backup. If the machine eats a card, if a card gets stolen, or if you lose your purse on a night out, a backup card will make all the difference between having mom fly you home and you continuing your travels.

 The cards you need are inside this code!

◇EMPTY SPACE IN YOUR BAG

It took me 5 years to learn that the less stuff you have, the more free you are. You are free to pick up and move around, free to shop for souvenirs, and free from relying on porters and taxis to help you carry your luggage. Plus, you're going to need space for all that extra shopping over here.

◇ WHAT NOT TO PACK

- ➤ Jeans
- ➤ High-heels (there's cobblestones everywhere so save yourself the sprained ankle)
- ➤ Hairspray (ya won't use it)
- ➤ A curling iron (with this humidity…no point)
- ➤ Too Many Bras (ya won't wear em')
- ➤ A Pharmacy of Medicine (you can get it all here)

WANT TO SEE WHAT I TRAVEL WITH?
GET MY PACKING LIST AT THESOLOGIRLSTRAVELGUIDE.
COM/PACKING-LIST …OR SCAN THIS CODE TO FIND IT.

How To Budget for Puerto Vallarta

How much money should you bring?

How much will you spend?

What is the least amount you can spend and still see it all?

When it comes to traveling, there are always 3 spending routes you can take.

BUDGET

Stay in hostels, eat local, and drink beer from mini marts.

BALANCED

Go cheap for half your trip and spend more towards the end. Or just stay middle-of-the road the whole way through by staying in Airbnbs, eating street tacos and going on the occasional boat trip or tequila tasting.

BOUGIE

Infinity pool resorts, yoga classes, and daily massages! Pamper yourself!

	BUDGET	BALANCED	BOUGIE
TOTAL PER DAY	$35	$80	$150+

All 3 of these options are possible, easy and will offer you the trip of a lifetime – as long as you plan it right.

Street Taco	$1
Restaurant Meal	$3.50
McDonalds (#BigMacIndex)	$4.75
Bottle of Beer	$1.50
Capuccino	$2.50
1 Night in a Hostel	$9.00
1 Night in a Private Budget Room	$24.00
1 Night in a Basic AirBnb (low season)	$60.00+
1 Night in a Basic AirBnb (high season)	$100.00+
1 Night in a Boutique Resort	$150+
1 Night in a Fancy Resort	$350+
1 Hour Massage	$40
Half-Day Private Boat Tour	$50
1 Hour Private Driver	$50

ON A BUDGET? TIPS TO SPEND LESS IN MEXICO

◊ Visit during "low season" when hotels are 30-50% cheaper

◊ Go to the ATM just once a week – the ATM fees are up to $8 per transaction

◊ Drink beer from mini marts or hole in the wall bars, rather than clubs

◊ Take the bus and go on DIY adventures

◊ Eat street food

◊ Take the bus

YOUR BIGGEST EXPENSES WILL BE...

◊ Alcohol

◊ Organized Tours

◊ Ubers & Drivers

Everything else can be tweaked to your wallet.

WHAT ABOUT TIPPING?

Some people tip, some people don't. When you like the service, tip 10% to 15% of the total. I usually tip my salon ladies and often my waiters.

Paying with a card? When the waiter brings the bill, hand them your card and ask them to add 10% (or whatever) and they'll add it on automatically.

Now that you know how much you'll be spending, let's talk about how to handle Mexican money like a pro (and not a tourist).

Money & Cards

YOU'RE GOING TO NEED CASH IN MEXICO!

Hotels and big restaurants may accept cards, but street food, transportation and haggling on anything requires cash-ola!

How much money to bring to Mexico: $0 USD.

Use the ATMs instead of the exchange counters. I'll tell you which ATMs give you the best exchange rates later in this section.

I suppose: If you are super pro-active and excited, you can exchange USD/ your currency for pesos at your local bank at home. Just double check that their exchange rates are close to the official market's exchange rates (at a bank, they should be accurate).

WHAT YOU NEED TO KNOW ABOUT MONEY IN MEXICO...

Mexican currency is called *pesos*.

However, in Puerto Vallarta, you will find some vendors or establishments that accept US dollars. The lady selling hats on the beach? She likely will give you a quote in USD.

But the street taco stand might only take pesos.

The ATMs will often give you the choice of taking out Mexican Pesos or US Dollars.

Personally, I only spend with pesos in Mexico. I feel like I get better value when the vendors charge me local prices in pesos. But if you have some extra US cash swimming around in your pocket, it won't hurt to use it.

When you land in Mexico, I recommend taking 2000-5000 ($100 - $250 USD) pesos out of the ATM depending on your plans. Going to an all-inclusive resort? Just take out 3000 ($150) pesos for tips and shopping. This way you avoid being charged the ATM fees over and over again.

KNOW YOUR

MONEY COLORS

Mexican Pesos are pretty! Each bills has a unique color, unlike the US dollar. Familiarize yourself with these colors to make sure you don't mistakenly hand over a 200 when you mean to hand over a 20.

> **100** is reddish

> **200** is green

> **50** is purple

> **20** is a kind of light teal / turquoise color

> **500** are either purplish or darker blue (old version and new version which will either have Frida Kahlo - you'll recognize her iconic unibrow - or some humpback whales on this one).

Money Pro Tip!

CONVERTING US DOLLARS

TO PESOS WITH YOUR BRAIN:

Take the number in pesos, cut it in half and take away a zero. Like this.

◊ *2,000 pesos = 100 USD*

◊ *100 pesos = 5 USD*

◊ *50 pesos = 2.5 USD*

WHAT ATM'S TO USE IN MEXICO?

Always use a bank-affiliated ATM (i.e. a bank-branded ATM instead of a weird generic ATM). You get the best exchange rate at official Bank ATM machines!

➤ Alexa-Approved ATMs:

Banco Azteca charges a flat 30-pesos ($2 USD) fee plus your bank fee.

Santander and Banamex offer great fees and fair exchange rates, as well.

➤ ATMs I Avoid:

Tangerine and Scotiabank. They charge 12% conversion rates. That's high!

MONEY SAVING TIP: In Mexico, ATMs will often ask you "Do you want to use the bank exchange rate?" Hit decline! DECLINE THE ATM EXCHANGE RATE which charges another 5% conversion. You want the default market exchange rage.

"Decline Conversion" at ATMs won't mean you receive no money. It just means that you'll get the rate your bank is offering, rather than one that may be a lot higher. So always decline!

PRO BANKING TIP FOR AMERICANS:

Open an account with Charles Schwab Bank. With Charles Schwab, I can use any ATM in the world without ATM fees. Every time you use an ATM that isn't your bank's ATM, you are charged a "foreign ATM fee" that can be $3-$12 depending on where you are. Lame. But at the end of every month, Charles Schwab reimburses all foreign ATM fees.

Pro Tip! Are you in the military? USAA also offers this "no ATM fee" service!

YOU NEED A TRAVEL-FRIENDLY CREDIT CARD

You are literally turning down free money if you're not taking advantage of travel credit cards when booking international flights and weeks of hotels.

Use a Travel Credit Card to...

◇ Book your flight with this card

◇ Book your hotels with this card

◇ Pay at restaurants with this card

Chase and American Express are the cards I can't live without. I explain why I love these cards here:

Internet & Cell Phone Plans

Almost everywhere you go in Banderas will have WiFi, but what about the places in between like when you're catching an Uber outside of a restaurant, in a car headed to a new city, walking and getting lost? You need cell phone data, *mija*.

JUST VISITING?

Get a SIM card when you land in Mexico.

In Mexico, I used a company called Telcel for my internet data.

How Much: The SIM card (the little chip they will put in your phone) was 300 pesos ($15 USD) and I pay around 200 pesos ($10 a month) for internet on my phone.

WHERE TO GET IT:

Just outside the airport parking lot is an OXXO mini mart where they sell Telcel SIM cards and data.

In town. Just put "Telcel" in your google maps and you'll find a location where you can buy the SIM card. The malls have Telcel kiosks, too.

To "top up" (add more internet on your card when you run out), you can go into an OXXO mini mart, tell them "200 pesos Telcel", give them your phone number and they will top up for you in a couple minutes time. And don't worry about where to find an OXXO. You'll see them everywhere!

IMPORTANT:

To use a Mexican data plan, please make sure your phone is "Unlocked". This means that you can use other company's data plans. You can just go to your cell-carrier's store, hand them the phone and say "I need this unlocked" and they should do it for you on the spot. If not, message me on Instagram and I'll give you some pointers ➤ @SoloGirlsTravelGuide

Pro Tip... **for Americans and Canadians:**

Your cell phone plan might already cover Mexico! Double check now.

Don't Get an "International Plan" on top of your current plan. That plan is expensive and doesn't guarantee good coverage. Besides! Mexican cell phone data is cheap, easy to get, and has great coverage.

SPENDING A LOT OF TIME IN MEXICO?

I have made the leap to T-Mobile's Magenta Plan which covers the US, Mexico and Canada. It's $70 USD per month, offers unlimited text, calling, and data with no contract (you can do month-to-month). I like this plan in the big cities, but once I stray off the beaten path I don't get much signal. Keep that in mind when choosing between T-Mobile and Telcel.

Want to get this plan for cheaper? Sign-up for a T-Mobile plan in Mexico instead of signing up for it in the US.

APPS TO DOWNLOAD ─────────────

WHATSAPP

The main messaging app and calling app out here. It's free to call and text whenever you have an internet connection (Wi-Fi or cell data).

INDRIVER

Like Uber, I use InDriver nearly every day. They provide an Uber-style service with a bidding-system. I explain how to use this app on page 43.

UBER

Just like at home. Connect your credit card inside the Uber App so you don't have to handle cash.

UBEREATS AND RAPPI

You can use the UberEats app and the Rappi app, but Pro Tip: many restaurants have a WhatsApp number where they take food orders and deliver for free or for cheap. Check their Facebook page or Instagram!

GOOGLE MAPS OFFLINE

This is a life saver when you don't have access to Wi-Fi. You can save Google Maps offline area-by-area. So open "Puerto Vallarta" on your Google Maps, type "Puerto Vallarta" (or any other area) and click "download". Now you can access the map without internet.

BUMBLE AND TINDER

Find a sightseeing partner with another traveler or link up with a local who knows all the best spots in the city. Mexico is very pro-dating app.

Fun Fact! *Bumble has a friend-mode called Bumble BFF where you can search for new friends to explore with!*

DUOLINGO

Start learning Spanish before you come!

XE

Currency Conversions in an instant so that you don't get ripped off while buying a cute hat at the market!

ACCUWEATHER

The most reliable weather app out there. Especially useful during the rainy season!

JOIN THESE FACEBOOK GROUPS

Girls in Puerto Vallarta

My girl-empowered PVR community

Girls in Global

My girl-empowered global community

The Solo Girl's Travel Guide

Know when new books and travelgoodies come out.

Transportation

It's easy to get around Puerto Vallarta but not always cheap. So, before you go spending an arm and a leg to explore, let me give you the best transportation options around.

You Should Know: Transportation options vary city by city. Some cities have Uber, some have buses, and some have golf carts! In each chapter, I'll tell you the best way to get around. But first, let me introduce you to the whole collection of options you'll encounter.

OPTION 1: UBER

Uber is mostly present in Puerto Vallarta but not always present outside the city center. Story Time: I easily got an Uber to drive me to a salon outside of town.

But when it was time to return to my Puerto Vallarta hotel, I couldn't find an Uber to pick me up! And that's when a friend told me about Option #2 which saved my butt...

OPTION 2: IN DRIVER

InDriver is similar to Uber but with a cool price-negotiation feature. You enter the price you want to pay and drivers accept or might offer you a higher price/lower price.

Let's say you bid 100 pesos to take you from the airport to centro. You might get three drivers that offer 120 pesos, 100 pesos or 90 pesos. You can choose based off their rating.

How do you know how much to offer on InDriver? Go on Uber, see the price you'd pay there. Then go on InDriver and offer a similar price.

Pro Tip! InDriver uses WhatsApp to communicate. I like to collect my InDrivers' WhatsApp numbers. I like these guys and love to have drivers' numbers saved in my phone.

Fun Fact! One of my drivers told me he was surprised to see me! "Not many "gringas" take InDriver". Usually, it's Mexicans who ride with this app. So don't be surprised if the driver calls you to speak Spanish. Just answer the call and simply state the name of your location.

Good-to-Know... Uber takes 30% commission from the driver while InDriver only takes 10% commission. Another reason I prefer InDriver.

OPTION 3: HIRE A PRIVATE DRIVER

I collected a few drivers' numbers in my phone who I message for long-distance adventures or day-trips. I like knowing my driver. It makes me feel safe, it makes the drives more fun and with the app commission taken out, the local drivers can give you a better price. Check out my list of local drivers in my Facebook Group, Girls in Puerto Vallarta here.

OPTION 4:TAKE THE CITY BUS

You can take the cheap city bus within cities and between cities. For example, the city bus is a great way to get around Puerto Vallarta, and also a cheap way to get from Puerto Vallarta to Sayulita. However, the bus can get crowded and you might now always have a place to sit.

The way it works: The bus comes every 25-30 minutes at designated stops. You hp on and pay as little as 10 pesos (30 cents) per ride. There are no round-trips or transfer tickets and each ticket is single-use.

Pro Tips...for Taking the Bus:
◊Have the correct change ready for the driver.

◊Sometimes, inspectors hop on and off to check tickets so keep your ticket available.

For Bus Routes, Prices and Times, use the website 1Map.com/routes which will make planning very easy for you.

HELPFUL SPANISH WORDS FOR BUS TRAVEL

Bus	Autobus
Driver	Chofer
Passenger	Pasajero
Schedule	Horario
Route	Ruta
Fare	Tarifa
Seat	Asiento
Destination	Destino

 However, if you'd like to familiarize yourself with the inner workings of the bus system in Banderas bay, I recommend bookmarking this article on your phone.

I'll give you more bus details in each chapter as we go along, as well.

OPTION 5: RENTA A CAR

Personally, I don't drive in Mexico because I prefer hiring driver (and I'm usually drinking Margaritas!) but here is Car Rental Wisdom from the expat girls in Girls in Puerto Vallarta:

➤ *National*

"They pick you up and drop you off wherever you need to go. And a friend of mine said that she totaled her rental car in a flash flood and they delivered a new car to her quickly. Just make sure you pay for the full insurance."

➤ *Gecko Car Rental*

"It's not the cheapest, but you don't want the cheapest when renting a car in Mexico. You want the company with reliable vehicles and good service. There are no hidden fees here and the customer service is super professional."

OPTION 6: BUY A CAR

Most expats that plan on staying in the area for a few months buy a car once they arrive in Mexico. Facebook Marketplace is a great place to find affordable cars for sale. Many of the cars are being sold by expats who are selling vehicles before they leave Mexico to go home. The benefit of buying here is that you're dealing with someone who speaks your language! When you go to check out the car, don't go alone with a wad of cash in your pocket. Bring a friend. Make sure before you buy, that the owner has the title of the car in hand.

If you're a tourist or a temporary resident here, you can actually use the drivers' license issued in your country just fine. Make sure you buy insurance, however. I recommend using Mexusinsurance.com as it's a trusted company with great prices.

OPTION 7: BRING YOUR CAR

If you're a tourist or a temporary resident, you can bring your US plated car here but you'll be required to pay a deposit to enter Mexico and get a decal for your windshield. Your car can stay as long as you can stay. You must return your car to the US by the end of your 180 day tourist visa or temporary residents visa. The consequence of not returning is losing your deposit or having your car impounded, so play by the rules.

Here is where to begin the process of bringing your car into Mexico temporarily: www.mexpro.com

If you are seeking permanent residency, your best bet is to buy a car here so that you can avoid the expensive import tax of bringing your car from home into the country.

For personalized help on this matter, search for Pat's Plates- Expat Help for Vehicle Registration and Driver's Licenses on Facebook.

Safe Girl Tip! Emilia is Mexican and a badass, but even she doesn't drive on isolated highways alone. When driving outside the city or between cities, avoid isolated roads and use toll road highways when possible. And when possible, drive with a man in your car rather than a car full of women.

Mexican Food Guide

I once found a Mexican restaurant in the isolated jungle mountains of Thailand. The whole world is obsessed and in love with Mexican food…but does the world really know Mexican food? I'd argue, not at all. There is so much more to Mexican food than tacos and quesadillas (although, I'm a slut for tacos and quesadillas). So, it is our goal in this guide to take you out of your Mexican shell (pun intended) and introduce you to a whole new world of Mexican cuisine. Emilia will be your Mexican food spirit guide starting now.

Pack your stretchy pants and get ready to eat.

LET'S EAT

TACOS

In case you've been living in a cult that doesn't allow fun food and have never had a taco, let me explain what a taco is. A taco is simply a tortilla that is folded to hold any kind of yumminess inside. The taco possibilities are literally endless but here are a few of the most common tacos you'll find.

◊ **Asada:** beef

◊ **Pastor:** spiced pork (usually served with a slice of pineapple)

◊ **Pescado:** fish

◊ **Camarón:** shrimp

◊ **Lengua:** tongue

◊ **Carnitas:** pulled pork

◊ **Cabeza:** head (yes, head meat sounds gross but I bet you we can get you to try – they're delicious!)

QUESADILLAS

One quesadilla folded or two quesadillas stacked with cheese, veggies and/or meat inside, which are grilled and melted together. But guess what! In Mexico, a quesadilla doesn't always have cheese! (What's the difference between cheese-less quesadillas and tacos? Not even Mexicans know. It's a nation-wide debate.)

BURRITOS

Flour tortillas rolled and wrapped around yummy fillings like beef, chicken, eggs…you name it. Real Mexican burritos, though, rarely include rice and beans and all of those Chipotle ingredients. Most burritos here will be stuffed with machaca (fried beef) or some kind of stew.

CHILAQUILES

Mostly a breakfast dish. Fried tortilla chips with salsa. You'll find chilaquiles both soft and crunchy and with either red or green salsa. They're served alone, with shredded chicken or with a fried egg on top. Pro tip...order them "divorciados" (divorced) which means you'll half with red salsa and half with green salsa.

GUACAMOLE

Mashed avocados with chopped tomatoes, onions, cilantro and sometimes a little bit of chili.

QUESO FUNDIDO

Molten cheese served on a hot plate. Sometimes served with mushrooms, or veggies or chorizo (see below), and an order of tortillas "para taquear" (to make tacos).

CHORIZO

Mexican spicy pork sausage that is fermented, smoked and curated. It's usually used with other dishes like scrambled eggs, queso fundido, enchiladas, etc.

ENCHILADAS

Rolled corn tortillas and stuffed with veggies, beans and meat (usually chicken) and bathed with red salsa and grated cheese. Yum.

TACOS

CEVICHE

TROMPO DE PASTOR

PHOTOS / UNSPLASH.COM

TAMALES

One of Mexico's most ancient dishes besides tortillas. Corn dough (called "masa) pockets" filled with chicken, cheese and even peppers. They are wrapped around in a dried corn husk (in the north) or a plantain leaf (in the south) and steamed to perfection

TORTA

Somewhat in-between of a Sandwich and a Burger, tortas are a street food icon. The base is: meat, cheese and veggies pressed between bread loaves called teleras. But the fillings can vary so much that you could never eat the same torta twice. From carnitas to tamales or chilaquiles.

BIRRIA

Birria is not as widely known as other Mexican dishes. Its stew made with meat (goat, mostly) and that is simmered slowly in a sauce and spices. And of course...tacos.

Pro Tip! Birria is one of the best things that can happen to you if you're hungover. You're welcome.

TOSTADAS

A hard tortilla shell topped with a mix of either seafood or shredded chicken/meat and veggies. Both totally different dishes, both insanely good.

CEVICHE

The recipe for ceviche varies from beach to beach but the base remains the same: raw fish, onion, tomato, chiles, cilantro and lime. The citrus cooks the fish and makes it ready for eating. To be eaten with corn chips and some "salsa marisquera" (spicy salsa made for seafood).

Pro Tip! Take a tostada and smear it with some mayo. Put the ceviche on top. Take a bite. Bonus points for extra avocado on top.

MOLE

One of the most iconic Mexican dishes as it takes over 30 ingredients. Starting from more than 1 kind of chilis, and including things like nuts and cacao. Mole is a marinade and a sauce used to bathe meat like chicken or beef. There are around 7 types of mole, but the most popular one is the "Poblano" (from Puebla).

Fun Fact! Mole is an ancient word for "mix". And one of Mexico's most famous Moles is chef Enrique Olvera's "Mole Madre", which is a plate of nothing but "Mole Viejo" ancient Mole that has been cooked uninterruptedly for over 2,000 days (at the time this book was written). And on top, a spoonful of fresh "Nuevo Mole".

GORDITAS

Gordita is a way to call someone or something chubby. In this case, a tortilla. Gorditas are smaller in diameter than a tortilla and also usually, thicker. They have a slit on one side where they are stuffed with cheese, meat or some other filling, creating a savory pocket full of Mexican goodness.

Fun fact: Mexicans add the suffix "ito" or "ita" to everything to make reference to size. A "plato" is a plate. A "platito" is a tiny plate. Sometimes it's more about making things sound sweet than actually indicating size. You'll hear this all the time.

SOPES

Fried masa base with different toppings like meat, chicken, veggies and even seafood. It's similar to a tostada, but smaller and with a mushier and fluffier base.

CHICHARRON

Chicharron is not only the best way to practice rolling those "r"s when ordering. It's a dish made of seasoned and fried pork belly, skin or rinds. You can find it soft or crunchy, as a dish itself or as a snack. But most likely, in tacos, gorditas, soups and as a part of many Mexican recipes.

MOLCAJETE

The word molcajete actually refers to a cooking utensil and not a dish. Molcajetes are volcanic stone mortars that are used to hand-make salsa. Molcajetes are used as hot plates to serve a mix of meat or seafood.

PESCADO EMBARAZADO

A typically local dish in Puerto Vallarta. This translates in English as "pregnant fish", and while it sounds strange, it's just a roasted fish on a stick marinated with lime and served with spicy salsa "Huichol" (a salsa brand from this region!).

POZOLE

A traditional Mexican stew made with hominy and meat and many seasonings. Topped with different elements like onions, cilantro, cabbage, chiles, etc. In the Banderas Bay area, you'll find a shrimp variation of pozole.

FLAN

A baked custard dessert covered with a light caramel sauce. You may also find "choco-flan", a chocolate variation of flan.

ARROZ CON LECHE

Sweet rice pudding made with milk, evaporated milk and sweetened condensed milk. Sometimes you'll find a cinnamon stick in it, or ground cinnamon sprinkled on top.

CHURROS

Churros were inherited to Mexico from Spain, but they've become the staple dessert in Mexican cuisine. They are sweet, deep-fried dough snacks sprinkled with sugar and cinnamon and filled with caramel or chocolate. Or to be dipped in "chocolate caliente" (hot chocolate).

TAJÍN

Tajin is a brand of powdered dried chilis that's become an actual term. It's sprinkled on top of fruit and snacks like watermelon, mango, coconut, cucumber and jícama.

Fun fact! In Mexican beaches you'll often find that coconuts are opened up and the meat is eaten with lime, salt and some chilis like Tajin. Try it. Your life will never be the same.

Mexican Pro Tip! Even though I'm Mexican, I'm the worst at handling spicy food. So, if you're like me, and you ever find yourself with your mouth on fire...eat some mayonnaise. It'll fix you right up. - Emilia

Drinks ─────────

MICHELADA

Micheladas are a whole different debate because you'll get something different depending on where you are. The basic michelada is a beer with lime and salt. But in some places, it also means Worcestershire sauce and Tabasco. And in some others, it even has Clamato (tomato and clam juice). Ask before you order, but here is the quick guide to ordering these drinks in Banderas Bay:

◇**Michelada:** lime and salt

◇**Cubana:** lime, salt, Worcestershire sauce & Tabasco

◇**Cielo Rojo (red sky):** lime, salt, Worcestershire sauce, Tabasco & Clamato (clam and tomato juice)

TEQUILA

Mexico's most iconic drink...and probably even the most iconic word. Tequila is made from one specific kind of Blue Agave, which goes through a lengthy process of cooking, fermentation and distillation. You can drink it straight or mixed in cocktails.

Fun Fact! Tequila is named after a town named, you guessed it, Tequila in central Mexico. If it's not produced in the area, it cannot bear the name of Tequila and has to be labeled as "Destilado de Agave" (distilled from agave).

Pro Tip! If you pour some tequila in your hands, rub them together, and feel sticky afterwards...you're drinking low-quality Tequila. And you have a guaranteed hangover. You're warned!

MARGARITA

The staple Mexican cocktail, it's prepared with tequila, orange liqueur and lime juice. Served with salt on the rim of the glass, and either shaken or blended.

MEZCAL

Mezcal is tequila's cousin as they both come from agave. However,

Tequila can only come from one kind of agave, while mezcal comes from over 20 types of agave. Mezcal is clear colored and its notes can go from spicy to smokey. All Tequilas are considered mezcal, but mezcal is not Tequila.

Fun Fact! There's an expression in Spanish for mezcal that goes: "Para todo mal, un mezcal Para todo bien, también." which says that mezcal is ought to be drunk both to drown sorrows, as to celebrate life as well. Cheers!

RAICILLA

A cousin of mezcal and tequila, Raicilla is another distilled from agave that is about 300 years old. Raicilla is made from the roots of the agave and goes through a single-distilled process. It's usually fresh and crisp to the tongue, and softer than you'd imagine. Once considered a humble drink, because it was originally drunk by farmers, Raicilla is nowadays the up-and-coming spirit in Mexico.

CAFE DE OLLA

Traditional coffee beverage. It's black coffee with cinnamon and sweetened with "piloncillo" (unrefined whole cane sugar). Cafe de olla needs to be prepared in a clay pot (olla = pot) as it gives a special taste to the coffee. It is commonly served in tiny clay mugs as well.

AGUAS FRESCAS

Non-alcoholic drinks made with fruits like tamarind, and flowers like hibiscus (Jamaica). One of the most common ones is Horchata, made of rice, milk and cinnamon. You'll find these pretty much everywhere and they're great to fight off the heat.

CHOCOLATE CALIENTE

Mexican hot chocolate is different than any that you've ever tried. What makes it special? Spices like cinnamon and nutmeg in the mix. Besides, every hot chocolate can be different, and sometimes people will even add a dash of chili. No worries, it doesn't make it spicy, but ti does makes the flavors way more intense.

CARAJILLO

Allow me to introduce you to your new favorite drink. A carajillo consists of espresso and a shot of Licor 43, sweet, citrusy spanish liquor, poured over ice. This drink is like a boozy dessert in a glass, it's usually served after meals as a digestif. But you can drink it at any time, and it's a wonderful pick-me-up to keep on sight-seeing through your afternoon. In some places you'll find some alternate Carajillo versions served with Kahlua or Brandy.

Spanish Language Guide

GREETINGS

Hello	Hola
My name is _____	Mi nombre es _____
How are you?	¿Como estás?
Good morning	¡Buenos días!
Good afternoon	¡Buenas tardes!
Good evening / night	¡Buenas noches!
Thank you	Gracias
You're welcome	Denada / Por nada

DAY TO DAY

Yes	Si
No	No
Can I _____?	¿Puedo _____?
No problem	No hay problema
I don't know	No se
I am finished	Terminé
What is this?	¿Que es esto?
Great	¡Muy bien!
I'm sorry!	¡Lo siento!
Excuse me...	Disculpa...

SHOPPING / ORDERING

Do you have?	¿Tienes _____?
How much?	¿Cuanto es?
How many?	¿Cuantos _____ ?
People	Personas
How many people?	¿Cuantas personas?
I want _____	Quiero _____
I don't want _____	No quiero _____
Big	Grande
Small	Chico
I like	Me gusta
I don't like	No me gusta
Do you have change?	¿Tienes cambio?
The check, please	La cuenta, por favor
One more, please	Uno mas, por favor

Pro Tip! Call your server male "joven" (pronounced ho-ven), instead of "señor". If it's a lady, you can call her "señorita". - Emilita

Food / Meal	Comida
Water	Agua
Drink	Tomar / Beber
Coffee	Cafe
Tea	Te

Beer	Cerveza
Wine	Vino
Red Wine / White Wine	Vino Tinto / Vino Blanco
Delicious	Delicioso
Corn	Maíz
Avocado	Aguacate
Fruit	Fruta
Vegetables	Vegetales
Juice	Jugo
Chicken	Pollo
Pork	Puerco
Beef	Carne / Res
Shrimp	Camarón
Fish	Pescado
Octopus	Pulpo
Clams	Almejas
Oysters	Ostiones
Tofu	Tofu
Vegetarian	Vegetariano
Vegan	Vegano
Rice	Arroz
Beans	Frioles
Spicy / Not Spicy	Picante / No Picante

USEFUL WORDS & PHRASES

Where?	¿Dónde?
Where is the toilet?	¿Dónde está el baño?
Room / Hotel Room	Habitación / Habitación de Hotel
Boat	Barco / Bote
To	A
From	Desde
Today	Hoy
Tomorrow	Mañana
Yesterday	Ayer

EMERGENCY PHRASES

Go away!	¡Aléjate!
Help!	¡Ayuda!
Police!	¡Policía!
Stop!	¡Alto!
Not safe!	No es seguro

Mexican Pro Tip! Rolling your r's is a big part of speaking Spanish. Bring the tip of your tongue to the roof of your mouth. Now blow some air strongly. Rrrrrrrrrrr. You're ready to order a burrito like a local.

Tips & Advice

DO'S AND DON'TS...

Just because you can do it, doesn't mean you should do it.

DON'T

X Don't Do Drugs

At some, you'll be walking down a Malecon and will inevitably be offered drugs. Please know that drugs are highly illegal in Mexico and if you're caught and can't pay the bribe, you can expect to sit in a Mexican jail for months before you get a fair trial. Stay off drugs, kids. Drink Tequila instead.

X Don't Try to Buy anything Illegal

Drugs. Exotic animals. Babies. Remember that if you go looking for trouble in Mexico, you'll find it. Just be prepared to bribe your way out of a situation if you get caught.

X Don't Support Animal Tourism

Dolphin shows. Iguana pictures. Feeding manta rays. If you want to be an ethical traveler, don't give money to people or industries that exploit animals.

X Don't Drink the Water

In general, Mexico's tap water is safe to shower in and brush your teeth with, but it's not usually safe to drink. While the water in Puerto Vallarta is the exception as one of only 2 cities with tap water approved for human consumption, you never know the condition of the pipes this water runs though. So still, stick to bottled water.

X Don't Talk to Time Share Salesmen

They are ruthless and relentless with their hustle. Don't agree to go to a showing. Just don't.

X Don't drive on isolated highways alone.

When possible, drive with a buddy (and male buddy is best for long inner-city drives).

✗ Don't Get a Temporary Tattoo on the Beach

While these tattoo slingers claim to be using henna, some of them are actually using a black ink chemical which can give you a nasty chemical burn. I just saved you from a scar and a fashion faux pau.

DO ───────────────────────

✓ Haggle

For all street products (except food), you can haggle. Sarongs, sunglasses, motorbike rentals, even taxi drivers that you find on the street! The first price is rarely the final price. If a lady offers you a 200 pesos for a shirt, know that the acceptable price is most likely closer to 125 pesos. Be playful and be reasonable so that everybody wins.

✓ Tip Your Salon Lady or Restaurant Server

Tipping isn't always customary in Mexico. But when it comes to beauty services and restaurants, a 10-15% tip is appreciated.

✓ Ask for your Bill

Maybe you want five more beers! The server won't drop your check until you ask for it! When you're ready for your bill, you can say, "La cuenta, por favor".

✓ Use Airbnb Experience Tours

Jungle hikes. Surf lessons. Food tours. I love to Link up with locals excited to show you around their backyard via Airbnb Experiences. Tours are with love and the profits go directly to those who deserve em'.

✓ Practice the Safe Code BEFORE Locking the Safe

Before you put your belongings in your room's safe, practice the code. You can reset a safe code with the button inside the safe, near the hinge of the door. Always reset the safe, enter you pin and then practice opening and closing the safe a couple of times before you lock your stuff in there. OH and make sure the safe keys aren't INSIDE the safe

Okay, you are no longer at risk of being a naive tourist. You, my darling, are ready to plan!

the Puerto Vallarta Airport Guide

To get to Banderas Bay, there's just one airport to fly into: PVR (Puerto Vallarta). It's a small airport making it relatively quick to get from the gate, out the door and vice versa.

BUT there are some survival tips you need to know so that you don't get lost or scammed on the way.

THE LAYOUT:

The Puerto Vallarta Airport has two terminals, A and B. Terminal A is usually used for domestic flights and Terminal B is used for international flights. These terminals are in the same building and connected by a hallway. This airport is super easy to navigate.

Arriving in Puerto Vallarta

HERE ARE THE STEPS TO FOLLOW WHEN FLYING TO PUERTO VALLARTA, STARTING JUST BEFORE YOU LAND.

Note: At the time this book was published, you do not need a COVID test to enter Mexico.

STEP 1: FILL OUT YOUR ARRIVAL CARD
AND THE DECLARATIONS CARD

On the flight, the flight attendant will hand you an arrival form that asks you to fill out basic information like your name, passport number, how long you're staying and your address in Mexico.

How long you're staying can be up to 6 months (on a tourist visa). If you don't know the exact date you're leaving, just write the date 1-2 months from your arrival date.

Your address in Mexico is your hotel, Airbnb, etc.

And they'll ask for your flight number which is on your boarding pass.

Your flight attendant will also hand you a Declaration Form that asks you if you're bringing over a liter of alcohol, tobacco, uncooked meat/plant products and/or commercial quantity of something. I recommend you don't do that and pack light.

STEP 2: SCAN THE COVID APP

At some point in the airport, you'll be asked to scan a COVID app and answer some questions about COVID contact.

STEP 3: LAND AND PASS IMMIGRATION

Follow the crowd to the immigration counters. When it's your turn, the immigration officers will ask for your arrival card, your passport, and may ask you some basic questions like how long you're staying and what you're doing here. An easy answer is to just tell you're on vacation. They might ask for specific plans, and after you've read this book, you'll have a little bucket list of what you want to do.

Important! Do not tell the immigration officers "I don't know yet" or "I want to live here" because that requires a different visa. I've made this mistake before and the lady stamped my visa saying that I had to leave after three months, instead of six months! So have a plan for this immigration moment.

STEP 4: COLLECT YOUR BAGS AT BAGGAGE CLAIM

STEP 5: GO THROUGH CUSTOMS

And hand the officers your Declaration Card. Depending on where you're coming from, you might be asked to press a button! Ooo fun! This is the customs lottery! If the button gives a green light, you can pass through. If it gives a red light, the officers will ask to inspect your bags.

STEP 6: ENTER THE SHARK TANK

After customs, pass through the sliding glass doors and enter the arrival hall, also known as the "Shark Tank".

Why the Shark Tank? Because you, my darling, are the innocent minnow in a sea of timeshare salesmen and taxi drivers who are ready to devour you. These guys will try to trick you in every way in order to get you to talk to them. They might ask you for your hotel reservation documents or offer you free transportation. Just ignore them.

Repeat After Me: **DO NOT ENGAGE. KEEP WALKING.**

STEP 7: GET MONEY, HONEY

The only thing you need to do now is go to the ATM machine in the arrival hall. You'll spot them quickly. Take out some cash to get you started on your trip. I usually take out 1000-3000 pesos (or $50 - $150 USD). I'll explain more in the money section on page 37.

Pro Airport Money Tip: Don't exchange money at an exchange counter in the airport. You get better rates at an ATM, bank or a money exchange counter in the city.

STEP 8: GET A RIDE

Taxi drivers are expensive at the airport and Uber is not allowed in the airport. So how do you get a ride?

Here are the options I recommend for getting from the PVR airport to your accommodation.

◊ *Option 1: Arrange a driver beforehand*

Have a driver waiting to pick you up with your name on a sign and everything! #YouFancy. To do this, you can...

 ➤ Arrange Pick-Up Online Here

➤ Get a private driver by checking out the quick list of private drivers in my Girls in Puerto Vallarta Facebook Group here

➤ Arrange Pick-Up with Your Hotel

◊ *Option 2: Walk Outside the airport to Get an Uber or InDriver*

Don't have WIFI yet? Order the Uber and drop your pin at Tacón de Marlin. Walk outside the airport parking lot, go left and walk over the highway on the pedestrian bridge. Go to Tacón de Marlin restaurant. Have your Uber pick you up there.

◊ **Option 3: Take an Airport Taxi.**

This might be the most convenient option if you have lots of luggage and don't want to walk to get an Uber.

See the booth in the arrival hall that says Taxi Autorizado"? Go there and they'll arrange your ride from the airport to your hotel or Airbnb. The airport taxis are "authorized" fixed prices according to which zone you're going.

Pay in pesos. You'll be handed a ticket. Walk out to the curb where the taxis are lined up. The taxi manager will take your ticket and assign you a taxi.

Have 1-3 people in your group? You'll be put in a car. 4 or more? You're getting a van.

Have exactly 4 people and little luggage? Negotiate for a car.

➤ Here are the general airport taxi rates for reference.

FROM PVR AIRPORT TO:	TAXI (1-3 PEOPLE)	VAN (UP TO 3 PEOPLE)	COLLECTIVE SERVICE
NUEVO VALLARTA	$25 USD	$49 USD	$10 USD
FLAMINGOS	$30 USD	$58 USD	$11 USD
BUCERIAS	$32 USD	$68 USD	$11 USD
LA CRUZ DE HUANACAXTLE	$63 USD	$90 USD	--
PUNTA MITA	$97 USD	$144 USD	--
SAYULITA	$100 USD	$147 USD	--
SAN PANCHO	$132 USD	$168 USD	--

◇ *Option 4: Street Taxi*

You can find street taxis as you exit the arrival hall or outside Tacón de Marlin. This is a little cheaper than the option above but still, not my favorite as these guys are old school and don't always use GPS to find your hotel (ie. more likely to get lost). There are easier options.

◇ *Option 5: City Bus*

Up for an adventure? Traveling super duper cheap? Not in a hurry? Packing light? Cool. Head towards Tacón de Marlin again, cross the street and wait for the bus marked "Zona Romantica" or "Centro" if you're going to Puerto Vallarta. Buses come every 25-30 minutes and cost 25 pesos ($1 USD).

Leaving from the Puerto Vallarta Airport

Time to leave Puerto Vallarta? NO! Don't go.

But okay, if you insist. Here's what you need to know.

STEP 1. YOU NEED A COVID TEST

 Watch my "How to Get a COVID Test in Puerto Vallarta Before You Fly" video here.

✈ Going to America? You need an Antigen test. These results will be ready in 45 minutes.

✈ Going to Canada or anywhere else? You need a PCR test. These results take up to 48 hours.

Pro Tip! As you'll see in my YouTube Video "Where to Get a COVID Test in Puerto Vallarta", your airlines might allow you the chance to upload your COVID results to their app, which makes the check-in process smoother.

STEP 2: FILL OUT THE COVID DECLARATION FORM

Your airlines will send you this before you fly or you can scan a QR code at the airport and fill it out there.

STEP 3: CHECK IN

They'll ask for your passport and COVID documents (airline app verification and/or paper).

Pro Tip:

You don't have to hang out at this tiny airport after you check in. Either head to the priority pass lounge upstairs for beer and snacks (sign up for Priority Pass in this code) or head outside the airport to Tacón de Marlin for a last bite to eat - because the airport doesn't have many exciting food options.

And that's it.

LET'S GET TO
PLANNING YOUR BIG TRIP!

BUT FIRST...

ALWAYS REMEMBER...

THAT YOU ARE BRAVER THAN YOU THINK,

STRONGER THAN YOU KNOW, AND SMARTER THAN YOU

BELIEVE.

STILL NEED A PEP TALK?

REACH OUT TO ME ON INSTAGRAM

@SOLOGIRLSTRAVELGUIDE

CHAPTER ONE

Puerto Vallarta

—

TIME NEEDED:

4 days to 1 month (or infinite expat life)

KNOWN FOR:

All-Inclusive Resorts, Gay-Friendly Zones, Solo Female
Expats, Water Sports and Boat Tours

HIDDEN GEMS:

Street Food, Hiking, Quiet Beach Coves, Under-Explored
Neighborhoods, a Top-Notch Beauty Industry

MEET PUERTO VALLARTA

When my American friends think of Puerto Vallarta, they think of all-inclusive resorts and cheesy touristy activities. And they're not wrong but they're also not completely right. There is so much more to this city than the tourist path - you just need to know where to look.

Puerto Vallarta is home to some of my favorite street food in all of Mexico. Get lost in the local villages behind the town center and see what day-to-day local life looks like. Take a hike into the jungles to big waterfalls with pools below. Dive beneath the surface with a vast array of marine species like humpback whales, sea turtles, manta rays and even dolphins that live and play all around the islands of this mini-archipelago.

You can take a super easy vacation by staying in an all-inclusive resort and never leaving, or you can visit Puerto Vallarta's hidden gems and get the local experience. Personally, I'm a fan of both. And in this chapter, I'm going to give you both.

But first, a story about the amazing expat community here.

Before I even landed in Puerto Vallarta, I had made a friend in a Facebook group after asking for private driver recommendations. An hour after getting off my bus, I went to meet my new expat girlfriend, Tiffany, and her expat girlfriends for breakfast! As we sat there, nearly every other person that passed by got a hey, how are you? or a see you tonight! I was blown away by the sense of travel-community that flowed through the city center. And that was all it took to ignite my social life from day one! Within 48 hours, I'd been invited to a villa party on the beach, to live music, to secret taco spots, and best of all, to Costco.

You can have it all in Puerto Vallarta. So, got your suit on? Let's go on vacation!

Areas to Know

FOR VACATION...

1. MARINA
2. HOTEL ZONE
3. PITILLAL
4. CINCO DE DICIEMBRE
5. THE MALECON
6. CENTRO
7. ZONA ROMANTICA
8. MISMALOYA
9. BOCA DE TOMATLÁN

MARINA

A beautiful boat marina lined with sports bars and spas. Marina is a pretty place to walk around if you're in the area, but not really a "destination" unless you're coming here to visit MedSpa or to see the local crocodile that hangs out at the head of the marina.

HOTEL ZONE

The big, all-inclusive resorts live here, along with La Isla Mall that is home to H&M, Sephora, Starbucks and the other bougie shopping spots, just 10 minutes from the airport.

PITILLAL

This local neighborhood is street-food heaven located just east of the hotel-zone. It's five x five blocks of local food, shops, and the beautiful San Miguel Arcangel Cathedral and Square that is definitely worth a visit if you consider yourself a foodie. Start at Mariscos Pichi II and walk around from there.

CINCO DE DICIEMBRE

Or 5 December, this area has tons of Airbnbs, food and shops, and even Playa Camarones Beach which is easily accessed by walking or from beach clubs and restaurants.

THE MALECON

The long walking street along the beach which is lined with shops, artisans, vendors, performers and restaurants (and Mcdonalds).

CENTRO

Gastronomy central. The center of the city is unsurprisingly home to the best restaurants, shopping, and entertainment in Puerto Vallarta. The center of town is located just north of the river, which is where the Malecon begins! You can walk up Iturbe street to get the best view of the city here or get dropped off at Plaza de Armas to begin your foot-exploration.

ZONA ROMANTICA

Cross the river and you're in the very beautiful and very gay Zona Romantica (Romantic Zone) or sometimes called Emiliano Zapata. Here you'll find lively nightlife and gorgeous hotels filled with gay men and straight girls! From here, you can also access the public beach, Playa de Los Muertos. You'll also hear of micro-neighborhoods in this zone called Olas Altas, South Side, Emilio Zapato and Basilio Badillo (home to tons of great restaurants if you feel like exploring on foot).

MISMALOYA

This little cove is located about 40 minutes south of the Romantic Zone. Use Mismaloya Beach as your jumping off spot to visit the islands (Mariettas, Las Animas, etc). Or stay and hang out; the beachfront is lined with restaurants where you can rent a table and umbrellas for around 300 pesos for the day! To get here, take an Uber (200 pesos) or catch the orange bus at the corner of Badillo x Constitucion for 10 pesos.

BOCA DE TOMATLÁN

Here you'll find gorgeous beaches and scenery as the mountains of the Sierra Madre Occidental jet out over the Pacific Ocean, creating hidden coves and gorgeous views. Located about 30 minutes south of Puerto Vallarta by bus, this tiny town is famous for two things: boat taxis and hiking. Many DIY adventures will begin by taking a boat from this little cove. And if you're into long hikes with scenic views and hidden beaches, Boca de Tomatlan is worth a visit. Wanna hike? Here's a quick trail map with beaches to stop by.

MOVING TO PUERTO VALLARTA? HERE ARE SOME EXTRA EXPAT AREAS YOU SHOULD KNOW ABOUT.

Areas to Know

FOR LONGER STAYS...

1 FLUVIAL

2 VERSAILLES

3 ARAMARA

4 RAMBALES

5 LOWER ALTA VISTA

6 CONCHAS CHINAS

7 EL NOGALITO

FLUVIAL

One of the hot and upcoming neighborhoods for women and families at the moment. It's home to some of my favorite spas, nail salons and shopping centers that stretch up to La Isla Mall.

VERSAILLES

Again, another trending area for expats. I like Versailles because you're close to all the bougie amenities but still get a taste of local life. You're right between fluvial and Cinco de Diciembre which makes for a really easy balance between social and solo time.

ARAMARA

One of my good friends lives in this neighborhood, close to Walmart and Sam's Club. You get more bang for your buck in this little residential suburb, so if you're looking for a bigger house and plan to rent or buy a car, this location is suitable for you.

RAMBALES

Located behind 5 December is this less expensive neighborhood that is still walking distance to local shops and restaurants.

LOWER ALTA VISTA

About four blocks back from the beach, behind Zona Romantica is this conveniently located neighborhood which still gives you access to downtown sunsets and fireworks, but keeps you tucked away from the tourist scene.

➤ You can also check out Aralias 2 to live like a local.

EL NOGALITO

Five more minutes south of Conchas Chinas, El Nogalito is quaint and quiet with small shops, access to Playa Punta Negra beach, and beautiful hikes. You can easily travel in and out of town with bus access!

CONCHAS CHINAS

A six-minute drive down the highway from the Romantic Zone is this beautiful neighborhood where many expats choose to live. That quick freeway drive makes Conchas Chinas close enough to all the fun of Puerto Vallarta center but far enough from the tourists. You can find unobstructed views of the ocean here but with that comes higher rent! Conchas Chinas is one of the more expensive areas to live.

Fun Fact! It's said that Puerto Vallarta is filled with Ley Lines, energetic lines that bring peace and healing energy. Many women say that Puerto Vallarta calls them. If you feel the same call, it might just be the Ley Lines.

PHOTO / ANA PERDOMO

Islands
& Beaches

TO EXPLORE...

1

2

3
4

5

6
7

8

PLAYA DEL HOLI

This is the Hotel Zone Beach where the big all-inclusive resorts like The Hilton and The Sheraton sit on this big, long, sandy beach with little shallow spots where you can swim. Expect lots of vendors on this beach trying to sell you hats and hammocks!

ROSITA BEACH

This is the Malecon's beach! The big walking street lines the ocean where you can access this beach, and also restaurants overlooking this beach where you can catch epic sunset views.

Pro Tip: Bring a little sunset picnic or a sunset beer.

PLAYA LOS MUERTOS

The most popular beach in Puerto Vallarta is easy to access, is the best for people watching and is decent for swimming when the tide is right. It's super convenient to access this beach from the Malecon (just to the left of the pinnacle) but as you can imagine, this beach gets crowded at peak hours!

Beach Hop Alert!

Playa Los Muertos > Las Amapas > Conchas Chinas Beach

There's a path from the south end of Los Muertos beach that takes you over a rocky formation called El Pulpito and down onto this tiny hidden beach called Las Amapas. Walk to the south end of Las Amapas and you'll find a path to Conchas Chinas Beach.

LAS AMAPAS

An intimate beach located just south of the Romantic Zone with soft golden sand, gentle waves and emerald green waters! This is a hidden beach that not many tourists know about so take advantage of your alone time by bringing a picnic and some towels to set up under a shady tree for an hour or two.

CONCHAS CHINAS

Come splash around in the tiny blue pools nestled under the unique rock formation on this tiny beach. There is a cove of sand where you can lay, but it's small so plan on spending just a little bit of time here and then walk to one of the restaurants nearby. To reach this beach, you can either walk the path mentioned above or get on the orange bus, tell the driver "Conchas Chinas" and depart by the OXXO located right before Sagitario Street.

PLAYA PALMARES

I wouldn't have noticed this beach as I was driving past if it weren't for the locals carrying down folding chairs and coolers. Playa Palmares is a local spot located just before Mismaloya. The water is clear but the beach does get a bit crowded with local families. Come early in the morning and you're winning at life. To get here, get on the orange bus to Mismaloya, tell the driver "Playa Palmares".

PLAYA GEMELAS

This beach is so pretty that you have to plan your visit strategically to avoid the crowds. Weekdays are best when you can swim in peace! Vendors will come by offering your drinks and snacks at fair beach prices. And Pro Tip: the big condo on site has a restaurant by the pool, just tell the security guards you're going to the restaurant and they'll usually let you through. Bring towels! To get here, head to Girasol Sur Condominium by bus or Uber. The entrance leads to some stairs that go down to the beach. When in doubt, ask someone to point out the entrance.

MISMALOYA

It's a small beach. It's sometimes a crowded beach. But it's one of my favorite beaches to spend the day. This little cove beach is located about 30 minutes south of the Romantic Zone and is lined with little restaurants that will give you a chair as long as you buy something! Check out Restaurant Teo's or Ramada Camarena. I like this beach because it's relatively easy to access for a lazy day trip. To get there, take the orange bus for 10 pesos or an Uber for around 200 pesos.

Feeling less lazy? From this beach, you can rent a water taxi to take you to Los Arcos to snorkel amongst some of the most interesting biodiversity in the area.

THE NEXT BEACHES REQUIRE AN ADVENTURE BY BUS, WATER TAXI OR HIKE.

To reach these beaches, you will either start at Los Muertos Pier in Puerto Vallarta or in a tiny town 30-minutes south called Boca de Tomatlan.

Refer to this transportation info as you plan your trip.

How to Get to Boca De Tomatlan:

> **Option 1:** Take a 30-minute orange bus from the PVR corner of Basilio Badillo and Calle Constitution in front of the OXXO. Buses leave every 10 to 15 minutes.

> **Option 2:** Take a 40-minute water taxi from Playa de Los Muertos for 160 pesos one way.

WATER TAXI TO YELAPA, QUIMIXTO AND LAS ANIMAS

Simply tell the boat captain where you're going. Buy a one-way ticket. You can buy your return ticket at your destination. Less stressful this way.

◇ Departing From Boca de Tomatlan (more flexible time table)

Every 30 minutes for 200 pesos per person.

◇ Departing From Los Muertos Pier in Puerto Vallarta

Monday - Saturday: 10am, 11am, 11:45am, 3pm, 5pm

Sundays: 10, 11am, 1pm, 3pm and 5pm

Round Trip: 320 pesos

One Way: 160 pesos

> *Note!* The Last Water Taxi Returns around at 6pm

For Info on How to Hike from Boca de Tomatlan to Las Animas, see the hiking section on page 105.

More Beaches...

CABALLO BEACH

One of the most unspoiled beaches you'll find in the area is this gorgeous palm-tree lined beach called Caballo Beach. To get here, hike from Boca de Tomatlan. To get a boat back to town, hike down to Las Animas beach (about 2 hours). Or hike over from Las Animas.

LAS ANIMAS

A stunning beach with turquoise water where you can spend the day lounging, reading, and swimming. Just like Mismaloya, Las Animas is lined with restaurants that will offer you beach chairs when you buy something. Want an extra adventure? Find the trail at the north end of the beach and hike over to Caballo Beach, another hidden gem beach!

To get to Las Animas, you can take a boat taxi from Mismaloya, Boca de Tomatlan or Playa de Los Muertos. You can also hike from Boca de Tomatlan, or jump on a boat tour with Chica Loco Tours (Sayulita/La Cruz) or Ally Cat (Puerto Vallarta).

The water taxi from Boca de Tomatlan to Las Animas should be 50 pesos. To get back, take a 50-peso water taxi back to Boca de Tomatlan and catch the bus into town.

QUIMIXTO

The ultimate day trip for explorers that involve a boat, a beach, a waterfall and a horse. From Boca de Tomatlan, take a water taxi (80-100 pesos per person) to Quimixto. Buy a one-way ticket, not round trip! When you arrive, you'll be approached by the horse dude. He'll set you up with a horse for 250 pesos that will trek you through the jungle to the waterfall. Note that there is a restaurant before the waterfall where its obligatory that you buy something.

Afterwards, you can swim in the waterfall and if you dare, jump off the side of the cliff and swing with the big rope that throws you into the waters below. Afterwards, chill at the beach and when you're ready, buy a boat ticket home. Just be prepared, you might spend 200 pesos on the boat ride back but I recommend trying to haggle them to 100. Just don't lose your breath over it.

YELAPA

You will hear people talking about the waterfall in Yelapa, but many people don't realize that Yelapa is actually a quaint, walkable beach town that is only accessible by boat! The beach is touristy, I'll admit. It's covered in beach chairs from the restaurants but the restaurants are yummy, the chairs provide shade and the water is just steps away! After your Pina Colada, walk around the town and hike up to the waterfall. If you don't want to do a DIY trip, the boat companies mentioned in this trip offer day trips to Yelapa.

Pro Tip! To get the beach all to yourself, stay the night in Yelapa. Water Taxi service stops at sunset so you'll get the beach for the evening and morning minus the tourists!

MARIETAS ISLAND

A protected marine sanctuary and an enigma of a beach cave with a hole in the ceiling, Marietas is a must. As this is a Marine Park protected by UNESCO, only licensed boats can access Marietas with a limit of 116 people per day from Wednesday through Sunday.

The way to see Marietas Island is to jump on a boat tour with Ally Cat Sailing (Puerto Vallarta/Sayulita) or do a private trip with Off The Grid Mexico - Tours & Excursions on Facebook. Phew, that was a lot of beaches. Hope you brought sunscreen.

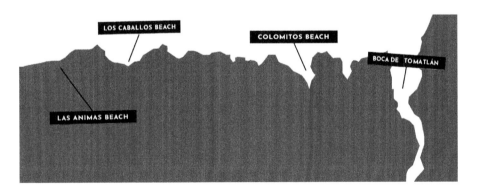

LOS CABALLOS BEACH

COLOMITOS BEACH

BOCA DE TOMATLÁN

LAS ANIMAS BEACH

HOW TO MOVE AROUND PUERTO VALLARTA

I recommend…

UBER

Know that Uber is easy to find in the city center but not always easy to find in the outskirts.

INDRIVER

More drivers everywhere! This is my rideshare go-to.

PRIVATE DRIVERS

Check out the list of Private Drivers in Girls in Puerto Vallarta here

BUS

The bus system in Vallarta is an easy and cheap way to get around within the city and between cities!

> ➤ To ride within the city or down to Mismaloya area, most trips start at Basilio Badillo & Constitution near the OXXO convenience store.

> ➤ To ride between cities, most trips start at the big bus stop in front of Walmart & Sam's Club. There will be a man with a clipboard there to help you get on the correct bus.

Use 1Map.com/routes to find your route.

If you want even more details, this article is extremely helpful:

Pro Tip... for taking the bus: To ask the driver to alert you when you've arrived at your destination, say this phrase: "Me puede avisar dónde bajar para ir a _____?").

Bonus! Check out the Hop-on-Hop-Off Bus on page 104.

WATER TAXIS

"Pangas" are the quick zippy boats that will take you to the off-the-beaten-path beaches!

Here are rates and timetables to refer back to as you plan your adventures.

◇ *For Yelapa, Las Animas, and Quimixto*

The Water Taxis will pick up anybody that is waiting at a pick-up pier no matter where you got dropped off, which is why I want you to only buy a 1-way ticket (especially if you're hiking and exploring).

Water Taxis from Puerto Vallarta are 380 pesos roundtrip and only includes bags you can carry. Have extra luggage? They might charge you a little extra.

PUERTO VALLARTA TO YELAPA

TIME	LOCATION	BOAT TYPE	COMMENTS
11am	Los Muertos Pier	Water Taxi	With Stops
11:45 a.m. (except Sundays)	Los Muertos Pier	Water Taxi	With Stops
3pm	Los Muertos Pier	Water Taxi	With Stops

YELAPA TO PUERTO VALLARTA

TIME	LOCATION	BOAT TYPE	COMMENTS
7:45am (except Sundays)	Playita Pier /Beach / Hotel Pier	Water Taxi	With Stops
9:30am	Playita Pier /Beach / Hotel Pier	Water Taxi	With Stops
12pm	Playita Pier /Beach / Hotel Pier	Water Taxi	With Stops

BOCA DE TOMATLAN TO YELAPA

TIME	LOCATION	BOAT TYPE	COMMENTS
8am	Pier Beach	Water Taxi	With Stops
9am	Pier Beach	Water Taxi	With Stops
10am	Pier Beach	Water Taxi	With Stops
11am	Pier Beach	Water Taxi	With Stops
12pm	Pier Beach	Water Taxi	With Stops
1pm	Pier Beach	Water Taxi	With Stops
2pm	Pier Beach	Water Taxi	With Stops
3pm	Pier Beach	Water Taxi	With Stops
4pm	Pier Beach	Water Taxi	With Stops

TIME	LOCATION	BOAT TYPE	COMMENTS
5pm	Pier Beach	Water Taxi	With Stops
6pm	Pier Beach	Water Taxi	With Stops
6:30pm	Pier Beach	Water Taxi	With Stops

YELAPA TO BOCA DE TOMATLAN

TIME	LOCATION	BOAT TYPE	COMMENTS
8am	Playita Pier /Beach / Hotel Pier	Water Taxi	With Stops
9am	Playita Pier /Beach / Hotel Pier	Water Taxi	With Stops
10am	Playita Pier /Beach / Hotel Pier	Water Taxi	With Stops
11am	Playita Pier /Beach / Hotel Pier	Water Taxi	With Stops
12pm	Playita Pier /Beach / Hotel Pier	Water Taxi	With Stops
1pm	Playita Pier /Beach / Hotel Pier	Water Taxi	With Stops
2pm	Playita Pier /Beach / Hotel Pier	Water Taxi	With Stops
3pm	Playita Pier /Beach / Hotel Pier	Water Taxi	With Stops
4pm	Playita Pier /Beach / Hotel Pier	Water Taxi	With Stops

Alexa's Top 10's

FOR PUERTO VALLARTA

TOP 10 MUST-DO EXPERIENCES

01 Whale Watching Between January and March
02 Street Food Tour with Vallarta Food Tour
03 Boat Tour to Marietas Island with Ally Cat Sailing
04 Horseback Ride to Quimixto Waterfall
05 Zip Line with Canopy River
06 Horseback Riding and Tequila Tasting
07 Yelapa Waterfall Hike
08 Spa Day at MedSpa
09 Cooking Class
10 Drag Show

TOP 10 PLACES TO EAT

01 Tacos de Birria Chanfay – *Order Birria Tacos*
02 El Brujo – *Order the Soft Shell Crab Enchiladas*
03 Hacienda San Angel – *Go for Brunch*
04 Panchos Tacos – *Order the Alhambra Plate*
05 Barcelona Tapas – *Order the Paella*
06 Tacon de Marlin – *Order the Marlin Burrito*
07 Pepes Tacos, Puerto Vallarta – *Order anything al Pastor*
08 Taqueria "El Moreno", Puerto Vallarta – *Order Quesadillas con Carne*
09 Camarón en Barro – *Order the Aguachiles*
10 El Pechugon – *Order the best Rotisserie Chicken in the world, take it home*

Alexa's BEAUTY GUIDE TO PUERTO VALLARTA

◊ **BEST LUXURY MASSAGE & BODY SCRUB**

MedSpa - Make an appointment a few days ahead

🌐 www.medspa.com.mx

◊ **BEST FACIAL**

MedSp - Make an appointment a few days ahead

🌐 www.medspa.com.mx

◊ **BEST AT-HOME MASSAGE**

Betty

She comes to you with a massage table and oils!

📱 WhatsApp +322 122 5713

➤ Tell her Alexa West sent you for a 75-minute massage for 1,000 pesos

◊ **BEST MANICURES AND PEDICURES**

Uñas Norma - Locations in Marina, Fluvial, and Caracol

♥ @unasnorma

◊ **BEST HAIR SALON**

Salon Malecon - See Luis for a color, cut and a Brazilian Blowout

♥ @salonmalecon

◊ **BEST WAXING**

Artepil Spa - Locations in Fluvial and Marina

♥ @artepilspa

◊ **BEST EYEBROW MICROBLADING**

Adriano - I'm obsessed with my new eyebrows! Adriano doesn't speak English, but it wasn't a problem for me as her uncle helps her translate.

♥ @adrianomicroblading

◊ **BEST ENGLISH-SPEAKING EYEBROW MICROBLADING**

Gigi - Another great eyebrow option

♥ @gigiyarden

WHERE TO STAY IN PUERTO VALLARTA

Since the beginning of time, I've been booking my accommodations through Booking.com because they offer free cancelations on most properties and their reviews are verified. Scan the QR codes in this guide to book.

All-Inclusive Resorts ———————

HILTON HACIENDA

The aforementioned adults-only resort where you absolutely must book the private swim-out pool room! This hotel has a sexy, almost Vegas-vibe to it with a social swim-up pool bar, a glamourous Turkish style second pool, a grand library and a social restaurant right next to the pool.

Stay here and you have access to all the amenities at the big Hilton resort including the O'West Lounge, the restaurants, the gym and the beachfront lounge chairs!

- 💵 **Budget:** $$
- 📍 **Where:** Hotel Zone
- 🏨 **Address:** Av. de las Garzas 136-1

 BOOK HERE

Covid Pro Tip!

The nicer resorts and hotels often include your COVID test for free, meaning that they will pay for it and arrange it for you. Ask when you check in so that you can properly schedule before you fly out.

THE HILTON

My top pick for an affordable all-inclusive resort BUT only if you book the right room and know where to hang out. Let me tell you the secrets. You want to book a hot tub room facing the ocean. And you want to hang out at the adults-only O'West Sushi Lounge on the 4th story rooftop with a pool overlooking the water! The other adults-only pool is a couple steps next door at the Hilton Hacienda where you can get poolside service and hang-out at the swim-up bar in peace with no splashing children in sight. There are 5 restaurants on site (make reservations for both the day before), a spa, a Starbucks (free classic coffees) and a free guided kayak tour in the mornings. Make your dinner reservations and kayak reservations a day before!

Budget: $$$

Where: Hotel Zone

Address: Av. de las Garzas 136

Contact: @hiltonpvr

 BOOK HERE

PHOTO / ALEXA WEST

VILLAS PREMIER BOUTIQUE

Adults Only!

A super-favorite among expats who live in the area. When their friends and family come to town, they often recommend staying at Villa Premiere Boutique Hotel. The honeymoon suite has a hot tub and a hammock on the patio where you will spend most of your time! However, the simpler rooms are perfectly comfortable and still give you the entire experience of staying at a beachfront hotel with all the luxury amenities such as the spa with oxygen bar and pillow menu! The biggest selling point of Villa Premiere? The location. You can walk everywhere, including the Malecon just a few blocks away. And hey pro tip, Villa Premiere is the adults-only sister to Buenaventura Grand, so when given the choice, choose this one if you don't have kiddos.

💸 **Budget:** $$

📍 **Where:** 5 de Diciembre

🏛 **Address:** San Salvador 117

 BOOK HERE

HILTON FIESTA AMERICANA PUERTO VALLARTA

Adults Only!

Hilton Fiesta is off-the-beaten-path, far away from the tourist zone and instead, nestled into nature on one of the best swimming beaches in the entire bay. If you plan to hike, visit waterfalls, take water taxis to explore tiny villages, you are right around the corner from Mismaloya which can be used as a jumping off point. Or don't leave at all. Stay and enjoy the spa with massages and plunge pools and then move on to the swim up bar. Everything you need for a reset is here.

💸 **Budget:** $$$$

📍 **Where:** South, Between Puerto Vallarta and Mismaloya

🏛 **Address:** Hwy Barra de Navidad km 4.5-Sur

 BOOK HERE

MARRIOTT PUERTO VALLARTA

All Inclusive Optional

Solo girls, groups of girls and couples who are looking for a fun vacation without breaking the bank, this one's for you. The Marriott will keep you buzzed during your entire vacation with a ceviche bar, a sports bar, a lobby bar, and a bar by the beach. You can opt in for an all-inclusive stay or go ala-carte, but if you plan on drinking the days away, go all-inclusive. Oh, and did I mention that the Marriott is known for having one of the best ocean view pools in the entire city? You will love laying by this pool and are sure to leave with a golden tan (and tan lines). Don't forget to treat yourself to a massage on the beach while you're here.

Price: $$$

Where: Marina Vallarta

Address: Paseo La Marina Norte 435

 BOOK HERE

Hotels & Hostels

CASA KIMBERLY

Elizabeth Taylor's former palace is over-the-top beautiful. Casa Kimberly was a gift to Elizabeth Taylor from her beau, Richard Burton, (who she married and divorced twice). And now it's your turn to be pampered like Elizabeth in this chic boutique hotel with crystal chandeliers, pink marble bathtubs, a gorgeous pool and spa. Today, there are nine luxury suites, each with a private patio and a private hot tub. The location is romantic, the decor is breathtaking and the food at The Iguana Restaurant & Tequila Bar on-site is legendary. Want to stay at Richard Burton's casa? Hacienda San Angel is just down the street.

Budget: $$$$

Where: Centro

Address: Calle Zaragoza 445

 BOOK HERE

LAS ALAMANDAS

Are you willing to drive 2.5 hours from the airport in order to reach paradise? Featured in The New York Times, LA Times, and Conde Nast Traveler, Las Alamandas is a slice of vacation heaven worth every penny. Situated on 1,500 acres of unspoiled nature reserve, you and only 16-other suite guests get to enjoy private white sand beaches, nature hikes, horseback riding, kayaking and sweet-water lagoons that will take your breath away.

🏷 **Budget:** $$$$

📍 **Where:** Las Alamandas

🏨 **Address:** Federal Hway 200 Km. 82

 BOOK HERE

PHOTO / BOOKING.COM

Fun Fact!

The name, Bahia de Banderas, comes from when the Spaniards came to explore this area, they were met with the indigenous tribes carrying thousands of colorful flags.

VILLA LALA BOUTIQUE HOTEL

Boca de Tomatlan's most magical treehouse hotel is surrounded by nature and serenity. The property is small and private, so expect to be doted upon by the lovely staff. Stay in the charming suit or go for the private pool villa overlooking the ocean. The location is about 45-minutes from Puerto Vallarta center, but if you plan on taking the water taxis to secluded beaches like Las Animas, Yelapa or Cochintos, you're just a short walk from the panga pier! On your laid-back days, take the free kayaks for a spin to spot dolphins and whales.

🏷️ **Budget:** $$$
📍 **Where:** Boca de Tomatlán
🚉 **Address:** Carretera Barra de Navidad Km. 16 No. 5696

 BOOK HERE

XINALANI RETREAT

Looking to unplug and recenter? This yoga retreat is isolated and only accessible by boat, 12 miles south of the airport. Spend your days eating clean, doing yoga, hiking and playing on the water with paddle boards and surf boards. However, don't expect luxury. Expect more of a nature experience one step up from glamping. The rooms are breezy with hammocks and mosquito nets, but stylish like a Pinterest board. Xinalani Retreat is very solo female friendly. Don't be surprised if you meet a couple solo gal pals while you're here. And just a little FYI: three meals a day are included, but it's not "all-inclusive" when it comes to drinks and snacks. Sneak a bottle of wine and some snacks over with ya!

🏷️ **Budget:** $$
📍 **Where:** Boca de Tomatlán
🚉 **Address:** Playa Xinalani

 BOOK HERE

CASA MARIA MALECON

Budget but beautiful! Splashes of pink and yellow with vibrant Mexican murals covering the walls, the beds, the mirrors! Happiness and fun dance through the halls of Casa Maria Malecon. It's got Malecon in the name as you can walk to the Malecon and the beach just two blocks away! Oh and "casa" means house, or "guesthouse" in this case! Here you'll have a host (Hi, Abraham) to look after you and give you all the tips, advice, and support you need during your stay in Puerto Vallarta! Be sure to spend some time swinging in the hammocks on the rooftop while you read this book!

🏷️ *Budget:* $$
📍 *Where:* Boca de Tomatlán
🏛️ *Address:* Carretera Federal 200 Km. 82

 BOOK HERE

HOTEL BOUTIQUE RIVERA DEL RIO

One of the strangest hotels I've ever stayed in, yet one of the most memorable. Hotel Boutique Rivera Del Rio screams old Hollywood glamour and has been featured in Vouge and Italian Elle Magazine. The rooms are peculiarly tucked away in separate corners of the house and often require a walk down a winding staircase. Just go with it.

Enjoy a welcome margarita, then put your bags down and head to the emerald pool or the rooftop hot tub overlooking the city where I found it very easy to make friends. If you have an open mind, I recommend staying here for 1 or 2 nights just for the experience and history.

🏷️ *Price:* starting $89
📍 *Where:* Romantic Zone
🏛️ *Address:* Rivera del Río 104

 BOOK HERE

CHANCLAS HOSTEL MALECON

Nervous about making friends? Let the little Jack Russel Terrier who runs these halls be your first friend, and then hang out in the social areas like the rooftop terrace and make new human friends quickly! Stay in a (admittedly) super basic but comfortable private room or a dorm room.

Join in on daily group activities, boat trips, drinking games, and nights out on the town with other travelers who tend to be ages 30 and like to drink. Breakfast is included and the staff are always willing to help! And fun fact for you: Chanclas means "flip flops" or "sandals".

🎟 *Price:* $19
📍 *Where:* Boca de Tomatlán
🏛 *Address:* Carretera Federal 200 km 82

 BOOK HERE

OUTSITE PUERTO VALLARTA AND COWORK CAFE

Digital nomads, come hither. Finally, a hotel with internet speed fast enough for you to work and travel. This coworking hotel is a simple, clean, no-fuss (and no-frills) space for you to work during the day and explore the city on foot. Walk in any direction and you'll hit the best taco stands, markets, and bars. Staying here means that you don't have to deal with transportation or navigation; once you're here you're here. And bonus, one of the best Asian Fusion restaurants in town is located in the lobby, called Bonito Kitchen Bar.

🎟 *Price:* $ 45
📍 *Where:* Romantic Zone
🏛 *Address:* Calle Juárez 535

 BOOK HERE

RIVER BY THE SEA APARTMENTS

Cozy and affordable cabin style rooms on the river in Boca de Tomatlán. If you're an explorer on a budget (or even not on a budget), this charming hotel ticks all the boxes for a nature adventure that is one part relaxation and one part exploration. This place is great for a longer stay with good WIFI, a washing machine and a kitchen with all the amenities. Go for a long hike in the mountains just outside your door or take a boat to a waterfall for the day. When you return, it feels like you're returning home.

🏷️ **Price:** $ 45
📍 **Where:** Romantic Zone
🚏 **Address:** Calle Juárez 535

 BOOK HERE

HOTEL MOUSSAI

Tucked in the Sierra Madre Mountains on a private silky beach away from the hustle and bustle of the city, Hotel Mousai is an upscale getaway that I love! Sway in your balcony hammock with views of the oceans, indulge in the spa with massages and hydrotherapy, stuff your fancy face at the top-notch sushi bar and best of all, sip a sunset cocktail at the rooftop pool bar and lounge. This is what vacation is supposed to look like. And if you ever decide to put shoes on and leave the hotel, another perk of staying here is it's location near Mismaloya Beach where you can jump in a water taxi to the southern beaches like Yelapa and Las Animas.

🏷️ **Price:** $ 45
📍 **Where:** Romantic Zone
🚏 **Address:** Calle Juárez 535

 BOOK HERE

Airbnbs in Puerto Vallarta

If you're looking to hunker down in one spot for a week or more, you can often get more bang for your buck on Airbnb. You can find condos in big apartment complexes with pools next to the malls or you can find a tiny hidden gem of an apartment in local neighborhoods close to street food and churches. Take your pick.

⊕ Airbnb.com

How to Rent a House or an Apartment

Before you go hiring a real estate agent, check out the Expat Housing Facebook groups! There are many expats that live part-time in Puerto Vallarta and so their homes are already set up and ready for you to move in while they're out of the country!

If you do decide to work with a real estate agent, two things you should know:

1. The property owner pays for the agent fee, not you. Don't pay the agent anything.

2. Find a place you like? Make sure you speak to the owner to confirm the deal (not just the agent).

First, I recommend you peruse these Facebook Groups:

◊ Puerto Vallarta Today's Real Estate and Rentals Puerto Vallarta Yearly Rentals

◊ Puerto Vallarta Affordable Yearly Rentals!

◊ Puerto Vallarta & Beyond Expat Rentals & Sales

◊ Rentals In Puerto Vallarta for Locals and Long Term Visitors

◊ Renta De Casas Departamentos Y Locales en Puerto Vallarta

Next, try searching rental sites like Airbnb, VRBO and Vivanuncios.

Know that...

➤ Rentals are more expensive in the Romantic Zone and cheaper in outskirt neighborhoods like Conchas Chinas and Pitillal.

➤ Rentals are most expensive if you're shopping around in High-Season (Late November to Late March).

THINGS TO DO IN PUERTO VALLARTA

Top AirBnb Experiences

I am a huge fan of Airbnb experiences everywhere I travel. I love giving back to locals while seeing the area through a local's eyes. The list is never-ending but here is where to start!

01

Horseback Riding and Tequila Tasting

02

Bioluminescence Eco Experience Kayak & SUP

03

Hike to Yelapa Waterfall

04

The Arches Snorkel Photoshoot

05

I'll Be Your Personal Photographer in PV

To find them, simply use the QR codes above or type these keywords into Airbnb.com/experiences

Vallarta Local Food Tours

BY FOOD PHOTO TOURS

It's time to get your hands into some real local grub. For all my food and booze tours, I chose to explore with Vallarta Food Adventures led by the coolest local chick named Star. I walked away from my tours feeling smart, full, buzzed and cute! She teaches you about culture, takes you to the best taco stands, introduces you to alcohol you didn't know existed, and takes professional snapshots of your foodie adventure (so wear somethin' cute).

Here are my Top 3 Picks of
Vallarta Local Food Tours

◊ Mexico in Six Bottles
◊ Taco Tour in Old Town
◊ Off The Beaten Path in the Morning

💵 **Budget:** $$

📍 **Where:** Romantic Zone

🌐 https://foodandphototours.com/

🌐 www.vallartalocalfoodtours.com/

MEXICO IN SIX BOTTLES

There is more to drinking than just tequila! In this mini class, you sip a collection of Mexican spirits you may not even know exist!

TACO TOUR IN OLD TOWN

I have kept Star's street taco spots a secret, you will not find them in this book...and I wouldn't have found them without her. But I can tell you that my favorite taco in all of PVR is on this tour.

OFF THE BEATEN PATH

IN THE MORNING

One of the most magical layers of Mexican food culture exists once the sun sets when street stalls open for just a few hours to feed the after-work rush of hungry locals.

PHOTO / VALLARTA LOCAL FOOD TOURS

Psst. Star also offers photoshoots. Some of my most cherished memories and photos in PVR were taken by Star. Learn more on her website foodandphototours.com

Cooking Classes

There are dozens of remarkable cooking classes offered in Puerto Vallarta which offer a variety of experiences when it comes to what you're cooking! Tamales, enchiladas, churros! Most cooking classes will greet you with a margarita and then whisk you away to a local market to shop for fresh ingredients. Some classes last a couple hours and some last six! The options are endless so let me recommend a couple to you.

Upscale:
GABY'S RESTAURANT

🏷️ *Budget:* $ 60 USD per person

🕐 *Hours:* 9am to 2pm

📍 *Where:* Centro

🛏️ *Address:* Calle Mina 252, Proyecto escola

🌐 gabysrestaurant.com

Cultural Experience:
COOKIN' VALLARTA

🏷️ *Budget:* $ 85 USD per person

🕐 *Hours:* :10am-3pm

📍 *Where:* In the chef's home

🛏️ *Address:* Given on booking

🌐 cookinvallarta.com/cooking-classes/puerto-vallarta/

Home Cooking:
ROSIE'S COOKING CLASS

🏷️ *Budget:* $ 85 USD per person

🕐 *Hours:* 9am to 1pm

📍 *Where:* Meet at Starbucks inside Galerias Vallarta Mall

🛏️ *Address:* Blvrd Francisco Medina Ascencio 2920

🌐 rosiescooking.com

Outdoor Adventures

SWIM WITH DOLPHINS IN THE WILD

This is a once in a lifetime experience that you can feel good about. You'll set out on the ocean with a marine biologist who studies the pods of native bottlenose dolphins that live in the area. You'll see dolphins from the boat and when the time is right, you'll be able to hop in the ocean and swim with the dolphins from a respectable but close-enough-to-cry distance.

Want more wildlife? Wildlife Connection offers more nature excursions that include whales, birds, turtles and more at wildlifeconnection.com

💸 **Budget:** $45 for kids and $72 for adults

📍 **Where:** Marina Vallarta

🏛 **Address:** Av. Paseo de la Marina Sur 214

🌐 www.wildlifeconnection.com/dolphins-tour/

WHALE WATCHING

December – March is whale season where you can watch Humpback whales leaping out of the water. You'll find boat tours that offer whale watching excursions. I recommend Ally Cat Sailing for a fun, social experience and Wildlife Connection for a more educational experience.

💸 **Budget:** $45 for kids and $72 for adults

📍 **Where:** Marina Vallarta

🏛 **Address:** Av. Paseo de la Marina Sur 214

🌐 www.wildlifeconnection.com/whale-dolphin-watching-tour/

ALLY CAT SAILING

A 60' Catamaran yacht with lounge beds, a free flow bar and waterslides into the ocean. A boat tour with Ally Cat Sailing is a must, especially if you're a solo girl or a group of girls looking to meet other travelers! Ally Cat Sailing whisks you away on a social day of beach hopping, kayaking, SUP, and (yes of course) drinking while you tick places like Yelapa and Las Animas off your bucket list. And if you're here December – April, congratulations, it's whale season. Check out Ally Cat's Whale Watching Tours!

💸 **Budget:** $$

📍 **Where:** Romantic Zone

🏧 **Address:** Av Revolución 41

🌐 www.allycatsailing.com

ZIP LINING
WITH CANOPY RIVER

Go with the "River Expedition" Take this 2.5-hour tour where you'll zip line through the jungle, float down the river in inflatable rafts, ride horseback through trails, cross dare-devil bridges and rappel down cliffs. Women of all ages can do this! Not ready for the full wild woman experience? Slow it down and browse your options at CanopyRiver.com.

💸 **Budget:** $$

📍 **Where:** Playa De Oro

🏧 **Address:** Playa de Oro 126 F

🌐 https://canopyriver.com/

NOGALITO ECOPARK

I have friends who come here just to hang out for the day and work at the "River Club" which is just a simple little riverside hang out with some dinky chairs but a killer menu. If you're not working, go on a relaxed river trek tour (including a tequila tasting) or a zip line through the jungle. This day is more relaxed than Canopy River but still gives you a dose of adrenaline. If you join a tour, they'll pick you up in town!

💸 **Budget:** $$

📍 **Where:** Laurel 107, Buenos Aires

🌐 www.nogalitoecopark.com

♥ @nogalitoecopark

SNORKELING AT LOS ARCOS

Los Arcos National Marine Park is hanging out off the shores between two beaches, Mismaloya and Las Gemelas. Los Arcos translates to "the arches" referring to the arched openings on the side of this giant rock island that is now home to an underwater world teeming with sea life. Want to come snorkel amongst angelfish, clown fish, octopus, manta rays and other fascinating species? You've got a couple ways to do this.

➤ 1. Jump aboard a day-trip with Ally Cat Sailing which makes a stop here

➤ 2. Make your way to Mismaloya and hook up with Paddle-Zone who will take you on a 3-hour paddle board and snorkel excursion.

➤ 3. Sign up for an Airbnb Experience

underwater photoshoot here when you'll snorkel and model

🌐 AllyCatSailing.com or Paddle-Zone.com or search for The Arches Underwater Photoshoot on Airbnb Experiences Puerto Vallarta

SCUBA DIVING

The deeper you dive at Los Arcos, the more earthly magic there is to see in the reef marine life lying in the depth below. Octopus, Turtles, Seahorses, Parrot Fish, Eagle Rays, Lobsters, Zebra Eels, Moray Eels, and these strange eels that stick straight out of the sand like shy ribbons, waving gently in the current at the bottom of the sea. You can dive to depths of 26 meters (85 feet) along rock walls and steep underwater cliffs. Link up with Banderas Scuba Republic or PV Ocean Tours.

🌐 Banderas-Scuba.com or pvoceantours.com

SKYDIVE PUERTO VALLARTA

Certified, highly trained skydive instructors will give you the thrill of a lifetime with a bird's eye view of Puerto Vallarta! If you've never jumped before, don't worry, you're not the first newbie. The instructors will keep you calm and guide you through the entire experience step by step. You're in good hands. Oh and after your adrenaline dies down, their "Sky Bar" restaurant (located on the ground) is pretty damn good.

🕐 **Hours:** 7am to 7pm

🏷 **Budget:** Starts at $245 for a Tandem Dive

🌐 skydivevallarta.mx/en

VISIT THE WETLANDS

Estero de Salado is a 400-acre wetland just on the edge of town and is home to colorful snakes, crocodiles, iguanas, snakes, and tons of exotic birds. To explore, hop in a boat for 300 pesos that will take you to the mangroves where you can try and spot these creatures. The money goes towards preserving and protecting this natural habitat so consider it a donation to Puerto Vallarta! If you want more crocs, visit the little brother to this park called El Cora, the crocodile sanctuary, nearby.

🕐 **Hours:** 9am - 5pm

📍 **Where:** Av. Francisco Medina Ascencio, Villa Las Flores

🎫 **Address:** Type Cocodrilario el Salado into your maps.

VISIT THE BOTANICAL GARDENS

People are loving the Botanical Gardens in Puerto Vallarta right now. Exotic flora and fauna plus butterflies and hummingbirds! It's easy to see why Puerto Vallata's Botanical Gardens were recently named among the top ten Best Botanical Gardens in North America by USA Today! They came in at #4 and were the only gardens on the list which are not located in the continental US!

🏷️ *Budget*: $

🕐 *Hours:* Daily 9am-6pm (closed on Mondays)

➤To get there:

Get on the 50 pesos bus! Look up "Vallarta Botanical Gardens, Bus Stop" on GoogleMaps which will lead you to Carranza and Aguacate streets, in the Romantic Zone. Every half hour or so, you can catch the bus to "El Tuito". This bus will also return to Puerto Vallarta making for a fun adventure. Alternatively, you can take a cab from Puerto Vallarta, but expect to pay around 400 pesos each way.

HOP ON - HOP OFF BUS

Ride around on a big double-decker bus as a fun touristy way to see the city for a day! The bus starts on the Malecon next to the Caballo de Mar monument and stops at 16 spots that stretch all the way past Mismaloya. In between you can hop off and walk around historic streets, breezy beaches and areas you might not reach on your own. Sit up top to get panoramic views or sit below in the air conditioning and cool off. As you ride, you can listen to audio recordings that tell you all about the city. The ticket is $17 and includes a sunbed at Mangos Beach Club in PVR and beer on the bus! Plus a few touristy extras.

If you were to stay on the bus the whole time, it would take about 3 hours. But with hopping on and off, you could easily turn this into a whole-day event.

🕐 *Hours:* $

🕐 *Hours:* Monday to Sunday from 10:00 am to 9:00 pm

➤ How to get there:

The buses pick up every hour at each official stop, but hey, this is Mexico so I find it helpful to double confirm where you're going to be by calling 322 293 8563 just in case.

Book here:

Hikes in Puerto Vallarta

Pro Tip!

Join the Facebook group called Puerto Vallarta Digital Nomads where they often organize small group hikes or ask in my Facebook group, Girls in Puerto Vallarta, if any girls want to join you on a hike (bet you there will be some bites)!

CENTRO TO CERRO DE LA CRUZ

For panoramic views of the city, walk up Abasolo Street and keep your eye on the big antenna you see in the distance. That is the Mirador de la Cruz.

BOCA DE TOMATLAN TO LAS ANIMAS

A coastal hike that takes you to secluded beaches and eventually to the lively beach of Las Animas. To start hiking from Boca de Tomatlan, you'll see a little bridge close to where you're dropped off.

Cross the bridge and follow the signs to "Colomitos". The whole hike from Boca de Tomatlan to Las Animas takes about 2 hours. The path is defined so don't worry about getting lost.

COLOMITOS TO PLAYA ANIMAS

If you don't want to do the whole 2-hour hike then here's how to cheat. Simply take a 50 pesos water taxi from Boca de Tomatlan to Colomitos Beach. Hang out on the sandy shores for a while and then trek to Playa Animas. This is one of the most stunning scenic walks in the bay! You will be rewarded with restaurants along the way with fresh seafood and cold beers.

PALO MARIA HIKE

20 minutes south of Centro, you'll find the head of this serene trail starting right at Garza Blanca. Prepare for a moderate 40-minute trek that will lead you to a waterfall with a swimming pool below!.

 ## HIKE TO YELAPA

You can do this alone if you're up for taking a bus then hiking a 2-mile trail for about an hour which eventually leads you to Yelapa Falls. But I recommend going with a guide that is going to teach you all about the area and the flora and fauna that surrounds you. Join this guided Airbnb Experience Hike!

Art & Culture

SALSA DANCING CLASS

You can't leave Mexico without learning a few sexy moves! I'm telling ya, learning how to Salsa dance is a life skill we all need to learn! Come to La Bodeguita del Medio, a Cuban-style bar, for a free one-hour group lesson on Tuesdays and Thursdays at 7pm. You won't be out of your league, there are many newbies here and many great unofficial teachers. After class, there's live music and an opportunity to practice what you've just learned.

⊙ **Hours:** 3pm to 8:30pm

♥ **Where:** Palo Alto

🏛 **Address:** 463 S California Avenue

⊕ www.labodeguita.com

CINÉPOLIS VIP

Movies count as art and culture, right? You can escape the heat by ducking into this VIP movie theater in the hotel zone. Sink into a reclining chair where you can order sushi, burgers, or whatever you crave off the menu which will be delivered to your little table in front of you. They show premiere movies in English with Spanish subtitles. The tickets are cheap and the popcorn is great.

♥ **Where:** Hotel Zone

🏛 **Address:** Las Glorias

⊕ www.cinepolis.com

WATCH A DRAG SHOW

Puerto Vallarta is the international club house for gay men! A Drag Show is absolutely an intrinsic part of modern-day Vallarta culture, and baby, you've got Drag Show options galore. I recommend you start perusing the calendars of these four theatres and see which one has shows that match up with your schedule:

◇ La Noche Bar

◇ Act2PV

◇ Paco's Ranch

◇ The Palm Cabaret and Bar

Keep an eye out for Diva Divine's shows. She's PVRs drag queen icon!

Remember, a drag show is not for the politically correct or the buttoned up! Come ready to laugh, be shocked, and open your eyes to an inspiring world of untethered self-expression.

DIY ART WALK

Free and self-guided! Here is an art walk created by James and Sarah at TheWholeWorldOrNothing.com that I have been hearing about for years. It's a DIY graffiti walk through Puerto Vallarta and it's worth your time (especially if you make it a spontaneous taco walk, too). Use their search bar to search "Art Walk".

⚲ Where: Start Cinco de Deciembre neighborhood

PROFESSIONAL PHOTOSHOOT IN THE CITY

Photography is art, therefore this photoshoot experience is culture. If you've never had a professional photoshoot before, jump on this opportunity! Alonso is a professional photographer who has worked with women of all shapes, colors, sizes and backgrounds and makes even the most camera-shy girl have fun during this hour and a half photoshoot with gorgeous Puerto Vallarta backdrops

 💸 Budget: $

VISIT OUR LADY GUADALUPE CHURCH

A neoclassical main building and renaissance-style towers surrounded by a big square with surrounding streets teeming in local life, this church is a main pinnacle of the city of Puerto Vallarta. The next time you're on a rooftop with a view on el centro, you'll see Our Lady Guadalupe Church standing tall before the sunset

And at the very least, you'll hear the church's bells at sunset. The church's small beginnings were built in 1883, and then developed into a more grand structure in 1913 and kept being developed upon every few years up until 1963. This history alone is worth a visit, even if you're not religious.

☉ Hours: 7:30am –8:30am, 12–1pm, 7pm–8pm

⚲ Where: Center

🏛 Address: Hidalgo 370, Proyecto escolae

WATCH THE VOLADORES DE PAPANTLA

5 men climb up a pole and then jump off with rope attached to their feet. They spin around in circles while wearing traditional clothes while one guy sits atop the pole playing the flute. What's the meaning of all this?

A rainmaking ritual. Each "flyer" represents one of the four nature elements as they seek to appease the rain gods. You can see this show on the Malecon before sunset. The show is free but tips are welcome!

Volunteering in Puerto Vallarta

First, a note. I say this on a personal and professional level: Please don't volunteer at orphanages. Turning children into zoo animals for profit is a rising problem around the world. To have a revolving door of people come through these orphanages is not healthy for the children, emotionally or physically. And to allow strangers to interact with children without background checks is dangerous. Please don't support these orphanage opportunities anywhere in the world.

VALLARTA FOOD BANK

Behind the vacation veil, there is a hunger crisis in Puerto Vallarta and Vallarta Food Bank is doing something about it. To date, Vallarta Food Bank has distributed 67,186 food bags and served 60,343 hot meals to the community. Bravo to them! Vallarta Food Bank is volunteer-run and would love for you to volunteer as a kitchen helper, soup kitchen server or pantry packer as they cook and serve 400+ hot meals Monday-Friday!

An added bonus is that you undoubtedly will make connections with other women living or traveling in PVR with big hearts who volunteer here often.

Note: Vallarta Food Bank asks that volunteers have self-quarantined for two weeks after traveling. If you can't volunteer, small donations help and 100% of your donation will go towards families in need.

♀ **Where:** 5 de Diciembre

⊕ vallartafoodbank.com

SULA SOCIETY

A dog-shelter that needs dog walkers! Sula Society is located about 30 minutes out of town.

So on a day that you want to visit, post in Girls in Puerto Vallarta and gather a couple more volunteers who want to share the 400 pesos (approx.) round-trip taxi ride.

⊕ facebook.com/thesulasociety/

PURRPROJECT

This no-kill feline shelter needs donations and volunteers! Pay 400 pesos and you will be picked up and whisked away to a cat ranch where your inner cat lady will be absolutely overjoyed as you tour the facility through a sea of cats!

This is a win-win-win. You get cats, the cats get cuddles, and the Purrproject gets much needed financial support to keep caring for these kitties.

⊕ purrproject.com

TURTLE CONSERVATION CAMP

This environmental conservation organization hatches and releases up to 500 baby turtles per day each hatching season. You can support this organization by donating to them. Those who donate get to be part of the turtle releases. The releases are spontaneous so to catch the opportunity, you must follow their Facebook page while you're in town. They'll post when they have a release coming up!

📍 *Where:* Nuevo Vallarta near the Airport

⊕ Facebook at Campamento Tortuguero Boca de Tomates

Did You Know...

Only 1 out of 10 turtles grows to be an adult? Most turtles fall prey to ocean predators. And worse... human predators in the form of fishing boats, abandoned fishing nets, and of course, plastic. This is why their conservation is so important.

hey!
YOU CAN TOTALLY DO THIS.
YOU'RE GONNA HAVE A GREAT TIME.

Pool Clubs & Beach Clubs

THE MARRIOTT HOTEL

Go around 10 or 11am. Walk in straight towards the beach and you'll find a little palapa (bungalow with straw roof) where you'll pay $30 for a day pass. $20 of the $30 goes towards food!

Snag yourself a lounge chair near the glittering pool overlooking the ocean and enjoy brunch, a mariachi band, mimosas, and pool access until 6pm!

🎟 **Budget:** $

🕐 **Hours:** 9am - 9pm

📍 **Where:** Marina Vallarta

🏛 **Address:** Paseo La Marina Norte 435

🌐 @marriottpv

THE SHERATON HOTEL

No pool at your hotel? Come spend the day at the Sheraton. Day passes are 650 pesos on Sundays, which includes a 350-pesos food voucher!

Enjoy eating and drinking from 9-2pm, then you can hang around the pool and enjoy the mariachi band until 6pm. Pretty good deal!

🎟 **Budget:** $

🕐 **Hours:** 10am - 6:30pm

📍 **Where:** Hotel Zone

🏛 **Address:** Blvd Francisco Medina Ascencio No 999

🌐 sheratonvallartaallinclusive.com

BUENAVENTURA GRAND HOTEL

If you don't mind children in your midst, Hacienda Buenaventura's beachfront location near the center of town is such an easy location to roll out of bed and mosey over to. With a day pass you get to food, drinks, the gym, pool & beach area. And you've got options.

➤ BREAKFAST DAY PASS: $580 pesos per person from 7am to 12pm

➤ LUNCH DAY PASS: $680 pesos per person from 12pm to 5pm

➤ FULL DAY PASS: $949 pesos per person from 8am to 5pm

➤ RELAXING DAY PASS: $1,649 pesos per person from 8am to 5pm and includes both breakfast, lunch, snacks and drinks plus yoga class and a 50-minute massage.

Just make sure you book a day ahead.

♀ Where: 5 de Diciembre

🏛 Address: Av México 1301

⊕ hotelbuenaventura.com.mx

Insider Tip!

They don't advertise it, but you can also get an evening pass from 6-10 for about 450 pesos which includes a buffet and free drinks, and allows you to watch evening entertainment. Inquire when you arrive.

SAPPHIRE BEACH CLUB

The best Chicken Club Sandwich in the city! Okay, maybe that's not that impressive to you, but it was to me! I love the food at Sapphire Beach Club. Their menu and portions blow the other dinky beach bars out of the water.

Order something to eat or drink and you can sit beachfront in one of their beach chairs on the iconic Playa Los Muertos! If you're not hungry, don't order anything and pay just $10 for a beach chair. And hey, when the massage lady comes by offering you a foot massage, give in!

🏷 Budget: $

⊙ Hours: 6am - 6pm

♀ Where: Romantic Zone

🏛 Address: Malecón 1

⊕ https://www.sapphire.mx/

CHICTINI BY PINNACLE

For $40, you can use the pool and you get $20 drink credit and a towel. lobby and ask for the place. Stay til 8 for sunset. One of the most sublime rooftop pool bars with panoramic views of the city!

For $40, you can use the pool and you get $20 drink credit and a towel. Let it be known, however, that the drinks here can get a little pricey so you'll want to make good use of their Happy Hour which runs from 5:30pm – 8:30pm

🏷 Budget: $$

⊙ Hours: 1pm to 9pm

♀ Where: Go to the Pinnacle Hotel Lobby and ask for a Sky Bar Pass

🏛 Address: Púlpito 179

♥ @chictinipv

LA PALAPA BEACH CLUB

La Palapa, or "The Umbrella", in English is sits right on Los Muertos Beach with sugary sand and warm waters excellent for swimming. You'll lounge in a beach chair while the friendly staff wait on you hand and foot!

This place is known for their excellent service! Expect never to have an empty drink! I recommend staying for dinner as the La Palapa Restaurant is legendary in Puerto Vallarta.

Hours:: 11am - 9:30pm

Where: Playa Los Muertos

Address Pulpito 105-3 Col. Emiliano Zapata

lapalapav.com

SWELL BEACH BAR

Some people call this place a beach "club" but it's more of a frenzied bar on the beach where your #1 entertainment is people watching! Embrace the vendors that offer you hammocks and jewelry. Make friends with the servers.

Order a Pacifico beer and some fish tacos and now you can say that you've officially been a tourist in Puerto Vallarta, but blissfully so! I totally recommend it.

Hours: 9am to 8pm

Where: Romantic Zone

Address: Amapas 182

f Swell Beach Bar PV

CANOPY RIVER

Okay, not a beach club but a river club! Hang out at Canopy River where the Wi-Fi is decent (10m up and down) enough to bring your laptop for some work or a book to unplug. There's a restaurant with fabulous food and drinks.

You can chill out in the hammocks or dip in the beautiful pool for 200 pesos! To get there, take an InDriver to get there (around 80 pesos) and then take their free shuttle back down into town at 2:20pm or 4:20 pm.

Hours: 7am - 8pm

Where: Los Almacenes
Camino Los Llanitos Km 4.5

https://canopyriver.com/

"IF WE WERE MEANT TO STAY IN ONE PLACE, WE WOULD HAVE ROOTS INSTEAD OF FEET."

- Rachel Wolchin

WHERE TO EAT & DRINK

Coffee & Coworking

THE LIVING ROOM BOOKSTORE & CAFE

Browse the bookshelves, find a new vacation read, and then sit down to enjoy scrumptious baked goods and pastries, handcrafted coffee, or take a refreshing lemonade or berry smoothie to go as you stroll along the marina. Best of all, we are supporting a fabulous female-owned business here. If you see Kelly in there, tell her you found her in this book and it will make her day!

🕑 *Hours:* 8am to 9pm

📍 *Where:* Marina Vallarta

🏛 *Address:* Local N, Av. Paseo de la Marina Sur 245

🌐 thelivingroombookstore.com

f facebook.com/TheLivingRoomPV

PUERTO CAFE

Coffee snobs will appreciate this coffee shop that operates with high standards. A little hipster goes a long way when you're looking for the best beans handled with expertise. Bring your laptop and post up at the little windowside table or at the coffee bar. You're more than welcome to chill and work here for a couple hours.

🕑 *Hours:* 9am to 7pm

📍 *Where:* Central

🏛 *Address:* Morelos 540, Proyecto escola

♥ @delpuertocafe

MYSTIC CIRCLE

Coffee first. Tarot card reading second. All of my witchy friends and intuitive sisters will love to discover that Puerto Vallarta has a café that doubles as a mini community center where you can join guided-meditation sessions, workshops and lectures all in spiritual nature. You can also learn about things in the human realm with Spanish Conversation Club on Fridays from 3:30pm to 5pm. Follow along on their Facebook page to see which activity you can join.

🕐 **Hours:** 9am to 6pm (except Sunday, 6am to 12pm)

📍 **Where:** Romantic Zone

🏛 **Address:** Lázaro Cárdenas 421

f facebook.com/MysticCircleCafe

BARRA LIGHT VALLARTA

Healthy food, strong coffee, calming décor and good WIFI. It's easy to see why you'll often see digital nomads sipping their lattes and working away at Bara Light Vallarta. Pro tip: Order the Matcha Latte.

🕐 **Hours:** 9am to 7pm

📍 **Where:** Romantic Zone and Marina

🏛 **Address:** Romantic Zone - Calle Rodolfo Gómez 134 and Plaza Neptuno / Marina - Francisco Medina Ascencio Km 7.5

f facebook.com/barralight.vallarta

STARBUCKS

Don't get mad at me! I know this is supposed to be a local guide but the Starbucks at La Isla Mall in the hotel zone is my favorite place to work!

They have a huge back patio where the sun shines down beautifully and the tables are extremely socially distanced. I find myself the most productive with my laptop and iced americano sitting right here!

🕐 **Hours:** 6am to 10pm

📍 **Where:** Marina Vallarta

🏛 **Address:** Av Paseo de la Marina 121-Local 25

🌐 starbucks.com.mx

INCANTO VALLARTA

My go-to for morning work and coffee sessions is Incanto, right on the river in the center of town. I love to start my morning outside in the breezy air under big billowing trees. However, Fridays through Sundays, I've got to either get out of there by 11 or prepare to get drunk with their awesome weekend promo which I'll tell you about next…

🕐 **Hours:** 9am to 11:30pm

📍 **Where:** Romantic Zone

🏛 **Address:** Insurgentes 109

🌐 incantovallarta.com

Brunch

Some brunches in PVR are flat-fee all-inclusive and others you just show up and order like a normal person.

———

ANDALE'S RESTAURANT & BAR

Fun Fact: I landed in Puerto Vallarta and went straight to Andale's Restaurant (last night's makeup and all) where I ordered a huge stack of pancakes and a Bloody Mary with my new expat girlfriends! It was the most joyous way to start my Puerto Vallarta experience. The servers act like they've known you for years and the owner came over to say hello. I loved feeling like family from the moment I sat down.

⊙ *Hours:* 7:30am to 11pm

♀ *Where:* The Main Drag in Centro

🛏 *Address:* Olas Altas 425

f Andale's Restaurant & Ba

SHERATON BUGANVILIAS

Perhaps it's the bottomless mimosas and sparkling wine that makes this the most popular brunch spot amongst my lady friends in Puerto Vallarta. La Villita restaurant is located inside the Sheraton Hotel with an impressive brunch buffet where you can fill your plate with seafood, ribs, cheese, sweet treats and more while you listen to mariachi and marimba play in the background! Come around 10am, pay 499 pesos…and you can stay all day. Just remember to drink water. As you can imagine, it's easy to get carried away here!

⊙ *Hours:* 9am to 2pm for brunch

♀ *Where:* Hotel Zone

🛏 *Address:* Blvrd Francisco Medina Ascencio 999

⊕ buganviliasclub.com/restaurant/la-villita/

INCANTO VALLARTA

Start your weekend right! Friday-Sunday starting at 11am, prepare to be dazzled by the live band that plays on the riverside while you dine! You can either watch the show and eat breakfast/brunch for 100 pesos or you can watch the show, have brunch and (drum roll please) enjoy unlimited mimosas for 400 pesos!

⊙ *Hours:* 11am

♀ *Where:* Romantic Zone

Address: Insurgentes 109

🌐 incantovallarta.com

HACIENDA SAN ANGEL

You're going to climb some stairs to work up an appetite before brunch, but I promise it's worth it. This legendary restaurant was literally built for past Hollywood stars and the service reflects that. November 1st through April 4th, every Sunday morning you can treat yourself to this bougie brunch complete with a violinist serenade and 180-degree views of Banderas Bay.

⊙ **Hours:** 10:30am - 12:30pm

📍 **Where:** Centro

Address: Calle Miramar 336

🌐 haciendasanangel.com

BARCELONA TAPAS

Easily one of the most talked about restaurants in Puerto Vallarta, Barcelona Tapas has a fabulous reputation for food, ambiance and unbeatable views. So it's a no brainer that you'd want to put this Sunday Brunch on your foodie bucket list.

Shake off that hangover with live, traditional music and a breeze from the open-air restaurant. On the menu you'll find sweet stuff like French Toast and Mexican fare like Chilaquiles!

⊙ **Hours:** Sunday from 10am - 2pm

📍 **Where:** Central

Address: Calle Matamoros 906

🌐 barcelonatapas.net/en/

FREDY'S TUCAN

A massive hit with the gay community - you know this place is going to be up to standard! This place is known for having the most delectable breakfasts. There is something for everyone with decadent omelettes, eggs benedict, smoked salmon bagel pastries - oh and the fruit plate is to die for! Ps. Cash only.

⊙ **Hours:** Daily 8am - 2:45pm

📍 **Where:** Romantic Zone

Address: Basilio Badillo 245

𝗳 Restaurante Fredy's Tucan Puerto Vallarta

LINDO MAR RESORT

Beachfront brunch right over Conchas Chinas beach! La Playita Restaurant located within Lindo Mar Resort offers a breakfast buffet every Saturday and Sunday from 10am to 1pm for 199 pesos per person!

⊙ **Hours:** 10:30am - 12:30pm

📍 **Where:** Centro

Address: K 2.5 Carretera a Barra de Navidad

☐ +52 (322) 221 5556

MR. CREAM PANCAKES AND WAFFLES

This place is always buzzing with tables of chit-chatting expats and travelers, whether they're casually sipping an early morning coffee or going to town on a fluffy stack of strawberry-topped pancakes for brunch. When you're finished, take a walk in the Marina and see if you can spot the massive crocodile that hangs out on the rocks.

◔ *Hours:* 8am - 2pm

♀ *Where:* Marina Vallarta

🚉 *Address:* Condominios Marina Sol S/N

f Mr. Cream, Waffles & Pancakes

LITTEN BROD

Laptop. Coffee. Pastries. You are all set for a productive morning of work at this unexpected Danish café that uses ancient baking techniques to bring you authentic European treats...in Mexico.I know it sounds strange to have come to Mexico to eat European but after you've been eating nothing but cheese and tortillas for a week, you're going to be craving this!

◔ *Hours:* 8am - 2pm

♀ *Where:* Romantic Zone

🚉 *Address:* Lázaro Cárdenas 311

♥ @littenbrod

Street Food & Local Spots

The most polarizing question of all time in Mexico is Where is the best taco stand?! Everyone has a must-try spot...including me. Actually, I have about 20 must-try spots but I'm going to narrow it down to five. Okay maybe 10. 10 street food stands and hole-in-the-wall restaurants.

And PS. When we refer to "taco stand" it doesn't necessarily mean you're going for tacos...

PEPES TACOS

Tacos that are stuffed so fat that you will barely be able to make it through two, three max. Here at Pepes, it's all about the Tacos al Pastor and the Mango Margaritas. The sweetness of the pineapple with the pastor pairs exquisitely with the Mango Margarita.

◔ *Hours:* 1pm - 6pm

♀ *Where:* 5 de Diciembre

🚉 *Address:*Calle Honduras 145 C Col. Cinco de Diciembre

f facebook.com/PepesTacoVallarta

TACOS SAHUAYO

Look at the wall. There's the menu. It's simple and easy to order from. And you see those prices? Oh, that's cheap! Less than a dollar per taco means that you should absolutely order one of each! Plus a Torta al Pastor if you're extra hungry. Look on the side of the grill and that's where you'll find the salsas!

⊙ **Hours:** 7pm - 3am

♀ **Where:** La Vena

🛕 **Address:** Benemérito de las Americas 290, La Vena

f facebook.com/ sahuayotacosalpastor

EL BRUJO

Your life will never be the same after you try the soft shell crab enchiladas and the taco de chicharron de queso with shrimp. Actually, order two of those tacos. This place is the definition of local and is such a hidden gem! What I remember more than the incredible food was the warm, friendly service. The server seemed to really enjoy helping me order. Overall, 5 stars for food and service!

⊙ **Hours:** 1pm - 10:30pm

♀ **Where:** Romantic Zone

🛕 **Address:** Venustiano Carranza 510

TACOS DE BIRRIA CHANFAY

It's a rite of passage when you come to Mexico. You must find and try the best Birria spot in town. Birria is stewed meat and can be eaten in a variety of ways. At Tacos de Birria Chanfay, I want you to try two things: Tacos de Birria and Tacos Dorados or "Doraditos" here (golden fried tacos). As always, look for the salsitas (little salsa cups) on the side. Order a Guava Juice for spicy emergencies.

⊙ **Hours:** 10am - 4pm

♀ **Where:** Romantic Zone

🛕 **Address:** Venustiano Carranza 373

TACÓN DE MARLIN

Remember that I told you that marlin is "the bacon of the sea"? Well, now is your time to see if I'm right. Which one strikes your fancy? Marlin tacos or the smoked marlin burrito? Or maybe just try both. There is no reason to skip this hole in the wall as it's located right next to the airport. Stop by when you land and order your Uber from here, or grab a burrito to go and eat it at the gate!

⊙ **Hours:** 10:30am - 5:30pm

♀ **Where:** 5 de Diciembre

🛕 **Address:** Honduras 145

⊕ tacondemarlin.com

MARISCOS LA TÍA

My mouth is watering just thinking about the Coctel De Mariscos! The food here reminds me of super over-the-top sushi rolls that are topped with sauces and meat and colorful treats…but in Mexican form. Now I may be starting a war, but some people claim that THIS is the best spot for marlin tacos. I'll let you order and decide. Ps. Mariscos la Tía also has a second location in Marina called Mariscos La Tía II

⊙ **Hours:** 10am - 7pm

♥ **Where:** 5 de Diciembre

🏠 **Address:** Calle Honduras 215

f facebook.com/latiadosoficial/

CAMARÓN EN BARRO

Welcome to shrimp heaven! Juicy, flavorful and cheap! Get ready to eat your shrimpy heart out. If you've never tried Aguachiles, now is the time! Aguachiles is raw shrimp (wait wait) that is cooked in lime with chiles and spices and topped with onion and herbs to create the freshest, most vibrant dish. Another must while you're here: Tostada de Mariscos.

⊙ **Hours:** 1pm - 7:30pm

♥ **Where:** 5 de Diciembre

🏠 **Address:** Guatemala 311

♥ @camaronenbarro

CENADURIA CELIA

Do you trust me? Ready to try something new? I promise it's nothing weird, just follow my lead. One chicken pozole (Pozole Pollo). One chicken sope (sope pollo). One flan (for dessert, you're not allowed to skip dessert). Not sure if you trust me yet? Just order the chicken taco;

you can't go wrong there. Keep in mind that portions are generous and the food is cheap!

⊙ **Hours:** Wednesday to Sunday 7pm - 11pm

♥ **Where:** Romantic Zone

🏠 **Address:** Lázaro Cárdenas 506

f facebook.com/cenaduriacelia/

PANCHOS TAKOS

Vegetarian friends, here's a gift for you wrapped in a tortilla. Panchos Takos not only makes the most indulgent quesadillas but they are also quite well known for their vegetarian tacos. Order the "Alhambra" plate for tacos stuffed with sautéed mushrooms, onions, and bell peppers. And if somehow you're still hungry, try the stuffed avocado.

⊙ **Hours:** 4pm - 12am

♥ **Where:** Romantic Zone

🏠 **Address:** Basilio Badillo 162

f Pancho's Takos

MARISCOS CISNEROS

Unpopular opinion here but I'm not a fan of the food at this place…except for two things which I absolutely love and adore and dream about: The quesadillas with the most melty cheese in the world and the frosty-cold Michelada (beer with lime and salt). Grab a table on the hidden patio in the very back of the restaurant and you've got the perfect afternoon snack-siesta in the most convenient location in the Romantic Zone.

⊙ **Hours:** 10am - 8pm

♀ **Where:** Romantic Zone

🏛 **Address:** Aguacate 271

f facebook.com/MariscosCisneros/

A couple more local places in Puerto Vallarta that I can't resist mentioning

◊ **Food Park PV**

◊ **Taqueria Las Güeras**

◊ **El Cuñado Taco Stand**

◊ **Cervecería Chapultepec**

◊ **Doña Raquel**

Pro Tip!

For a spontaneous taco hop, start on the corner of Naranjo and Venustiano Carranza (in front of El Brujo), and walk west towards the beach. You'll pass by many taco stands!

PHOTO / EMILIA IGARTUA

Restaurants

…rather than quick hole-in-the-wall spots.

HACIENDA SAN ANGEL

One night, I was walking through my whimsical neighborhood and heard the most enchanting mariachi band I've ever heard. I stuck my head through a kitchen window and asked, What is this place?! And that's how I discovered Haciend a San Angel. Step back in time with this 1960's romantic-era hacienda once owned by Richard Burton where he'd entertain his A-list friends on the terrace for sunset dinner with the most spectacular 180-degree sunset views.

The food is fine-dining with an upscale Mexican menu using the freshest local ingredients from the area. The Jewel of Mexico Mariachi Band plays five nights a week; Sunday, Tuesday, Wednesday, Thursday and Friday at 7:45pm and 9:15pm. There is a dress code and reservations are recommended.

🕐 *Hours:* 9am - 2pm / 5pm - 10pm

📍 *Where:* Centro

🏛 *Address:* Calle Miramar 336

🌐 haciendasanangel.com/dining/

BARCELONA TAPAS

What do you get when you mix the American son of a Cuban immigrant with Mexican traditions and ingredients? This! Barcelona Tapas is one of the most respected and adored restaurants in all of Puerto Vallarta, from the wood fire grill to the artistic plating, Barcelona Tapas isn't just feeding you, they're creating an experience!

The restaurant itself is another masterpiece of Chef William who converted the roof of his house into this impressive restaurant with jaw-dropping city views where live music and artisan cocktails go hand in hand.

🕐 *Hours:* 12am - 12pm

📍 *Where:* Centro

🏛 *Address:* Calle Matamoros 906

🌐 barcelonatapas.net/

GABY'S RESTAURANT

You might remember this place from the cooking class I mentioned earlier. The food here is so authentically delicious that people beg for the recipes! The dish I recommend most is the Chile Relleno Traditional. Take one bite and you, too, will be asking for the recipe.

But it's not just the food that makes this place famous, it's also the old town setting. You'll be sitting on a balcony surrounded by romantic architecture and a view of the ocean a few blocks away. Don't skip this place

🕓 **Hours:** 1pm - 10pm

📍 **Where:** Centro

🏛 **Address:** Calle Mina 252, Proyecto escola

🌐 gabysrestaurant.com

EL RIO BBQ

Come for the comfort food, stay for the party. El Rio BBQ is the famous gathering spot for expats in Puerto Vallarta who come for the best ribs in town paired with live music and dancing!

Music days tend to book up quickly and times change according to the day so make sure you check them out on Facebook and make a reservation! Bring your dog, and bring your swimsuit! You can take your bucket of beers down to the river for a little swim!

🕓 **Hours:** Wednesday to Sunday 11:30am - 7pm

📍 **Where:** Up into the mountains along the river, you'll need to take an Uber to get there

🏛 **Address:** Felipe Angeles 245, Paso Ancho

🌐 elriobbqbar.com

RIVER CAFE

Hidden in plain sight, this is the most charming little restaurant in town perched right over the river. With a bit of a pricier menu (175 pesos for Guacamole), I recommend coming here for a slow meal, rather than grabbing a quick bite to eat. Make a reservation and request a table under the river gazebo. And if you've got a sweet tooth, try the Bananas Foster!

🕓 **Hours:** 8:30am - 11pm

📍 **Where:** Romantic Zone

🏛 **Address:** Isla Rio Cuale 4

🌐 rivercafe.com.mx

EL BARRACUDA

Beach Bar Alert! If you like oysters, this is the place to come and suck em' back with your toes in the sand! The shrimp tacos and octopus chicharron are also to die for. Seafood lovers, you'll be in heaven.

Stay after dinner and this place turns into a reggae bar with live music and the occasional fire dancer. Be sure to hit the ATM before you come because this place is cash only!

🕓 **Hours:** 1pm - 10pm

📍 **Where:** 5 de Diciembre

🏛 **Address:** Paraguay 1290

🌐 elbarracuda.com/en/

DINNER IN THE SKY

I've always wondered how you pee when you're strapped into a restaurant chair 45 meters in the sky. Well it turns out, this dining experience is only one hour, so you won't have to worry about that. Dinner in The Sky is a restaurant lifted up by a crane, with dinner guests seated around a big chef's table for an up-close-and-personal cooking show and a beautifully presented set menu. Now we know.

◷ *Hours:* Breakfast 9am / Lunch 4pm / Dinner 6pm

♀ *Where:* Marina Vallarta

🏛 *Address:* Pelicanos 311

⊕ dinnerinthesky.com.mx/vallarta/

◇ *Comedor Versalles*

◇ *Bonito Kitchen & Bar*

◇ *Ah Camamba*

◇ *El Sazón de Amá*

◇ *Kensao Sushi Bar*

◇ *Joe Jack's Fish Shack*

◇ *The Iguana*

◇ *La Traviata*

◇ *Abbraccio*

◇ *Layla's*

EL SANTO TACO

Solo Girl Approved! My favorite way to eat out is at a bar top instead of a big half-empty table. Pull up a stool at El Santo Taco's bar where the bartender will entertain you and you've got a chance that a fateful stranger will sit next to you. Oh shoot, I didn't even mention the food yet! For me, it's all about the al pastor tacos!

◷ *Hours:* 9am - 2pm / 5pm - 10pm

♀ *Where:* Centro

🏛 *Address:* Basilio Badillo 219

f facebook.com/elsantotacopv

A few more restaurants worth mentioning for my super-foodie friends...

Drinking Day & Night

Besides the beach clubs, here is where you can come to get your buzz on…

MARGARITA GRILL

Solo girl approved! Whenever I travel solo, I look for social bars where I can plop down in a chair, order a margarita and easily start talking to the people next to me. This is that kinda place. Plus, the drinks are strong. That'll get you talking in no time! And if you don't meet anyone of interest, I can promise you that the people watching will keep you fully entertained. Pro Tip: Order a Basil Margarita for an unexpected delight or a Frozen Cucumber Daiquiri and add rosemary! You're welcome.

⊙ **Hours:** 11am to 1am

♀ **Where:** Romantic Zone

🏠 **Address:** Pino Suárez 321

f facebook.com/margaritagrill.vallarta/

MONZON BREWING CO.

Get your craft beer fix! Monzon's got a selection of rotating beers that are brewed right here in Puerto Vallarta! So, you don't have to consider this "day drinking". You can call it a cultural experience sampling native hops. Order a beer flight so that you can try a few and order a huge pizza with every intention of taking a couple slices home. Ps. You can feel good about drinking here with Monzon's charitable initiative called Drops in a Bucket. Look for it when you visit.

Last thing, I promise. Monzon Brewing has a really cool promo called When it Rains it Pours. When it's raining heavily, check their social media as they'll announce a 25% off rain promo.

⊙ **Hours:** 12pm to 12am

♀ **Where:** Romantic Zone

🏠 **Address:** Venustiano Carranza 239

f MonzonBrewing

NINE NINETY 9

You have to drink when you're watching sports. So come to this classy sports bar and pretend to watch something while you drink before noon. Located inside the Sheraton Buganvilias Resort Vacation Club where the fancy people stay, this is a great place to come and pick up men. Yeah, I said it. Happy Hour is all day on Wednesday. Just remember: drink water, too.

- **Hours:** 1pm to 1am
- **Where:** Hotel Zone
- **Address:** Blvrd Francisco Medina Ascencio 999
- ⊕ nineninety9.com/en/

LA PLAYITA

Today is a total write off because Happy Hour starts at noon and then there is another Happy Hour at 5pm. It's half off drinks…and they're strong. La Playita is located on Conchas Chinas Beach just south of the Romantic Zone but be careful walking home over the rocks…these margaritas are strong.

- **Hours:** 8am to 10pm
- **Where:** Conchas Chinas Beach
- **Address:** K 2.5 Carretera a Barra de Navidad
- ⊕ lindomarresort.com/Ocean-Front-Restaurant.aspx

NACHO DADDY

Don't know what to do with your day? Feelin' a little social? Start with a drink at Nacho Daddy and see what happens. Happy Hour is Monday – Friday from 4-6pm. They've got live music scattered throughout the week, 3pm on Tuesdays and 8.30pm on Friday. Also a sports bar, Nacho Daddy always has some kind of game on their screens. To stay up to date on what's going on, check out their Facebook page below!

- **Hours:** 11am to 12am
- **Where:** Romantic Zone
- **Hours:** Basilio Badillo 287
- ⊕ nachodaddy.mx/
- **f** facebook.com/NachoDaddyPV/

BLONDIES

"Every day we are hosting our version of the perfect cocktail party where everyone is on the guest list!". This quote from Blondies says it all! I've been going to this funky little slushy bar (yes, frozen slushy alcohol) in the Romantic Zone for years. It's sat on a busy corner that just seems to collect people as they walk by! It's social, full of good vibes, sweet people, and much-needed icy drinks!

- **Hours:** 11am - 2am
- **Where:** Romantic Zone
- **Hours:** 115 Pulpito
- ⊕ blondiespv.com

Cocktails & Nightlife

MEZCAL Y SAL

Actual art. You've never seen anything like this, I guarantee it. What feels like cartoon cocktails and appetizers come to life is absolutely dazzling. Grab a table with a view of the bar so you can watch the bartenders passionately create and design their miniature masterpieces. No one will judge you here if you take half a dozen photos of your drinks and bites. #PhoneEatsFirst

⊙ **Hours:** 6pm - 11pm

♥ **Where:** Romantic Zone

🏛 **Address:** C. Francisco I. Madero 176

f facebook.com/Mezcalysal

EL COLIBRI COCKTAIL BAR

A cocktail lounge where solo girls can feel safe and comfortable. This bar is owned by good people who hire and attract good staff. The vibes here feel relaxing, warm and welcoming. The dim lighting and chill music is soothing. The candle lit tables are romantic. So whether you're coming for a solo date to treat yourself or looking for a safe spot to bring your Bumble date, El Colibri gets my vote.

⊙ **Hours:** 8pm - 2am

♥ **Where:** Centro

🏛 **Address:** Morelos 582

⊕ elcolibri.com

LA NOCHE

A gay bar with go go dancers and a drag show! Ladies, welcome to Puerto Vallarta's fabulous gay nightlife scene! The thing about gay men is that they have high standards so you can expect fantastic music, cocktails and energy.

The drag show starts every night at 6pm and the sexy dancing starts at 9pm and goes on until 3am. Are you ready for this?

⊙ **Hours:** 3pm - 3am

♥ **Where:** Romantic Zone

🏛 **Address:** Lázaro Cárdenas 267D

⊕ lanochepv.com

INCANTO PIANO BAR

Famous. Incanto Piano Bar is absolutely famous in Puerto Vallarta for hosting the most incredible talent! Come during the evenings to the piano bar to listen to singers so incredible that I can hear their voices gently reverberating throughout the valley of Puerto Vallarta from my balcony six blocks away like a siren song. Sometimes there's a cover charge, and sometimes not. Check their website for showtimes and prices!

🕑 *Hours:* 9am - 11:30pm

📍 *Where:* Romantic Zone

🏛 *Address:* Insurgentes 109

🌐 incantovallarta.com

IK MIXOLOGY BAR

Get your camera ready for a bar full of human-sized bird's nests where you can drink or have a mini photoshoot! This place feels like a fairytale, especially when the sun fades away leaving twinkle lights and a view of the glittering pier over the water.

🕑 *Hours:* 4pm - 11pm

📍 *Where:* : Romantic Zone

🏛 *Address:* Olas Altas 380

🌐 theikbar.com

LA LULU RAICILLERÍA

So local that it's almost hidden. This bar is a Raicillería. Raicilla is a traditional Mexican spirit (a cousin to Mezcal and Tequila) and a Raicillería is what you call a place that distills their own Raicilla. To add to the fun, they have a salsa band and Ladies

Night. Check them out on Facebook to see what events are coming up!

🕑 *Hours:* 8pm - 2am

📍 *Where:* Centro

🏛 *Address:* Morelos 582

🌐 elcolibri.com

BAR MORELOS MEZCALERIA

Hey Party Girls. If you're the nightclub kind of gal, here's a mini nightclub that will give you a taste of what you're craving without going full-on Vegas. Expect low lighting, weird entertainment antics, and bumpin' music.

🕑 *Hours:* 7pm - 3am

📍 *Where:* Centro

🏛 *Address:* Morelos 589

f facebook.com/ BarMorelosPuertoVallarta/

Check out These Spots for Live Music

◇ *Roxy Rock* / Rock

◇ *Whiskey Kitchen PV* / Blues

◇ *Garbo Piano Bar* / Piano Bar & Jazz - Plus the best martinis in town

◇ *La Bodeguita Del Medio* / Salsa (and dancing)

SHOPPING IN PUERTO VALLARTA

Street shopping. Beach vendors. Mexican Mall Shopping. American Mall Shopping. And…Walmart. You need a strategy.

Shopping in the Center of Town

STREET SHOPPING

You'll pass by little shops on the street with completely open fronts with dresses and swimsuits hanging in front, maybe even some inflatable pool toys. You can often find sunglasses and souvenirs here. Just know that the first price is never the final price. If she offers you 100 pesos, counter with 50% at 50 pesos. You will probably meet somewhere in the middle around 75 pesos. Haggling is all part of the game!

MERCADO MUNICIPAL

RIO CUALE

A good spot to fill your bag with little trinkets and souvenirs to take home. Keychains, ukuleles, homemade (and wrapped) snacks. This little market is just before the river making it a convenient stop on your way to the next market.

⊙ **Hours:** 7am - 8pm

♥ **Where:** Centro

🏠 **Address:** Agustín Rodríguez s/n

CUALE ISLAND FLEA MARKET

Where I like to buy my gifts for home. This is one of those markets that you leisurely stroll through on a sunny afternoon as you peruse little trinkets sold at one colorful stall after the next.

You'll find everything from boho-style hand woven hammocks to winter scarves with American Football Team logos on them. It's a touristy market, for sure, but a gorgeous one with colorful flags strung over the paths and vibrant colors everywhere you look.

⊙ **Hours:** 9:00 AM - 9:00 PM

♥ **Where:** Center, right before the

bridge that crosses over into the Romantic Zone

🏛 *Address:* Emiliano Zapata

OLAS ALTAS SATURDAY MARKET

Handmade beaded necklaces, homemade breads and soups, fresh squeezed juice! This is Puerto Vallarta's version of a Farmer's Market and you must come to sample some local treats! Sometimes there's even a live band, creating the perfect weekend atmosphere.

🕐 *Hours:* 9am - 2pm

📍 *Where:* Romantic Zone

🏛 *Address:* Lázaro Cárdenas

M VALENTINA VALLARTA

A trendy shoe store in the center of Puerto Vallarta with high-quality sandals and sneakers that are fashionable but also practical to match the cobblestone terrain of Puerto Vallarta!

🕐 *Hours:* 11am - 7pm

📍 *Where:* Center, right before the bridge that crosses over into the Romantic Zone

🏛 *Addres:* Morelos 799, Centro

♥ *Contact:* @ mariavalentinavallarta

BEACH VENDORS

While you're lying on the beach, you'll have vendors approach you carrying an impressive amount of inventory on their head, their backs,

their arms. After a few drinks, it's easy to beach shop. Don't want to shop? Say "No, gracias. Buena Suerta" (no thanks, good luck). That "good luck" part is the trick to get them to leave you alone.

And please be wary of buying "silver" from these guys. If you are buying silver in Mexico, make sure it is stamped 925 somewhere on the piece. This is close to pure silver. However, even then, you can't be sure it's real silver. Your best bet is to shop at physical stores, but still look for the stamp.

Malls

LA ISLA MALL

A huge outdoor LA-style shopping motel in the hotel zone with H&M, Apple, Starbucks and my favorite shop of all time called Stradivarius. This mall is worth it just to go to that shop with the most stylish, affordable clothes!

🕐 *Hours:* 11am0 - 10pm

🏛 Avenida Francisco Medina Ascencio No. 2479

You can walk from La Isla to Plaza Caracol in 10 minutes!

PLAZA CARACOL

I love this mall filled with local Mexican brands, shops, nail salons, and a huge Soriana grocery store. If you like a hunt and a bargain, you can easily spend an hour inside the air conditioned maze of shops! Inside here, you'll also find Unas Norma nail salon which is one of my favs.

⊙ **Hours:** 7am - 11pm

♀ **Where:** Las Glorias

🏛 **Address:** Av. Francisco Medina Ascencio

GALLERIA VALLARTA

A big mall with mostly local shoppers. You can find book stores, athletic stores, clothing stores, a TelCel counter, and a big food court on the top floor with Burger King, McDonalds, Chinese food...you get the picture. There aren't many American name-brand shops here, however, I think this mall is worth a stroll. They've got cute stuff of good quality!

⊙ **Hours:** 11am - 9pm

♀ **Where:** Educación

🏛 **Address:** Av. Francisco Medina Ascencio 2920

Food Shopping

MERCADO EMILIANO ZAPATA

Shop for your produce like a local! Get the fresh tortilla chips and juicy tomatoes for the cheapest prices here! This market quadrant is home to several shops (tiendas) where you can buy produce, meat, eggs, and more. Challenge yourself by ordering chicken from the butcher. It's intimidating at first but these guys know how to help us gringas eat!

Speaking of eating, to feed the hungry shoppers, there are several little hole-in-the-wall local restaurants selling everything from quesadillas to pozoles. Pro Life Tip: The fastest way to integrate into your community is to make friends with the shop owners. Learn their names and remember them!

⊙ **Hours:** 6:30am to 3pm

♀ **Where:** Romantic Zone

🏛 **Address:** Mercado Emiliano Zapata local 31

WALMART

This was such a weird concept to me! Why did I come all the way to Mexico just to shop at a Walmart?! Well, when you run out of your favorite shampoo, have a random (but strong) Pop Tart craving or need new makeup, you'll start to appreciate having a Walmart in town. #LifeSaver

Walmart Locations:

🕐 **Hours:** 11am - 8pm

📍 **Where:** Near the Marina

🏬 **Address:** Blvrd Francisco Medina Ascencio 2900

🏬 **Address:** Av. Francisco Villa 1526

COSTCO AND SAM'S CLUB

If you already have a Costco card or Sam's Club Card, good news! You can use them here. If you don't have these cards, even better news! You can buy one here for cheaper than back home...and it's got valid worldwide use meaning that you can use it in Mexico and at home. The Costco and Sam's Club here is just like anywhere else with bulk paper towels and lots of wine!

Sign-up here:

🌐 **Mexican Costco:** costco.com.mx/membresias

🌐 **Mexico Sam's Club:** sams.com.mx

Costco

🕐 **Hours:** 10pm - 8:30pm

📍 **Where:** Fluvial Vallarta

🏬 **Address:** Av Fluvial Vallarta 134

SAM'S CLUB

🕐 **Hours:** 7am - 10pm

🏬 Blvrd Francisco Medina Ascencio 2880

LA COMER

Need a taste of home? La Comer is full of international goodies that will cure your homesickness. Easily the most upscale grocery store in town, you'll find wine from all over the world, gorgeous produce, a section for home goods and beyond. Everything is laid out so beautiful that it's a joy to come shop here in the air conditioning!

🕐 **Hours:** 7am - 10pm

📍 **Where**: Fluvial Vallarta

SORIANA

If Target and Walmart had a Mexican baby, this would be it. Soriana is a local grocery store with (slightly) cheaper prices and lots of miscellaneous isles and departments to peruse. Better yet, Soriana is attached to Plaza Caracol which is one of my absolute favorite Mexican-style malls with great shopping and super friendly people! Everything you could ever need is here.

🕐 **Hours:** 8am - 10pm

📍 **Where**: Plaza Caracol

Shopping Pro Tip!

You can order from Amazon.com.mx but of course, try to shop local first!

Souvenir Ideas

◊ Vanilla

◊ Tequila (buy with star)

◊ Spices or sauces like Tajin

◊ Mexican snacks from Oxxo (really!)

◊ A Bag of Fresh Mexican Coffee Beans

◊ A Hammock (but you'll have to check it in when you fly home!)

◊ Glass-blown Kitchenware from Mundo de Cristal

◊ Native Mexican Art from Peyote People: Huichol Indian and Mexican Folk Art Gallery

◊ And when in doubt, just wander The Rio Cuale Island Market or Mercado Municipal de Artesanias

Pro Tip! If there's no extra space in your bag, bring a small foldable duffle bag that you can stuff with extra souvenirs (for you and the fam) on the way back.

hey!

DO YOU HAVE YOUR TOTE BAG YET?

GET IT AT

THESOLOGIRLSTRAVELGUIDE.COM/TRAVEL-SHOP

In case you forgot where you're going next...

FROM SOUTH TO NORTH

1. AIRPORT
2. PUERTO VALLARTA
3. NUEVO VALLARTA
4. BUCERIAS
5. LA CRUZ DE HUANACAXTLE
6. PUNTA MITA
7. SAYULITA
8. ISLAS MARIETAS

STATE OF NAYARIT

- *Pacific Ocean*

CHAPTER TWO

Nuevo Vallarta

—

TIME NEEDED:

For vacation, skip it. For expats and digital nomads, stay a
month of more.

KNOWN FOR:

Big houses and golf courses

BEST FOR:

Unpacking and living the expat life

INTRODUCTION TO NUEVO VALLARTA...

Nuevo is Spanish for "new" and the newer styles of gated communities, condos, and apartments, interspersed with the all-inclusive resorts have created a comfortable community for expat families. This community concept began as a place to provide a sunny, seaside escape for tourists and snowbirds wanting to relax. But over the last few years, Nuevo Vallarta has become quite the hub for expats looking to make more of a home base for themselves. This area benefits remote workers too, as the newer buildings offer better and stronger WIFI speeds than most other areas in Banderas Bay.

If you're on vacation, however, it only makes sense to stay in this area if a) you're a big golfer or b) you're coming to stay at one of the awesome resorts which I list below. And with that being said, this is going to be a short and sweet chapter.

Fun Fact!
Mexico has over 500 beaches along its coasts.

Areas to Know in Nuevo Vallarta

AND A SUPER QUICK MAP
FOR YOU TO START GETTING AROUND

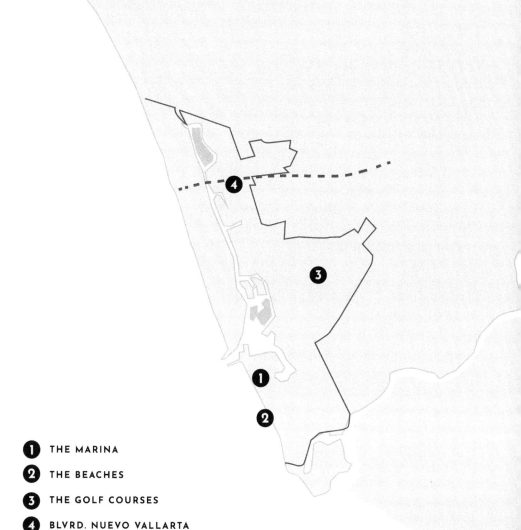

1 THE MARINA

2 THE BEACHES

3 THE GOLF COURSES

4 BLVRD. NUEVO VALLARTA

Unlike Puerto Vallarta, Nuevo is relatively simple to map out. You've got…

THE MARINA
Not a huge marina, but a busy one. You can walk the small boardwalk to find a handful of restaurants with a view or just spend some time sitting on the dock of the bay, watching the boats float away!

THE BEACHES
Unlike Puerto Vallarta, with its many smaller beaches carved out with rock formation borders, the beach in Nuevo is mile after mile after mile of uninterrupted, hard-packed sand. A lot of locals call it Playa Dorado (Golden Beach), due to the way the sun shimmers off of it.

Just south of the marina, there is a smaller beach called Playa Nopal where the Grand Mayan, Mayan Palace and Sea Garden resorts sit. Playa Dorado is where the beaches in the chapter are located.

THE GOLF COURSES
Just behind the marina is where Mayan Palace Golf Course and El Tigre Golf Course sit. Remember the name El Tigre and is used often as a point of geographical reference. There's also Flamingo's Golf Course home to the Crocodile Sanctuary.

BOULEVARD NUEVO VALLARTA
This is the main vein which cars drive to access Nuevo Vallarta. At the very top of this road is where you'll find Sam's Club, Walmart, the big bus stops/stations, and you're way into Puerto Vallarta.

HOW TO GET HERE

Nuevo Vallarta is super close to Puerto Vallarta - just a straight shot down Highway 200. This road is also known as Carratera Pacifico and is the main road through both PV and Nuevo.

Take an Uber or InDriver which should cost you about 200-300 pesos depending on where in PV they pick you up. When using apps like InDriver and Uber, however, you'll want to make sure your driver can bring you back again - because sometimes they cannot pick you back up if you're in a gated area. In that case, you'll need a private driver. Add some Puerto Vallarta private drivers into your phone now. You can find them on page 292.

Take a Bus from Puerto Vallarta which costs 13 pesos and takes about a half an hour. An easy route is from Plaza Genovesa to Las Garzas where buses come every 16 minutes. Another easy way to calculate your route is to jump on mapi.com to find the most convenient option for you.

Pro Tip: Some gated communities have their own shuttle services, so if you're taking a bus, coordinate with the shuttle service to pick you up where the bus drops you off.

HOW TO GET AROUND

Unless you're staying in a gated community with its own onsite shops and amenities, you'll want to get out and about for shopping, beaches and hot dates. Here's how to make that happen.

BUY OR RENT A CAR

If you're planning to jump into an expat life in Nuevo Vallarta, investing in a reliable used car once you get to town is a smart idea. I break down this whole topic in the Survival Guide on page 25.

BUSES AND TAXIS

They are available...but might not always be available to pick you up in your exact location. You'll often have to walk to reach a pick-up point.

PRIVATE DRIVER

Like I mentioned in the section above, Uber and InDriver can't always pick you up in Nuevo - however, they can drop you off. For pick-up, have a few private drivers' numbers in your phone ready to go for the hot days when you don't feel like walking.

WHERE TO STAY IN NUEVO VALLARTA

GRAND VELAS RIVIERA NAYARIT

Often ranked as the best all-inclusive resort in the Nayarit (even including Puerto Vallarta), the Grand Velas is known for having impeccable service, some of the most beautiful beach space in this side of the bay and a luxurious spa that has been named among the best spas in the world by Condé Nast Traveler.

🏷️ **Budget:** $$$

🏨 **Address:** Av. Cocoteros, Paseo de los Cocoteros 9

 BOOK HERE

HARD ROCK HOTEL VALLARTA

With several pools and hot tubs, four bars, six restaurants and tons of beach space, staying at the Hard Rock Hotel means that you won't have to fight for room to enjoy your vacation.

During the day, tan in the sand and swim in the pool. At night, enjoy live music with bands covering rock classics in their live amphitheatre or at the Sun Bar Monday- Sunday. And yes, this place is all-inclusive!

🏷️ **Budget:** $$$

🏨 **Address:** Paseo de los Cocoteros 19 Villa 8 Fraccion

 BOOK HERE

CASA VIRGILIOS BNB

A very quiet and peaceful bed and breakfast surrounded by tropical trees and hosted by the loveliest local couple who will make you feel at home, Casa Virgilios is a great choice for those of you coming to Nuevo and want to take it slow. If you want to explore on foot, you're just a 15-minute walk from the beach and a 5-minute walk from places to eat including sushi, italian and a bakery!

💸 *Budget:* $$$

🏚 *Address:* Jacarandas 69, 63735

 BOOK HERE

MARINA BANDERAS SUITES HOTEL BOUTIQUE

One of the most affordable boutique hotels, this quaint little place overlooks the marina where you can watch boats come in and out from your balcony suite.The junior suite has a microwave and a fridge, while the more lux suites have full kitchens - but you might not decide to cook seeing as how you're within walking distance to quite a few little restaurants and cafes with a view.

💸 *Budget:* $$$

🏚 *Address:* Calle 16 de Septiembre #42

 BOOK HERE

AIRBNB.COM

So many expats buy luxury condos in Nuevo Vallarta but only spend a fraction of the year living in them. You win at life when you use AirBnb to book your stay in the area.

My pro tip is to use the map feature and see how close to the beach you can get.

WHERE TO EAT IN NUEVO VALLARTA

LA SAZÓN DE AMA

A hidden gem perched on the top floor of Paradise Plaza, this is Mexican fine dining but with reasonable prices which is popular with both expats and locals! But hey, just because this restaurant is in a mall doesn't mean it's fast food! You can taste that the chef at La Sazón puts a lot of love into each plate. Make sure you save room and order the churro cart for dessert!

⊙ *Hours:* Daily 8am - 10pm
♥ *Where:* Top floor of Paradise Plaza
🏛 *Address:* Paseo De Los Cocoteros Local J2 Y J3

MAIZUL

The most picture-perfect food in Maizul, everything here is plated like a piece of art! The portions are massive and if you don't leave stuffed, you will leave with leftovers! For breakfast, order the rojo y verde chilaquiles. For lunch, ask to look at the ceviche menu! For dinner, if fish with a head doesn't freak you out, order the red snapper plate. And did I mention this place has a view of the marina? Don't skip it if you're in the area.

⊙ *Hours:* Daily 10am - 10pm
♥ *Where:* Marina
🏛 *Address:* Calle 16 de Septiembre 42

TINOS LA LAGUNA

Watch alligators swimming by, turles poking their head up for air and tropical birds flying around all while chowing down on some really good local food. Tinos la Laguna sits on the lagoon in Nuevo Vallarta for an immersive nature experience. Just a heads up: there is no aircon here, only fans.

I recommend coming during the evening while it's still light out so that you can enjoy the scenery and the breeze.

🕐 *Hours:* Daily 12pm - 9pm
📍 *Where:* Southern border of El Tigre
🏛 *Address:* Boulevard de Nayarit #393

EDDIE'S PLACE

Identifying as "Mexican/Lebanases/Seafood" is admittedly weird, but I still want you to give Eddie's Place a try. Come for breakfast where you can order all the morning comfort foods from pancakes to omelettes.

Come back in the afternoon for some Mahi Mahi tacos or a big juicy burger. This menu requires no thinking, just eating. Ps. Cash only.

🕐 *Hours:* Daily 8am - 10pm
📍 *Where:* Marina
🏛 *Address:* Boulevard Nayarit 70

hey....
**HAVE YOU JOINED
GIRLS IN PUERTO VALLARTA YET?**

THINGS TO DO IN NUEVO VALLARTA

WALK THE BEACH

Take an easy morning stroll along the beach. If you're up for an adventure, you can walk all the way up to Bucerias and never take your toes out of the sand. The walk between Nuevo and Bucerias is about 4 miles and depending how fast you walk, takes around 2 hours.

GO SHOPPING IN PARADISE

Paradise Plaza is always a must. It's a two-story, fully air-conditioned mall with over 100 active businesses ranging from coffee shops to restaurants to bars to boutiques to clothing stores to gift shops to you name it!

It's great fun to walk around and see everything on offer and escape the heat for a few hours. It's quite literally the be all/end all of any Nuevo shopping excursion.

EXPLORE THE NEIGHBORHOODS NEARBY

There are also smaller towns scattered just a few minutes outside of Nuevo that offer an escape from gringo-land. In areas like Mezcales and San Vicente you can find traditional artisans, authentic restaurants, tons of street food (you haven't lived until you've had elote out of a Chile Relleno from a roadside stand), and locally owned tiendas. Just plug these neighborhoods into GoogleMaps and you'll be on your way.

WHERE TO NEXT...

When it comes to exploring other parts of Banderas Bay, Nuevo Vallarta follows the same transportation methods as Puerto Vallarta. Check out page 81 for all the details and remember that you're right near the big bus station outside of Sam's Club which makes for easy DIY adventures.

CHAPTER THREE

Bucerias

—

TIME NEEDED:

1-2 days. Unless you want to become a resident, or a kitesurfer. Or both.

KNOWN FOR:

Tranquil waters and windy shores (aka, kitesurfing paradise)

BEST FOR:

Staying away from the hustle and bustle of PVR and Sayulita

INTRODUCTION TO BUCERIAS

If you're a young girl traveling alone, you might want to skip the next two chapters. Don't get us wrong, both Bucerias and La Cruz de Huanacaxtle are lovely, but these micro destinations are all about(very) quiet and chill time. And watersports.

Bucerias is your typical mexican town postcard: cobblestoned streets, bright facades, friendly locals and 5 miles of sandy beach. It's a quaint little place that you can explore by bike and stop along the way to enjoy the restaurants, cafes and the lively music scene.

Or, if you like adrenaline, Bucerias is the perfect spot to learn how to Kitesurf. It's often windy and the shallow waters make it a hub for kitesurfers of all levels and from all around the world.

As in many other locations in Banderas Bay, Bucerias is also home of a thriving international community, conformed mainly by Canadians. It is also a very family and kid-friendly place.

Fun Fact! The name Bucerias comes from the spanish word for diving - bucear. It comes from the town's origins of pearl fishing and it's pronounced: "boo-say-ri-uz"

Areas to Know in Bucerias

AND A SUPER QUICK MAP
FROM NORTH TO SOUTH

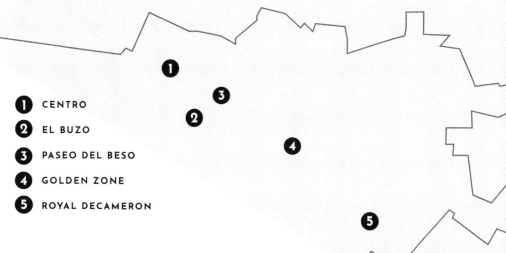

1. CENTRO
2. EL BUZO
3. PASEO DEL BESO
4. GOLDEN ZONE
5. ROYAL DECAMERON

Bucerias is divided in two main neighborhoods that spread along the coastline. However, on the other side of the highway and towards the east, Bucerias still goes on for quite a few blocks. In this chapter we'll focus on the two main neighborhoods known as the Golden Zone and the Centro (downtown area), as it's here where most things to see, do and eat happen.

THE GOLDEN ZONE

The southern and more residential and international part of town with a large concentration of expats and foreigners. The Golden Zone is known for its streets lined with art galleries, coffee shops and boutiques. This area goes from the Royal Decameron Complex (a massive resort that's my worst nightmare) to Paseo del Beso. Most shops and restaurants are located on the streets of Lazaro Cardenas and Francisco I Madero. I recommend you walk these streets when you get to town to get a lay of the land. Pro Tip: The beach in the Golden Zone is usually less crowded, except for the kitesurfers, paddle boarders and windsurfers.

PASEO DEL BESO

Paseo del Beso translates into "Alley of the Kiss". This little alleyway serves as the gateway between The Golden Zone and Centro.

CENTRO

The older, more local side of town. Walk up Lazaro Cardenas street until you reach the bridge. Cross over and you'll reach the Paseo del Beso. Keep going and you'll find yourself in the Flea Market right away. When you reach the end, turn left on Alfredo V. Bonfill street and you'll reach the ocean. And a statue of a diver, called "El Buzo". This is the heart of Bucerias. Right across, you'll find Plaza Bucerias, the town's main plaza and the church.

You can then explore up and down Av. Mexico and Av. Pacifico to see all the restaurants and shops around. This area is a bit more touristy than the Golden Zone, so you'll see more beach vendors and tourist-trap restaurants. But it's also where local life happens. You'll see residents enjoying the beach, children playing in the plaza, and older people catching up as they exit the church. And you'll find many more local businesses as well.

PHOTO / EMILIA IGAR...

HOW TO GET TO AND FROM BUCERIAS

UBER OR INDRIVER

Bucerias is a less than 40 min drive from Puerto Vallarta, and around 22 min from Nuevo Vallarta. You can take an Uber or an In Driver for approx. $270 MXN ($13 USD).

From Sayulita, San Pancho, or other locations, you most likely won't find an Uber so a Taxi or a Bus will be your only option.

BUSES

The bus takes from 30 to 40 minutes. You can take the Compostela bus or ATM bus from Las Glorias or Walmart in Puerto Vallarta. They run every 15 minutes and cost $25 MXN (less than $2 USD).

The drop off is at Bucerias Centro (Downtown). If you're staying in the Golden Zone area and are carrying around big bags, you can take a taxi right at the Main Plaza, on the side of the church. This ride will cost around $70 MXN ($3 USD).

HOW TO GET AROUND

UBER AND INDRIVER

Same as in Puerto Vallarta and Nuevo Vallarta, these riding apps are also available in Bucerias. There might be less drivers available at times, and sometimes the waiting time for a pick-up can be a bit long, so plan to order your rides with time to spare.

BIKE

Bucerias on a bike! Some streets are smooth and some streets are covered in bumpy cobblestones - but both are easy to navigate on two wheels. Know that the blocks closer to the shore are totally flat and there are some steep hills closer to the highway. Some areas are very sandy and dusty, so be mindful when you turn and girls...always, always, wear your helmet. Safety is cool.

> *Bike rentals:*
SURF MEXICO

💸 ***Budget:*** Hourly rentals from $200 MXN ($10 USD)

☉ **Hours:** Mon - Fri 9:00 AM - 6:00 PM / Fri - Sat 9:00 AM - 4:00 PM

♀ **Where:** Golden Zone

🚏 **Address:** Lazaro Cardenas 86

🌐 **Contact:** www.surfmexico.com

BICI BUCERIAS

💸 ***Budget:*** Hourly rentals from $200 MXN ($10 USD) (I know, that's a bit expensive)

☉ **Hours:** 8:00 AM - 2:00 PM

♀ **Where:** Golden Zone

🚏 **Address:** Lazaro Cardenas 40

🌐 **Contact:** http://bicibucerias.com/

TAXIS

As in most traditional Mexican towns, you'll find a Taxi Driver Site in one of the corners of the Main Plaza. In Bucerías, you'll find it on the plaza's corner towards "El Buzo" (the diver) statue. On Av. Alfredo Bonfil, right across from the Flea Market.

There's another Taxi stand on the far end of the Golden Zone, near the Royal Decameron Complex. Rides are not metered and prices depend on the area or distance you're headed to.

You know by now, that I always recommend trying Uber or InDriver first. Taxis should be your backup plan.

You can book your taxi ride on the following numbers:

◇ Golden Zone: +52 329 298 3959

◇ Centro: +52 329 298 0714

WHERE TO STAY IN BUCERIAS

REFUGIO DEL MAR LUXURY HOTEL BOUTIQUE

Let's be honest: you will most likely end up staying at this vibrant, charming boutique hotel in downtown Bucerias. It's the best in town with colorful rooms (some with kitchens), a breezy rooftop and a refreshing pool all within walking distance from the beach. There are golf carts you can use to explore around town and there are beach chairs for guests when you want to spend the day with your toes in the sand.

💵 **Budget:** $$$
📍 **Where:** The Golden Zone
🏛 **Address:** Benito Juárez 51

 BOOK HERE

AVENTURA PACIFICO BOUTIQUE HOTEL

One of the most unique Mexican-style places to stay in Bucerias is the Open-Air Palapa at Aventura Pacifico. "Open Air" means no walls! Just a palapa roof where the breeze blows through at night to give you a glamping meets hotel experience like you've never had before. Need walls? This hotel has rooms with those, too. During your stay, hang out at the pool or take a little stroll down to the beach just a few blocks away.

💵 **Budget:** $$
📍 **Where:** The Golden Zone
🏛 **Address:** Franciso I Madero, 132

 BOOK HERE

VALLARTA GARDENS RESORT & SPA

This place is technically in La Cruz de Huanacaxtle, but it's actually way closer to Bucerias than La Cruz center, so I have included it in this chapter. Vallarta Gardens is a series of luxury villas with a private terrace each. They include a kitchenette and living room area. Private pool optional. Or you can just enjoy the 2 shared pools, spa and an outdoor restaurant with international cuisine.

🏷️ **Budget:** $$$
📍 **Where:** North Bucerias Town
🏨 **Address:** Km 1.2 Hwy to Punta Mita

 BOOK HERE

HOSTAL BUCERIAS

If you're traveling on a budget, look no further. A hostel with a homey vibe four blocks away from the beach. Daily breakfast is included and there are free lockers and wifi access. This place also has a shared TV area, kitchen and garden for guests to enjoy.

🏷️ **Budget:** $40 private, $ 8 dormitory
📍 **Where:** The Golden Zone
🏨 **Address:** Blvd Riviera Nayarit 148

 BOOK HERE

Random Mexico Fact!

Color T.V. was invented in Mexico in 1942 by 17 year old engineer Guillermo Gonzalez Camarena. The first color transmission was broadcasted from Mexico City in 1946.

WHERE TO EAT & DRINK

Coffee & Brunch

EL CAFÉ DE BUCERÍAS

A local coffee spot and cafe that will become your home away from home. No matter what you're craving, they've got it...especially for breakfast. Pastries galore, crepes, eggs benedict and of course, chilaquiles (which by now you understand is somehow a breakfast food). Warning, this place does get crowded so get here early or you might have a little bit of a wait to get your food or table.

⊙ **Hours:** 8am to 9pm

♥ **Where:** Golden Zone

🛏 **Address:** Benito Juárez 51

♥ facebook.com/ ellcafedebucerias/

MR. CREAM WAFFLES & PANCAKES

When you wake up with a sweet tooth, this is where you come. As the name suggests, Mr. Cream is the place to go for fresh waffles and fluffy pancakes topped with all the goodies. The coffee is hot and the service is friendly. As with most popular places in this tiny town, come early to beat the hungry wave of humans.

⊙ **Hours:** Monday - Sunday 8am - 2pm

♥ **Where:** Golden Zone

🛏 **Address:** Abasolo #86-Int. A

♥ @mrcream_pancakesandwaffles

LA CABRA Y LA MATA COFFEE ROASTERS

If a plain old cup of coffee doesn't do it for you, come to this coffee roastery where you can get the best artisan coffee in Bucerias. Unlike the other cafes that get really crowded, this place is great because it's not very widely known. La Cabra y La Mata serves and sells coffee sourced from small family-owned cooperatives in different states of Mexico. Come and order an espresso or a cold brew to kick start your day.

🕐 *Hours:* 7:30 am - 2:00 pm

📍 *Where:* Golden Zone

🏬 *Address:* Lázaro Cárdenas 34 A

Street Food & Local Restaurants

EL CAFÉ DE BUCERÍAS

A local coffee spot and cafe that will become your home away from home. No matter what you're craving, they've got it...especially for breakfast.

Pastries galore, crepes, eggs benedict and of course, chilaquiles (which by now you understand is somehow a breakfast food). Warning, this place does get crowded so get here early or you might have a little bit of a wait to get your food or table.

🕐 *Hours:* 8am - 9pm

📍 *Where:* Golden Zone

🏬 *Address:* Benito Juárez 51

♥ facebook.com/elcafedebucerias/

MARISCOS VILLARREAL

Shrimp, octopus, oysters - this is where you get your seafood fix in Bucerias! If you want to eat fresh mariscos like a local, visit this little restaurant where you'll sit at plastic tables under a big umbrella next to Mexicans savoring their ceviche, tostadas or the super popular seafood salad...which is just a huge plate of in-season seafood of all kinds.

🕐 *Hours:* Fri - Wed 12pm - 6pm

📍 *Where:* Centro

🏬 *Address:* Dr. Abraham Gonzalez 22

LOS DORADOS DE VILLA BIRRIA

When you have a second, take a look at this Instagram: @los_doradosdevilla. This is what real birria tacos and birria soup look like. The benefit of staying in such a small local town is that you're going to get the most authentic versions of Mexican specialties. This place is case in point. Pro Tip: Go with the crispy taco (instead of the soft) and don't forget the salsa.

⊙ **Hours:** 8am - 2pm

♀ **Where:** Centro

🏠 **Address:** Corner of Av. Mexico and Cuahutemoc

EL REY DEL MAR

In English, this place means "The King of the Sea". It's a quirky seafood spot that specializes in aguachiles: a traditional coastal dish that consists of raw shrimp cut open "butterfly" style and cooked with lime. Served with avocado, cucumber and onion and a very spicy green salsa.

⊙ **Hours:** 1pm - 8pm

♀ **Where:** Golden Zone

🏠 **Address:** Av. Las Palmas 22

Pro Tip! When ordering aguachile, ask for the salsa on the side. That way you can decide how spicy you want to eat.

Restaurants

KENSHO

The date spot in Bucerias is an Asian and Thai-inspired restaurant owned by an American family. While the food is insanely good here at Kensho, what makes this place truly special is the friendliness and the fun the staff have while preparing and serving your meal. They make you feel like part of the gang. The experience plus the awesome food create an atmosphere you just can't get enough of. Ps. Try the Yellow Thai Curry.

⊙ **Hours:** Tue - Sun 3pm - 10pm

♀ **Where:** Golden Zone

🏠 **Address:** Calle Lázaro Cárdenas 108

⊕ kenshobucerias.com.mx/

OCEANS RESTAURANT

Seafood on the beach! Come for a day of sun tanning in lounge chairs in the sand while munching on guacamole and chips. Or come for lunch or dinner, sit at a table and order fresh lobster while watching the sunset. This is the little slice of restaurant paradise that you've been looking for. Beachfront, affordable and fresh.

⊙ **Hours:** 11am

♀ **Where:** Centro

🏠 **Address:** Av Pacífico #202

♥ facebook.com/

oceansrestaurantbucerias/

MR. & MRS. FISH

The name is going to spoil this surprise, but Mr. & Mrs. Fish has the best fish and chips in Bucerias! You also must try the fish tacos! Don't expect anything fancy here. Mr. & Mrs. Fish is a humble local eatery where they focus on fantastic food and service rather than frills.

♀ Where: Centro
🏛 Address: Avenida Del Pacifico #17
🌐 http://mrmrsfish.restaurantsnapshot.com/

LA POSTAL

The best pizza and pasta in town set in the cutest backyard picnic style courtyard surrounded by plants and twinkling lights. La Postal is a must visit for the food and the atmosphere! For oven fired pizzas, try the Sabriosa with brie cheese, cherry tomatoes and prosciutto. For handmade pasta, go for the La Fresca and let the pasta speak for itself!

☉ Hours: 10am - 10pm
♀ Where: Golden Zone
🏛 Address: Jose Maria Morelos 11
♥ facebook.com/lapostalbucerias

N'WOK COCINA ASIÁTICA CASUAL

Pad Thais, gyozas, curries, noodles... this is the place for all your asian food cravings. Even though Chef Norman is from Colombia, this place is known for its spot-on authenticity and amazing service. N'WOK closes

seasonally and usually remains closed from April through October, saving all their love and talent for you when they reopen.

☉ Hours: Mon - Sat 4:30 pm - 10:30pm
♀ Where: Centro
🏛 Address: Av. Mexico 30B
🌐 https://mmugazz.com/

LE BISTROT

An unexpected French restaurant in Bucerias founded by french couple, Sandrine and Jean-Christophe. Their menu is built on a balance of local and imported ingredients and including French classics like beef bourguignon and even snails. A night here feels like a mini vacation (within a vacation) to France! Take advantage!

☉ Hours: Thu - Tue 6pm - 10:30pm
♀ Where: Golden Zone
🏛 Address: Galeana 11
🌐 http://lebistrotbucerias.com/en/

IXI'IMI VEGANO

Jackfruit and hibiscus tacos, tofu chorizo, and delicious (but spicy) homemade salsas...this place is going to make you believe in the magic of vegan food. If you're still suspicious, start slow with a chocolate banana smoothie or the waffles!

☉ Hours: Mon, Tue, Wed, Thu, Fri, Sat 6pm - 10:30pm
♀ Where: Golden Zone

Address: Agustin Melgar 6

facebook.com/ixiimvegano

MEZZOGIORNO

During the day, Mezzogiorna has more of a beach club casual vibe. But as the sun goes down and torches and candles are lit, it turns into a romantic spot for wining and dining your honey (or yourself). Day or night, however, the food is undeniably sensational. Try the calamari and/or the gnocchi bolognese.

Hours: Tue - Sun 5pm - 11pm
Where: Centro
Address: Av. del Pacifico 33
mezzogiorno.godaddysites.com

Drinking

KAREN'S PLACE

The hangout spot. Karen's place has live music on the weekends from 7:00 PM to 9:00 PM and happy hour everyday from 3pm to 5pm. It's a casual and cozy spot where you can take your shoes off, sink your toes into the sand and get a little tipsy with an ocean view. Ps. This chapter of this book was written while sitting at Karen's Place...the wifi here is great.

Hours: 9am - 9pm
Where: Zona Dorada
Address: Benito Juárez 12
karensplacebucerias.com

SUKHA BEACHHOUSE

Sukha comes from the "sanskrit" term for "everlasting happiness". And to put their money where their mouth is, Sukha has an ongoing happy hour with special 2x1 cocktails everyday. Yes, this is where to get your Margarita fix.

Hours: 9:30am - 10pm
Where: Golden Zone
Address: Lazaro Cardenas 17
sukhabeachhouse.com/

THINGS TO DO IN BUCERIAS

AirBnb Experiences

BIKE + BOOZE

The quickest way to understand Bucerias is to ride around on a bike! On this tour, you'll ride around the most iconic landmarks while sampling food, beer, wine and traditional Mexican spirits. Don't worry, you'll just be tasting. This won't be enough to get you wasted while driving. Safety first!

Book here:

BIKE + FOOD

A must! This Bike + Food Tour will take you around town and even a little bit offroad in the countryside where you'll stop to try some of the best local food and most authentic food in town. During your leisurely 6-mile ride, you'll hear stories that will teach you about the history, culture and people of the area with breathtaking scenic views included.

Book here:

Outdoor Adventures

CHILL AT THE BEACH

Playa Bucerias is a 5-mile strip of soft sandy shores where you can bring a book, towel and sunscreen and go have a dip in the ocean. Or if you'd rather stay dry, you can sit at one of the restaurants on the beach and enjoy a beer with your toes in the sand. I recommend Karen's Place or Sukha Beachhouse (see our Where to Eat and Drink section for more deets).

LEARN HOW TO KITE SURF

The best time to learn to kite surf in Bucerias is between January to June when the weather stirs up the most wind. Check out the kitesurfing shop called The Kite Zone. They offer lessons, camps and even kite trips to other areas of Mexico. Come to learn or if you've already got the basics down, you can just rent the gear.

💸 **Budget:** Beginner lessons from $90 USD an hour (equipment included)
🕐 **Hours:** Wednesday to Sunday 10am - 6pm
📍 **Where:** The Golden Zone
🏛 **Address:** Lazaro Cardenas 86
🌐 thekitezone.com

STAND UP PADDLE BOARDING

Also known as SUP, stand up paddle boarding is a full body workout that takes a few tries to really get the hang of. Keep trying as you travel, especially in Bucerias. When the water is calm, SUP is a great way to explore the bay and get a viewpoint of the town from the water. Rent your board at Surf Mexico or join one of their SUP lessons or excursions where you'll hopefully spot some dolphins swimming right by you.

💸 **Budget:** One day rentals from $800 MXN ($40 USD)
🕐 **Hours:** Mon - Fri 9am - 6pm / Fri - Sat 9am - 4pm
📍 **Where:** Golden Zone
🏛 **Address:** Lazaro Cardenas 86
🌐 www.surfmexico.com/

Art & Culture

WALK AROUND DOWNTOWN

The downtown area of Bucerias looks like a Mexican postcard with pink, yellow and blue buildings, flags, paintings and handicrafts everywhere you turn. Get delightfully lost in the maze of cobblestone streets, then cross over the Paseo del Beso alley and explore the flea market. Shop around for Mexican crafts and continue on to the main plaza where locals just hang out enjoying the day. Carry on exploring up and down Mexico Avenue and Pacifico Avenue, which run along the ocean shore where you'll find many coffee shops and restaurants along the way.

VISIT THE ART DISTRICT

Every Thursday from 6pm during the months of November to April, Bucerias streets get crowded. People come out to join the Art Walk, a weekly event where resident artists open up their studios, galleries and boutiques for people to see their work and shop. And when they're finished, wine and dine in the restaurants in the area.

The Art District is the area encompassing the Art Walk. It spans across the Golden Zone, from Agustin Melgar street all the way to the Paseo del Beso. And includes over 20 restaurants, 10 galleries, boutiques, art galleries and studios. But you don't have to come to Bucerias only during Art Walk season. Check out the map and have your own DIY walk around the Art District. You can find the map here:

➤ https://beachpleasemexico.com/art-walk-bucerias.

⊙ *Hours:* High Season (November - April)

♀ *Where:* You can start at any of the map's locations, but the unofficial starting point is at Lazaro Cardenas 60a

SHOPPING IN BUCERIAS

Street Shopping

AROUND THE GOLDEN ZONE

All along Lazaro Cardenas in the Golden Zone, you'll find boutiques and art galleries with both traditional Mexican art and contemporary high-end pieces. You'll also find beautiful clothing and accessories along the way. Just have a stroll and window shop until you see something you can't resist.

WEDNESDAY'S FOREVER SPRING FARMER'S MARKET

A seasonal Farmer's Market that runs from mid-fall to mid-spring where you can find all kinds of local vendors selling everything from fresh juices and produce to traditional (and-not-so-traditional) arts and crafts.

⊙ *When:* November through April, every Wednesday 9am - 1pm

THE FLEA MARKET

Located right in the middle of the Downtown Area and the Golden Zone, this market is a few blocks of stalls packed with colorful Mexican crafts from the region and from all over the country. Vendors are usually open to barter but please be respectful of their prices, too. Pro Tip! The famous Alley of the Kiss is right in the middle of this market so you'll likely pass it as you explore the town.

⊙ *Hours:* Daily 10am - 6pm

♥ *Where:* Right in the middle of downtown and the Golden Zone

➤ Start at Alfredo V. Bonfil street, right next to "El Buzo".

BUCERIAS SUNDAY TIANGUIS

Tianguis is Spanish for "flea market" and this one is truly authentic. You can peruse this market every Sunday along the Arroyo del Indio with stall after stall of knicks and knacks, fruit, veggies, electronics, clothing items, and every random item you can imagine.

⊙ *Hours:* Sundays 7am - 2pm
♀ *Where:* Across the highway on the truly local side of Bucerias.
🛕 *Address:* Arroyo del Indio S/N

Souvenir Ideas

◊ Huichol art and crafts
◊ Ojos de Dios
◊ Talavera style tiles
◊ Blown glass tableware
◊ Colorful beaded jewelry
◊ Woven fabrics and "zarapes"

Food

MEGA SORIANA

The biggest, full-sized supermarket in the area. No membership needed.

⊙ *Hours:* 8am - 10pm
♀ *Where:* On the highway (so a drive or a bus is needed to get here)
🛕 *Address:* Hway Tepic - Puerto Vallarta 1297

CHEDRAUI

Another full-sized supermarket. A tad smaller than the Mega, but a little bit closer to town. No membership needed.

⊙ *Hours:* 7am - 11pm
♀ *Where:* Golden Zone (right beside the highway)
🛕 *Address:* Corner of Blvd Riviera Nayarit and Av. Las Palmas 596

PHOTO - UNSPLASH.COM

CHAPTER FOUR

La Cruz de Huanacaxtle

—

TIME NEEDED:

1-2 days

KNOWN FOR:

The Marina, the sailing life...and a particular taco place
which we'll tell you about later

BEST FOR:

Relaxing, beach time, watersports

INTRODUCTION TO LA CRUZ

This little unpronounceable town has been a fishing community for generations and still remains so today. Here you can witness the vibrant local fishing life puttering along as boats come to shore, carrying their shiny, fresh catch of the day. La Cruz's life and essence is so embedded with the ocean that even the streets are named after seafood.

La Cruz de Huanacaxtle means the cross of huanacaxtle (huanacaxtle is a type of wood). This little boat town represents life's intersection between local life and luxury yacht life (with a yacht club and all). It's this high-end development that has earned the town the title "the Nautical Capital" of the Riviera Nayarit and has turned it into a hub for seafaring life, especially sailing. This little bay is where many sailboats stop here to rest, stock up and refuel before continuing their journey along the coast. So...Tinder is pretty good here, just sayin'.

But La Cruz is not juuust a cruising pitstop on the way north or south. It's also a little expat hub, especially during the winter (high season). During this season, there's a Sunday Farmer's Market that's well known around the area and attracts residents from all around Banderas Bay.

La Cruz is also a great spot for fishing and even surfing when the waves get high enough. And because of its privileged location, you'll find the best panoramic view of the Bay, Puerto Vallarta and the mountain range beyond.

Ps. It's pronounced "wha-nah-CAX-slee". And yes, it takes some practice.

Areas to Know in La Cruz de Huanacaxtle

...AND A QUICK MAP TO MAKE THIS EVEN EASIER

1 MESA QUEMADA

2 LA CRUZ DE HUANACAXTLE

3 THE MARINA

4 EL TIZATE

5 LA MANZANILLA

6 CRUZ DE HUANACAXTLE BEACH

7 PIEDRA BLANCA

8 ARENA BANCA

You could easily walk around the entire town of La Cruz in one day. The town runs along 3 miles of beach, right between Bucerias and Punta Mita. And while most of it is referenced as La Cruz de Huanacaxtle, there are a few names you'll see around. So for easier understanding, let's break them down, shall we?

MESA QUEMADA

Mesa Quemada is the neighborhood at the far end of La Cruz towards Punta Mita and Playa La Manzanilla. You'll see this area mentioned as a part of many addresses in GoogleMaps and other platforms.

LA CRUZ DE HUANACAXTLE

The rest of the town is mostly referenced just with the town's name. You'll also notice that in the addresses. The whole town is a grid of picturesque cobblestoned streets where local life meets expat life - which is pretty damn easy to navigate.

THE MARINA

Located south of the Mesa Quemada neighborhood, La Cruz's high-end marina is a busy area that's fun to observe. Come grab a bite to eat at one of the restaurants, check out the fish market, and the seasonal La Cruz Farmers Market.

Fun Fact! La Cruz de Huanacaxtle's marina is the most modern marina in all the Mexican Pacific Coast and has 341 slips for boats up to 400 feet.

THE BEACH

The beach of La Cruz is a stretch of 3 miles of golden sand and clear waters, divided into 5 areas. You'll find

> **El Tizate** - on the southern side of town (towards Bucerias)
> **La Manzanilla** - on the northernmost edge of town (towards Punta Mita)
> **Cruz de Huanacaxtle** - right next to the Marina, on the Mercado del Mar side
> **Piedra Blanca** - a private beach north from La Manzanilla
> **Arena Blanca** - another private area after Piedra Blanca, surrounded by condos and new developments.

HOW TO GET TO AND FROM LA CRUZ

La Cruz is right between Bucerias and Punta Mita, 30 - 40 minutes North from Puerto Vallarta.

UBER OR INDRIVER

From Puerto Vallarta or Nuevo Vallarta you can take an Uber or an InDriver which will take around 40 min. It will cost a little less than 300 pesos (15 USD). From other locations further North, you'll most likely won't find an Uber so a Taxi or a Bus is your only option.

BUSES

The bus will take around 40 minutes. You can take the Compostela bus or ATM bus from Las Glorias or Walmart in Puerto Vallarta. They run every 15 minutes and cost 25 pesos (less than 2 USD). Make sure the bus you take says "LA CRUZ" on the windshield.

To leave La Cruz, walk towards the La Cruz de Huanacaxtle - Punta Mita Highway (the little highway that connects to the main highway, Riviera Nayarit Boulevard) to catch the bus. ATM buses run every 15 min and you'll see Puerto Vallarta or Mescales written on the windshield. They both will take you back to Puerto Vallarta and drop you off at the Walmart stop. If you're going to the downtown area of Puerto Vallarta, you'll have to change buses on that stop.

Pro Tip! You can always ask bus drivers "Para en (insert your destination here)?" to make sure you don't end up somewhere unexpected.

WHERE TO STAY IN LA CRUZ

GRAND MATLALI HILLS RESORT & SPA

All-inclusive Optional

Ready to make your friends jealous? Located on top of a panoramic hill, Grand Matlatli has one of the most sensational views in the area. A view which you can enjoy from your private pool villa.

If that's not in your budget, just book a private villa and enjoy the shared pool areas, plus... two adult-only jacuzzis, and even a unique natural pool with spring water from the mountain. This place also has their own private Beach Club, Eva Mandarina, which they will shuttle you to and from so you can get a bit boozy.

🏷️ ***Budget:*** From $$$

📍 ***Where:*** La Cruz de Huanacaxtle

🛏️ ***Address:*** Carretera Punta Mita Km 0.2

 BOOK HERE

B NAYAR

All-Inclusive Optional

A high-end exclusive resort with stunning Pacific Ocean views! Located on the southern end of town, this resort allows you to feel a little more isolated while still being super close to town to explore.

B Nayar offers suites and full-sized ocean-view villas plus - not one - but three pools, a jacuzzi, two restaurants, a gym and a spa AND fun amenities like kayaks are available to guests. This place has literally everything you could ever need on vacation.

💵 **Budget:** From $$$

📍 **Where:** Cruz de Huanacaxtle

🏠 **Address:** Blvrd Riviera Nayarit Km 1

 BOOK HERE

VILLA BELLA BED AND BREAKFAST INN

How does an infinity pool with panoramic views of the Sierra and the Pacific Ocean sound? How about intimate villas with ocean views and lush garden views? This Inn has been around since 1999 and has been run by the owner ever since. The whole place has been decorated with love over time and has a clean, crisp and cozy feeling with a sprinkle of luxury.

💵 **Budget:** From $$

📍 **Where:** Mesa Quemada

🏠 **Address:** Calle Monte Calvario 12

 BOOK HERE

CASA VILLA MAGNOLIA

Just a few blocks from the ocean, Casa Villa Magnolia is a set of colorful, rustic-style villas with palm trees and tropical vibes that really make you feel like you're on a Mexican vacation. There's a big pool waiting for you to jump in after your La Cruz adventures - and tennis lovers, you'll be pleased to find tennis courts waiting for you here.

💵 **Budget:** From $$

📍 **Where:** Cruz de Huanacaxtle

🏠 **Address:** Pampano 9

 BOOK HERE

JARDIN DEL MAR

Jardin del Mar has its own private beach access, shared pool, rooftop terrace and kayaks for you to explore the coast. A beachfront hacienda-style estate turned hotel with 7 villas (or "casitas") filled with mexican antiques and quirky trinkets, each casita can host up to 4 people and range from palapa studios to a full sized house!

🎟️ *Budget:* From $$$

📍 *Where:* La Cruz de Huanacaxtle

🏛️ *Address:* Playa Tiyazate, Casa Jaramillo

 BOOK HERE

PUNTA ESMERALDA BY DESTINO

Punta Esmeralda is almost right in the middle between La Cruz and Bucerias, so it's a great option if you want to explore both areas. Located on top of a hill, the views from their eight pools (yes, eight!) are gorgeous. Just imagine the sunsets!

The rooms have fully equipped kitchens which is convenient since the location is a bit of a walk to either town centers. If you're not in the mood to cook or go out, they've got a hotel at the restaurant to keep you content.

🎟️ *Budget:* $ (min. Booking of 3 nights)

📍 *Where:* La Cruz Huanacaxtle

🏛️ *Address:* Highway to Tepic KM 138

 BOOK HERE

WHERE TO EAT IN LA CRUZ

Coffee & Coworking

EL CAFE DE DON SIMON

A family-run little hidden gem in La Cruz that feels like home. Come here for the coffee and Mexican food, stay for the warm and homey service. Although this is mainly a coffee/breakfast spot, you can also come for lunch or dinner. Ps. Try the burritos.

⊙ *Hours:* Wed - Sun 8:30am - 10pm
♀ *Where:* Mesa Quemada
♀ *Where:* Delfin 19A
f @cafe.donsimon.1502

CAXTLE PASTELERIA Y CAFE

Sweets and coffee are the best way to start your day (especially when you're on vacation). Here is where I come for my frappuccino and cinnamon rolls fix...and usually end up taking some brownies home for later.

⊙ *Hours:* Wednesday - Monday 8am - 10pm
♀ *Where:* Mesa Quemada
♀ *Where:* Coral 8-18
♥ @caxtle.panaderia.y.cafe

Street Food & Local Restaurants

TACOS ON THE STREET

Meet the taco stand that inspired us to visit La Cruz in the first place. So many friends recommended this place that we just had to try it out! The carne asada tacos and quesadillas were, in fact, the best in the area and made the stay totally worth it. This place is Mexican Girl Approved!

🕑 **Hours:** Wednesday - Sunday - 5pm 10:30pm

📍 **Where:** Mesa Quemada

🏪 **Address:** Huachinango 9

f Contact: Tacos On The Street

PHOTO / EMILIA IGARTUA

THE LITTLE HOT GRILL

Real Mexican food created by locals for locals. But not exclusively. Everyone's welcome at The Little Hot Grill. The menu is short which is the mark of a great restaurant. This place is so local, even prices here are Mexican prices (aka cheaper than what you'll usually find.) Try the chilaquiles any time of day!

Hours: Mon - Sat 8pm - 9pm

Where: La Cruz de Huanacaxtle

Address: Corner of Atun and Camaron

RINCON DEL BUZO

You must stop at this place on your way in or out of La Cruz! While the menu is seafood-centric, the burgers are ah-mazing. Especially the shrimp burger which is a mix of the two evils! Come hungry and prepare to get a little juicy as this is a "I need more napkins" kind of place.

Hours: 12pm - 9pm

Where: La Cruz de Huanacaxtle (near the town's entrance)

Address: Av. Bahía de Banderas 24

rincondelbuzo.com

Restaurants

LA PESKA

Want to live the yacht life without the hassle of a boat? Come to La Peska for a fancy-yet-casual dinner with a view of the marina and beyond. It serves mainly, of course, seafood, but has international dishes on the menu too. And the best part? They have Skinny Margaritas (Alexa's go-to). Cheers!

Hours: 1pm - 10pm

Where: The Marina

Address: Malecon de la Marina 1B

https://lapeska.com/

FRASCATI

Tired of seafood? Just below La Peska you'll find Frascati. An Italian ristorante that shares the stunning Marina views but gives you a break from ocean creatures. Go full Italian with a caprese salada wood fired pizza and a big bowl of creamy pasta. This is also your opportunity to swap margaritas for wine!

Hours: 1pm - 9pm

Where: The Marina

Address: Malecon Marina 1A

frascatilacruz.com

MASALA BAR & GRILL

Mexican meets Mediterranean at Masala Bar & Grill. Seafood. Crab Cakes. Duck. Pasta. And you guessed it: locally caught fresh seafood. Masala Bar & Grill is often hailed as the best restaurant in La Cruz. Come see (and taste) for yourself.

Hours:: Wed - Sun 5pm - 10:30pm

Where: Mesa Quemada

Address: Coral 10

masalarestaurante.com

MARINA BAR & GRILL BY OSO'S

Live music on the waterfront and a 3-hour-long Happy Hour (3-7). Yep, this place is holiday heaven. Plus, Marina Bar & Grill by Oso's is located right within the Mercado del Mar in the Marina, so fish and seafood here are as fresh as it gets.

⊙ **Hours:** Daily 12pm - 9pm
♀ **Where:** Mercado del Mar
🚇 **Address:** Del Mar 4
f MarinaBarandGrillLaCruz

FALCONI

Ready for another seafood break? Falconi is all about freshly made pasta, pizza and calzones. They also deliver, so if you want to take a break from exploring and eat pizza in bed, these guys got you covered. (We won't judge. We do it all the time)

⊙ **Hours:** Daily 3pm - 10:30pm
♀ **Where:** Two blocks down from Mar Mediterraneo street towards the ocean
🚇 **Address:** Calle Sierra 28
⊕ http://falconilacruz.com/

TREEHOUSE BAR & GRILL

American meets Mexican in this menu filled with BBQ ribs and burritos. They've got live music and dancing nights every night of the week - so put on your dancing shoes and check out their Facebook page down below for their dancing calendar.

⊙ **Hours:** Mon - Sat 4pm - 11pm
♀ **Where:** La Cruz de Huanacaxtle
🚇 **Address:** Coral 68
f treehousebarlacruz

YIN YANG

With all the fresh seafood around, it'd be a crime to not have a sushi place in La Cruz. Luckily Yin Yang is just that. Their menu has both traditional sushi and what we call Mexican sushi. Mexican sushi is kind of a remix of japanese dishes into new and more elaborate ones. Baked rolls, toppings and even some spicy sauces...It's sushi reloaded. The only downside is that this place closes seasonally from July to October.

⊙ **Hours:** October to June / Tuesday - Saturday 5pm - 9pm
♀ **Where:** La Cruz de Huanacaxtle (right in front of the Catholic Church)
🚇 **Address:** Marlin 39
f fyinyangsushilacruz

THINGS TO DO IN LA CRUZ

Outdoors

LA MANZANILLA BEACH

Just 0.5 miles past the center, La Manzanilla is La Cruz's best known beach. The shore is calm and has a gentle slope, making it a super friendly place to swim. You can chill under the palapas (umbrellas) which are sprinkled along the beach or rent sun chairs from the restaurants on the beach. During high season, La Manzanilla can get quite crowded. When this happens, head toward the southern end of the beach for an emptier area.

DESTILADERAS BEACH

A beautiful long white stretch of white sand and dramatic rock formations, this beach sits on the bay right across from Puerto Vallarta. There are several palapas and local eateries along the shore and you can rent your own little palapa and sun chairs for the day which costs around 250 pesos (12.5 USD).

The water here is usually calm and great for swimming. However, swells are known to come into this beach when the tides change...which is not fun for swimming in. The swell is bigger on the southern end of the beach where you'll often see surfers riding the waves. Just be observant and pick the calmest area to swim.

To get here from La Cruz you can take one of the local buses that go towards Punta Mita. Just make sure that they don't go on the highway, because they will drop you off very far away from the beach's entrance. The ATM (Auto Transportes Medina) line runs along Nuevo Vallarta to Punta Mita and stops at Las Destiladeras beach too. A bus ride will cost around 20 pesos ($1 USD). For a more convenient way to get here, just get a driver.

GO FISHING

La Cruz is the best destination for fishing in the entire Banderas Bay. Many residents here are longtime fishermen and also offer local fishing excursions for tourists. If you're lucky you can come back to shore with tuna, sea bass, snapper or maybe some even some bigger game.

Environmental Tip! If you catch a small to medium size fish, please catch and release. Not only is it not healthy to eat fish that are too young, it's also not good for the ecosystem. We need to allow these fish populations to grow to their adult and reproductive stage. Let's keep our oceans thriving!

LEARN HOW TO SAIL

Did you know that having sailing experience on your resume is actually an incredible way to travel and see the world? All over the world there are open positions for boat crew in all kinds of sailboats and vessels. And La Cruz de Huanacaxtle is home to the International Sailing Academy, a world-class school for sailing, especially laser sailing (small sailboat dinghies). ISA has trained everyone, from junior sailor to Olympic qualifiers. So you can also come to La Cruz for a mix of fun and education.

➤ Visit https://internationalsailingacademy.com/ for more info.

Ps. If you already sail there are frequent WWS (Women Who Sail) meet-ups in the area.

➤ facebook.com/groups/WomenWhoSail/

Art & Culture

EAT, SLEEP, REPEAT.

Food is culture. And eating is exploring. So if sailing or fishing are not your thing, coming to La Cruz just for a food tour is totally worth it (and justified). Because of its fishing tradition and location, this town is known for its wide variety of super fresh seafood dishes in every form and recipe. And other local culinary surprises.

LA CRUZ MARKET

The most famous farmers market in all of Banderas Bay! Really! Residents from all around the area drive to La Cruz to do their shopping in this market. In this market, you can find a wide variety of local vendors offering local dishes, fresh produce, artisanal cheeses, homemade jams, mexican arts and crafts, handmade jewelry, local snacks, and all kinds of products.

If you're staying a longer period (and during market season) it's worth the visit to do your weekly shopping here. Or just to pass the morning and have a bite with views to the Marina.

This market is run by a local non for profit organization called Huanacaxtle A.C., and they make this Sunday occasion more than just a market. They run an array of activities, workshops and programmes all with the intention to continue developing the community in La Cruz in a positive way. So visiting this market is also supporting the community. Win-win.

⊙ *Hours:* November through April/ Sundays 8am - 2pm
♀ *Where:* The Marina
🚉 *Address:* Marlin 39A
🌐 www.lacruzmarket.com

MERCADO DEL MAR (FISH MARKET)

The local fish market. Developed as an alliance to the marina, this market has over 30 stalls where the local fishermen display their catch of the day. Even if you're not planning to buy and cook, it's still worth coming to see this essential part of the local life of La Cruz. And seeing the colorful sea goodies is always interesting. Weird, but interesting.

Pro Tip! English is not widely spoken in this market, so come prepared with some useful phrases, or bring along a bilingual friend.

⊙ *Hours:* 8am - 3:30pm
♥ *Where:* the Marina
🚉 *Address:* Marlin 39A

Pools & Beach Clubs

CLUB DE PLAYA B NAYAR

B Nayar Resort's own pool club. Not a guest? Fear not, my love. You can still enjoy the beach, sun chairs and both pools with a Day Pass. T

he cost? 500 pesos (25 USD). This includes credit towards food, use of the facilities and use of kayaks. Towels are charged extra (lame, we know), but you can bring your own.

⊙ *Hours:* 9am - 8:30pm
♥ *Where:* La Cruz de Huanacaxtle Beach
🚉 *Address:* Blvd Riviera Nayarit SN Km 1
⊕ www.hotelbnayar.mx

EVA MANDARINA BEACH CLUB

Hey Fancy Pants, welcome to Grand Matlali Resort & Spa's own beachclub, right on the crystal waters of La Cruz. You can come here and enjoy the private beach even if you're not a guest of the hotel.

Their Day Pass has a cost of 700 pesos (35 USD) which includes credit towards food and drink and use of their amenities like the sun chairs and wifi.

⊙ *Hours:* 12pm - 5:30pm
♥ *Where:* Right next to the Marina
🚉 *Address:* Pescador 37
⊕ https://www.matlali.com/en/beach-club

NAUHI (DESTILADERAS BEACH CLUB & RESTAURANTE)

Also on Destiladeras, Nahui serves as the entrance point to this beach. So there's no way you'll miss it. Order some food (with a cold beer on the side) and you can enjoy their sun chairs and palapas. Ready for some beach people watching?

⊙ *Hours:* 11am - 10pm
♥ *Where:* Playa Destiladeras
f NahuiDestiladeras

SHOPPING IN LA CRUZ

Food Shopping

If you want to visit a big supermarket, I regret to inform you there's none right in La Cruz but don't fret. You can head to the Mega Soriana or Chedraui in Bucerias, just 15 minutes away. (Check our Bucerias chapter on page 145). You might not need to even go to these grocery stores, however, as you can find all the essentials in the local "abarrotes" (convenience stores) around town.

LA CRUZ MARKET

You can get fresh produce and snacks from local vendors every Sunday at La Cruz Market. This is a great place to shop for unique and healthy groceries and in fact, many residents of the area drive here every week for their weekly supplies. But remember, this market is seasonal!

◷ **Hours:** November through April, Sundays 9am - 2pm
♥ **Where:** The Marina

⊞ **Address:** Marlin 39A
⊕ www.lacruzmarket.com/

MERCADO DE MAR

All the fish and seafood you could ask for, freshly caught by local fishermen. What's available will always depend on the fishing seasons, but La Cruz is mostly abundant in tuna, mahi mahi and snappers in addition to octopus and shrimp. Pro Tip! If you're good with Spanish you can always ask the fishermen for their local recipes and cooking tips for whatever you buy.

◷ **Hours:** 8am - 3:30pm
♥ **Where:** the Marina
⊞ **Address:** Marlin 39A

CHAPTER FIVE

Punta Mita

———

TIME NEEDED:

3+ days

KNOWN FOR:

A contrast between the fanciest resorts in the bay and a
laid back beach town with incredible seafood

BEST FOR:

An upscale luxury vacation or a surf getaway while
staying a hostel

INTRODUCTION TO PUNTA MITA

Luxury or low key, take your pick. Punta Mita is two worlds in one.

In Punta Mita you'll find some of the most high-end resorts in the world that have attracted big stars like Jennifer Aniston, Leonardo DiCaprio and Lady Gaga. But you'll also find budget-friendly surf hostels made from recycled shipping containers for everyone who isn't ballin' out on $1000 per night hotels. In Punta Mita, you can spend your day lounging in a private beach cabana at the Four Seasons or you can watch the fisherman carry in their daily catch from the main beach. Or you can do what I did: both.

Punta Mita is a peninsula that jets out into the Pacific Ocean with incredible surf breaks. Tides have created sugary white sand beaches on all sides. Humpback whales, dolphins, sea turtles and a plethora of wild birds can be seen off the coast of this protected marine habitat amongst some of the most beautiful sunsets.

In my humble opinion, Punta Mita is a must. No matter your budget, a week here is going to have the same result. You'll leave with a greater appreciation of local culture, nature and food - and probably make a few friends, both locals and expats. Nothing here is touristy, not even the resorts who do possibly the most eloquent job at immersing you into traditional Mexican culture. Punta Mita has preserved the essence of the Banderas Bay and found a balance between welcoming travelers while keeping local traditions alive.

Areas to Know in Punta Mita

AND A QUICK MAP TO GET TO KNOW THE LAY OF THE LAND

1 CENTRO & PLAYA ANCLOTE

2 THE RESORT COMPOUND

3 PLAYA CAREYEROS

4 FOUR SEAONS

5 ST. REGIS

6 PLAYA LA LANCHA

7 W PUNTA MITA

CENTRO & PLAYA ANCLOTE

Punta de Mita has one main road called Avenida Las Redes which will lead you to the main beach Playa Anclote. This beach is where you'll find restaurants, shops, and a couple of hotels and condos. This is also where you'll find pangas (boats) to take you on trips to places like Marietas Island. Centro and Playa Anclote melt together into one.

THE RESORT COMPOUND

Four Seasons, The St. Regis and the Bahia & Pacifico Golf Course share an entrance to their facilities. These resorts are home to the most beautiful beaches in all of Bahia de Banderas - but you can only visit them if you're a guest at the hotel or golf course.

PLAYA CAREYEROS

The beach north from Playa Anclote across the peninsula is Playa Careyeros. Depending on the tide, this beach can offer white sand and crystal clear water for swimming. You'll find several guest houses over here that offer you the chance to slow down, connect with yourself and connect with other souls looking for the same chilled out vibe.

HOW TO GET TO PUNTA MITA

Nestled on the Pacific Coast in the state of Nayarit, Sayulita is only 13.5 miles from Puerto Vallarta (and it's airport) and will only take you about 45-minutes to 1.5 hours drive to reach it depending on how you're traveling.

DRIVER OR HOTEL PICK UP

If you're staying at one of the luxury resorts here in Punta Mita, they will most likely include free-pick up from the airport or your hotel in another area of the bay.

If not, hire a private driver from my driver directory on page 292.

If you're in the center of Puerto Vallarta, you can try getting an InDriver or Uber when you're ready to leave.

BUS

Catch an "ATM" bus at Walmart. You'll see two waiting zones for buses. Once you're facing Walmart and Sam's Club, head over to the larger waiting area on the left. Look for a man with a clipboard. He is there to direct passengers to get on the correct bus.

Board the ATM bus that says Punta Mita. It will drop you in town (not at the resorts) and then you can walk to your hotel. Or you can board the green and white Compostela bus to Bucerias and take a cab to Punta Mita from Bucerias. Ask the man with a clipboard when both buses come and you can decide which option is most convenient for you.

HOW TO GET AROUND

This all depends where you're staying.

Staying at the resorts? You won't be within walking distance to town so most resorts offer either a shuttle or private driver to take you in and out of town on the days you want to explore.

Staying in the center of town? Walk! Punta Mita is only about 10 by 10 blocks and accessible by foot.

Want to beach hop or head back to your resort on your own?
Take a cab which you'll find in the center of town.

Note that there are not likely to be Ubers or InDrivers in Punta Mita so it's important to have some private drivers saved in your phone.

WHERE TO STAY
IN PUNTA MITA

FOUR SEASONS PUNTA MITA

Celebrities such as Selena Gomez, Jessica Simpson and...me (humble brag) have fallen in love with this 5-star resort in Punta Mita. Yes, me and Emilia spent one blissful week at this 5-star resort and it was a dream come true.

PHOTO / FOUR SEASONS

Wake up for yoga on the rocks overlooking the ocean or an intense AquaForza fitness class in the pool. Then, head to a breezy cabana on the beach where you spend your morning running from the warm ocean water on sugary sand to swinging chair beds beneath palm trees under the sun, and back to the cabana for a plate of fresh exotic fruit and repeat.

The staff happily wait on your every whim. There are paddle boards and kayaks to explore the waters and a golf cart waiting to take you back to your room where you can sip a coffee in your robe on the balcony with a view.

Or take it easy with a relaxing morning as you float the lazy river with a bloody mary in hand and then head to the spa for a blissful massage followed by a dip in the bathhouse with a collection of 3 different temperature pools. In the afternoon, join an intimate tequila blending class and return home with a bottle of your very own bottle of personally blended tequila.

For you golfers, Four Seasons Punta Mita is home to Jack Nicklaus-designed course featuring the world-famous Tale of the Whale hole and offers panoramic views of Bahía de Banderas.

This little slice of paradise offers you four restaurants to choose from, my favorite being Bahía, right down by the sand with a stunning view of the ocean. Dos Catrinas Restaurant is a close second where you can discover new agave spirits you never even knew existed through a Mexican Spirits Flight tasting experience. There's also a beach shack with cocktails, popsicles in the afternoon, an adults-only pool and the list goes on. Put Four Seasons Punta Mita on your vacation bucket list and tick it off as soon as you

💸 **Budget:** : $$$$$

📍 **Where:** The Resort Compound

 BOOK HERE

CASA KOKO

Coming with a crew? Casa Koko is a luxury villa where the celebrities often stay to enjoy an infinity pool overlooking the ocean, a fire pit where you can watch the stars and to be pampered by a full time staff including a chef and a driver. When you stay here you get access to the best resorts' beach clubs, golf clubs and tennis clubs, as well. This villa can accommodate 16 people and starts at $5000 per night.

💸 *Budget:* $$$$$
📍 *Where:* La Punta del Faro, Lote 5

 BOOK HERE

W PUNTA MITA

Now is your chance to snag a private pool villa where you can swim at night with a view of the stars above and the sound of waves crashing in the distance. W Punta Mita just screams sexy with a quirky colorful design set against the jaw-dropping background of crystal blue ocean and white sand beach. Bring your best outfits and get your camera ready. Go with the W Unlimited all-inclusive package to eat and drink through their 5 on-site restaurants and all the cocktails you need to totally unplug and unwind.

💸 *Budget:* $$$$
📍 *Where:* Hway La Cruz de Huanacaxtle - Punta Mita Km 8.5

 BOOK HERE

XIOBELLA BOUTIQUE HOTEL

One of the most pristine, untouched beaches in the area has just popped up with a brand new exclusive hotel. Xiobella is a small and intimate escape where you come with a book, a journal and tanning lotion (and maybe a boyfriend) and leave all your worries at home. When you get a sudden burst of adventure, Sayulita is only 20 minutes away.

💵 **Budget:** $$$

📍 **Where:** Playa Careyeros

 BOOK HERE

CONRAD PUNTA DE MITA

If you're the kind of girl that loves to live in the pool during her vacation while sipping a cocktail and meeting new people..this ones for you. Conrad Punta de Mita is luxury for a more social crowd of friends, couples and solo travelers. The pools, bars and beach clubs are spacious but also make it easy to meet other people. There's a spa, sauna, a gym, and hot tubs to tend to your vacation needs and the gorgeous ocean with white sand to tend to your mermaid soul! Solo girl approved!

💵 **Budget:** : $$$

📍 **Where:** Just North of Playa Careyeros

 BOOK HERE

HOTEL MESON DE MITA

Affordable and in the perfect exploring location right in the center of town but also right on the beach! This place is an absolute steal. You'll love the big refreshing pool, the lounge chairs in the sand, and the friendliness of the staff who are excited to make your stay as comfortable as possible.

💸 *Budget:* $

📍 *Where:* Playa Anclote

 BOOK HERE

PACIFIC NOMADS EARTHBAG HOUSE

Eco-friendly chic! This sustainable, solar powered "earthbag" house feels like Santorini meets Mexico! Big breezy balconies facing the ocean, hammocks, a swimming pool, surf boards that you can drag right down to the beach - this place is a dream. Come, chill, and meet new friends for adventures which Pacific Nomads will help you organize on the spot.

💸 *Budget:* $

📍 *Where:* Playa Careyeros

 BOOK HERE

Fun Fact!

Mexico's real and full name is United States of Mexico. It's divided in 31 states, plus the Federal District which you know as Mexico City.

WHERE TO EAT
IN PUNTA MITA

Coffee & Coworking

Local Restaurants

CAFECITO DE MITA

A coffee shop by the beach which most people find becomes part of their regular Punta Mita morning routine. At Cafecito de Mita, you're sipping local coffee from the state of Nayarit which is turned into your favorite fixes like cappuccinos, lattes, or simply over ice. They've also got smoothies, ice cream, and fresh pressed juice; everything you need to wake up or cool down in the Mexican morning heat.

⊙ *Hours:* Daily 8am - 5pm
♀ *Where:* By the beach
🏠 *Address:* Ave El Anclote 15
♥ *Contact:* @cafecito_de_mita

SAZÓN DE MITA RESTAURANTE

In Mexico, there's this popular breakfast dish called Chilaquiles. It's basically fried tortilla chips with fresh cheese and salsa - and it's totally indulgent. But when in Mexico, do as the Mexicans and order this for breakfast alongside a freshly squeezed "Jugo Natural". This is the place to come and eat like a local. Sazón de Mita is a tiny restaurant with just a few tables and locals popping in for their morning coffee fix.

Come back a little later in the day and try some of their other dishes for lunch. They've got all the classics: birria, ceviche, burritos, enchiladas, tacos, tortas and quesadillas - and it's all super affordable cheap eats.

Budget: Monday - Saturday 7:30-5pm (closes 3:30pm on Saturdays)

Where: Punta Mita Town, a 7-minute walk from the beach

Address: Otilio Montaño, Emiliano Zapata 6

MINA RESTAURANTE MEXICANO

What used to be known as Si Senor, Mina is a staple in the Punta Mita restaurant scene! It's the kind of place you'll find yourself coming back to over and over again because the food is exquisite and the servers become your friends. Come for a casual bite with a view or make an event of it with their gorgeous menu filled with steaks, lobster, and local delicacies. Ps. Keep an eye out for fishermen carrying massive fish through the restaurant!

Hours: 12pm-11pm

Where: By the Beach

Address: Ave El Anclote 200

♥ @minarestaurante

ROCIO

Eat your lunch and then run into the ocean, Rocio is a restaurant + activity in one. They are most well-known for their grilled fish, shrimp and lobster served with sides of bread, salad and potatoes. When you're done eating, go for a swim right in front of your table or rent surfboards and paddle boards directly in front of the restaurant. It's easy to spend a whole afternoon hanging out at Rocio.

Hours: Daily 8am-6pm

Where: Right next to La Rustica on the beach, it's kind of hidden so walk to the left of Rustica towards the sand and look for a simple little beach bar.

Address: Ave El Anclote

Restaurants

HECTOR'S KITCHEN

A former Four Seasons Chef creating the butteriest octopus, the most scrumptious grilled shrimp, mariscos risotto that will blow your mind and whatever else Chef Héctor Leyva is pulling out of the sea.

Come eat like a queen, order a bottle of wine, and treat yourself. On average, prices range from $7.5 to $27 USD - take advantage because this kind of dining experience would be twice the price back home.

Hours: 11 am - 6 pm

Where: Centro

Address: Ave El Anclote 202

♥ **Contact:** @hectorskitchen.mx

CASA TERESA

Romantic whether you are solo or coupled up. Dinner here is a love story. Lit by candlelight and adorned with chandeliers, this old European style Italian restaurant is actually set in the backyard and house of a local family here in Punta Mita. The dishes are made with love and use fresh ingredients like handmade pasta and meatballs and locally caught seafood. It was no surprise to discover that Casa Teresa was the scene for a dinner date on The Bachelor. This place is date-worthy.

⊙ **Hours:** 6 pm to 11 pm

♀ **Where:** Punta De Mita

🛏 **Address:** Calle Pez Vela 133

🌐 **Contact:** casateresapuntamita.com

LA CABAÑA

Local comfort food in a casual setting under a straw palapa with plastic chairs by the beach. You'll find no smoke and mirrors here. Just home cooking where each bite speaks for itself. If you like seafood and want to eat like a Mexican order the Coctel de Camaron; a big glass full of shrimp and avocado which you eat with a spoon. Or go classic with fish tacos and order a beer to go with em'. You'll leave spending around $5-$10 USD per person...depending on how much you drink.

⊙ **Hours:** Daily 10am-8pm (10pm on Sundays)

♀ **Where:** By the beach

🛏 **Address:** Ave El Anclote 341

LOBSTER PARADISE

When I think of a Mexican vacation, I think of sipping a margarita by the beach with some guacamole while waiting on my locally caught lobster and juicy coconut shrimp, while catching a breeze. Lobster Paradise delivers just that.

I recommend coming both during the day and at night for a total contrast in environment. The day feels ultra casual and the evening feels more elegant and sophisticated.

⊙ **Hours:** Daily 12pm-10pm

♀ **Where:** By the beach

🛏 **Address:** Ave El Anclote 7

RUSTICA PUNTA MITA

LA meets Mexico, I call this place "casual-cool". It's where you come to get a little dressed up and order a cocktail while watching the sunset. Rustica is one of the most popular dinner + drinks spots for the expats in the area so the people-watching is top notch. Coming alone? Walk straight in and go to the circular bar in the middle of the restaurant. Post up on a bar stool and alternate between watching the ocean and the Punta Mita whos' who

⊙ **Hours:** Daily 3pm-11pm (opens early at 1pm on Saturday/Sunday)

♀ **Where:** By the beach

🛏 **Address:** Ave El Anclote 222a

♥ @larusticamita

TUNA BLANCA BY THIERRY BLOUET

Fancy farm-to-table dining, Tuna Blanca is the kind of place you come for a 5-course tasting menu and wine pairing by the beach.

Of course you can also order off menu, with upscale dishes like Grilled Beef Medallions with Camembert Cheese Sauce and finish with a Milk Caramel Fondant for dessert. The plating is art and the flavors are divine.

⊙ **Hours:** Monday - Saturday 7:30-5pm (closes 3:30pm on Saturdays).

♥ **Where:** Punta Mita Town, a 7-minute walk from the beach

🛕 **Address:** Otilio Montaño, Emiliano Zapata 6

♥ @tunablancamita

DINNER MADE BY A PRIVATE CHEF

Have you ever had a private chef come to your place and create a dining experience just for you? Now's your chance with Chef Isaac, an international-traveling chef with an impressive kitchen resume.

He'll bring all the ingredients and tools he needs. You can watch him cook, put on an apron and help out or just wait for the gorgeous works of food art to be served. At $84 per person, this really is a once-in-a-lifetime experience.

 Book him here...

Foodie Fun Fact!

Even though you'll find burritos mostly everywhere, burritos are originally from the northern part of Mexico. And no, real mexican burritos are not filled with rice.

THINGS TO DO
IN PUNTA MITA

PHOTO / UNSPLASH.COM

On the Water...

SNORKELING, DIVING AND SURFING

When I travel to a small town like Punta Mita, I like to link up with one company that does it all. Getting to know the people you're going on adventures with makes them all the more fun. In Punta Mita, I recommend a company called Mictlan Surf for your water adventures. They've got lots to choose from - but here is where to start.

SURFING

Punta Mita is known for having some of the best surf breaks in the entire bay. Mictlan Surf offers surf lessons for beginners and lessons for surfers who want to advance their skills on the board. Want to get a little more adventurous? They also offer surfing boat trips where you head out to hunt down the best breaks according to the tides and weather. This means less crowded surf and more waves for you.

SCUBA DIVING
AND SNORKELING

Punta Mita is teeming with a gorgeous underwater world where you can see mantas, dolphins, octopus, sea horses and an array of colorful fish and coral in addition to pinnacles, underwater caves, channels and drop offs. For diving, snorkeling and Open Water Certifications, Mictlan Surf has you covered. You can trust their safety standards, boats, equipment and certified divers.

🕐 **Hours:** Daily 8am - 7pm
📍 **Where:** By the beach
🏛 **Address:** Ave El Anclote #151
🌐 **Contact:** www.mictlansurf.com
❤ @mictlansurfshop

FISHING AND SPEARFISHING

FISHING

Spearmex does all things fish-related starting with deep-sea fishing excursions. You can go Big Game fishing where you're hunting for marlin, yellow fin tuna, and more. Or go Inshore Fishing where you're looking for reef snapper, mahi mahi and mackerels. Want something a little more adventurous? Try Spearfishing.

SPEARFISHING

Spearfishing is a centuries old method of catching fish underwater with a harpoon-style tool rather than a pole. It takes some finesse and skill which you can learn in a beginners spearfishing tour with Spearmex based out of Punta Mita.

You'll hop on a boat with the experts who will take you to different areas in the bay where you'll hunt and catch fish which you will later grill up and eat. Snorkel gear, wetsuits and spearguns will be provided and your crew for the day will pick you up!

Spearfishing can be taken to even more extreme levels when you train as a freediver...

FREEDIVING

Freediving is what I often refer to as Mermaid Shit. Emilia is a free diver which means that she trains to hold her breath in a meditative state to dive to the depths of the ocean with no breathing gear or air tanks. This sounded impossible to me until I started taking lessons myself. Freediving unlocks a whole new world of possibilities in the ocean. Give it a shot and take a lesson with Spearmex while you're here.

☉ **Hours:** Daily 9am - 6pm

♥ **Where:** Playa Anclote

🏛 **Address:** Ave El Anclote 200
🌐 **Contact:** Spearmex.com
♥ @spearmex

DIY SUP PADDLE BOARDING

When the tide is low and the surf has mellowed, head to Rocio restaurant on the beach (right next to Rustica Cafe). Right in front of the restaurant is where you can rent paddle boards.

Before you take the paddle board into the water, ask the rental guys where to find the calmest waters. Usually this is just 100 meters up the beach. Afterwards, have a bite at Rocio restaurant and you've got yourself the perfect little afternoon.

☉ **Hours:** Daily 8am - 6pm
♥ **Where:** Playa Anclote
🏛 **Address:** Next to Ave El Anclote 222a

VISIT MARIETAS ISLAND

A fascinating site, come to snorkel, lay on the beach, explore little caves and catch some breathtaking views of the islands. Marietas Island is part of a protected marine sanctuary which only allows a certain number of people to visit per day, so I recommend going in the morning!

➤ **Ways to Get There:**

1. Take a Local Panga Boat

Rent a boat per hour to take you wherever you want, Marietas Islands included. Panga boats can be arranged by the Cooperativo in Punta de Mita, a local fishermen's co-op where all the boats are located in the same spot at the end of Ave Anclote (past all the restaurants).

You can hire a captain for around $70 USD per hour. Want to reserve a captain ahead of time? Call Captain Rudi at 322-228-7274

2. Link Up with an Adventure Company

Go on a laid back trip to Mariettas with Mictlan Surf School in Punta Mita or jump on a party boat with Chica Loca Tours leaving from Sayulita and La Cruz.

EXPLORE WITH CHICA LOCCA BOAT TOURS

A party boat that offers epic adventures in the bay on the most badass catamaran's around. Check out page 223 where I give you all the details of the adventures that Chica Loca Offers, including a day trip to Marietas Island, Yelapa Waterfall and Whale Watching (December to March). To hop on these tours from Punta Mita, you can meet them either in La Cruz or in Sayulita.

 Check them out at Chicalocatours.com

fun, educational and safe. Wildmex offers 3 tours which vary in length and difficulty, but all of which are worth the sweat!

9 _Where:_ $65 - $85 per group @wildmexadventure

 Check out Wildmex.com

On Land...

STROLL THROUGH TOWN

Where trucks ride through the town with speakers on the back advertising fresh fish they're selling out of the truck bed, kids play in the streets and little tiendas sell Micheladas out front. Punta Mita Town has a lot of local life to offer once you walk back into the neighborhood away from the beach. It's hard to get lost in Punta Mita but easy to find little gems that will delight you.

HIKING

The peninsula of Punta Mita offers some spectacular vistas especially if you're willing to hike to them. The hikes in this area, however, are not the easiest to navigate solo which is why I recommend going on a guided tour with some local guides who will make the experience more

PUNTA MITA GOLF CLUB

Golfers come from all over the world to tee off at this 36 hole course set on 380 acres of land. The course jets out into the Pacific Ocean giving you spectacular views of the Banderas Bay and features the world famous Jack Jack Nicklaus Signature Tail of the Whale hole. The Punte Mita Golf Club features the Pacifico Course and the Bahio Course, only accessible to guests of the Four Seasons and the St. Regis Hotel, and residents inside the gate.

 Check out GolfPuntaMita.com

WHERE TO NEXT?

If you recall, arriving in Punta Mita is **most accessible by car** and the same is said when departing. Your best bet to get to your next destination is to **arrange a driver ahead of time** to pick you up. Check out the **driver directory on page 292.**

However, if you're **staying at a resort,** they'll often **offer to drive you** to your next destination no matter where it is. The Four Seasons included this driver service with our stay, however the other resorts might charge a fee. Check with your resort when you arrive.

If you are traveling cheap, the bus is still an accessible option. You'll want to get yourself to the main highway 200. If you're heading to Sayulita (north) then you'll want to cross the street to be on the far side of the road. Look for the paper on the front of the buses driving through which will have their destinations clearly written. A simple wave is all you need to get their attention, as they'll be looking for passengers to pick up as they make their way through Punta Mita.

COVID TESTING

If you're staying at a fancy resort, they will often provide COVID tests for you.

Otherwise, go here...

The Punta Mita Hospital
➤ **Antibody Test** - $400MXN - Results in 15 minutes
➤ **Antigen Test** - $1,250MXN - Results in 4-6 hours
➤ **PCR Test** - $3,690MXN - Results in 12-18 hours

CHAPTER SIX

Sayulita

—

TIME NEEDED:

3+ days

KNOWN FOR:

Surfing, Boho Markets, Digital Nomad Scene

BEST FOR:

Beach life during the day and going out for cocktails at night.

INTRODUCTION TO SAYULITA

Safe safe safe safe safe safe safe. First and foremost, I like Sayulita because it's safe. Of course, keep your wits about you. Don't walk alone in the dark, don't get too drunk with strangers - you know the drill. But all in all, Sayulita is a place you can come to, let your hair down and allow your worries to melt away into a big icy margarita.

Sayulita is a solo girl's travel dream come true with bohemian markets, smoothie bowls, surfer dudes and a candlelit craft cocktail scene. Wander aimlessly through the markets, explore the maze of cobblestone streets, stop at tiny cafes to have a coffee or a cocktail - it's hard to get lost and easy to find your way around.

This quaint little surfers paradise caters to every budget. You can travel cheap while staying in hostels and eating $1 street tacos, or you can settle into a luxury suite with a hot tub overlooking the ocean. It's this flexibility that has made Sayulita so popular with long-term nomads. Some might say that Sayulita's new booming popularity has ruined it's small town charm...a statement that I find to be only half true.

At a glance, you'll see cafes packed with digital nomads on their laptops and nightlife sprinkled with bachelorette parties. If you're looking to join a community or a party, this atmosphere is good news for you. However, if you're looking for a more off-the-beaten-path experience, I've got you covered. This chapter will navigate you around the overrated spots and lead you to the places that are worth your time (plus a few hidden gems that tourists don't know about).

Areas to Know & Beaches to Expore in Sayulita

1. SAYULITA TOWN
2. NORTH SAYULITA
3. SOUTH END
4. GRINGO HILL
5. SAYULITA BEACH
6. NORTH BEACH
7. PLAYA LOS MUERTOS
8. PLAYA CARRICITOS
9. PLAYA ESCONDIDA

AREAS TO KNOW

SAYULITA TOWN

Home to Sayulita Beach and the town center, this is where all the action happens. You'll find nightlife, shops, restaurants, umbrellas on the beach, and everything else to keep you fed and entertained. Make sure to check out La Plaza principal where you can peruse native Huicol art stalls and galleries.

NORTH SAYULITA

Once you cross over the bridge at Jose Mariscal & Las Gaviotas, life tends to get a bit quieter with less tourists. Just over this bridge is also where you'll find the Hippie Market!

SOUTH END

Home to Los Muertos Beach (Playa de Los Muertos), this is the quieter corner of Sayulita. Staying here means less people but more walking when you want to explore the town center - something that is still easily done in 10 minutes by foot.

GRINGO HILL

Yup, that's what people call it. Gringo Hill is the hill right behind the main plaza. It got its name years ago when Sayulita started to get populated by expats who built houses in this area with the best views of Sayulita. This is mostly a quiet residential area with some Airbnbs and it's walking distance to downtown. If you consider staying here know that you're going to get a workout walking up these hills.

Pro Tip! Want to skip the crowds all together? Head to the next chapter: San Pancho - a town that is described as "Sayulita 10 years ago".

BEACHES TO EXPLORE

SAYULITA BEACH

PHOTO / UNSPLASH.COM

This is the main beach in Sayulita where you'll see clusters of surfers in the water trying to catch some waves and an insane amount of beach umbrellas huddled together where locals bring their speakers and beer coolers. It's madness. However, all you need to do is head to the very south end or the north end of the beach to escape the crowds.

NORTH BEACH

Just head right and keep walking. Once the beach starts getting quieter and you've passed over the mouth of Arroyo river that runs through town, you've reached North Beach. This is the best place to bring a towel and a book and chill out for the day. Vendors will come by and offer you snacks, too!

PLAYA DE LOS MUERTOS

Or in English "The Beach of the Dead" which got its name from the cemetery you'll pass to get here. This beach has fewer people in the water and on the shores, but don't expect total solitude. This beach is becoming more popular by the day. Playa de Los Muertos is a delightful 10-minute walk from town.

PLAYA CARRICITOS

If you keep walking along the dirt path from Playa de Los Muertos and into the jungle, you will eventually reach this isolated beach with no vendors, no nothing. It might be a bit confusing to navigate this path alone so I recommend doing this in the morning hours so you have plenty of time to get lost! Alternatively, you can go on this hike with a guide which you'll find on page 105.

PLAYA ESCONDIDA

Bachelor Nation! This is where Bachelor in Paradise is filmed! This beach is not open to public access, but for $100 you can get a day pass which gives you access to the pool, day bed, spa, restaurant and bar - but you'll still have to pay extra for food, drinks, massages, etc. If you're a Paradise fan, I say it's totally worth it.

Sayulita Pro Tip!

Carry cash. Sayulita doesn't always accept cards and ATMs are scarce but you can find one in Oxxo mini mart and another inside White Waves on the Beach.

HOW TO GET TO SAYULITA

Nestled on the Pacific Coast in the state of Nayarit, Sayulita is only 13.5 miles from Puerto Vallarta (and it's airport) and will only take you about 45-minutes to 1.5 hours drive to reach it depending on how you're traveling.

HIRE A PRIVATE DRIVER
Check out my private driver section on page 292 . You can hire a driver to take you from PVR Airport or Puerto Vallarta town to Sayulita for about 700 pesos.

INDRIVER OR UBER APP
If you're in Puerto Vallarta town, you should easily be able to hop on the app and find a driver to bring you to Sayulita. Expect to pay around the same price as above.

Pro Tip! Try InDriver first so you can set your price at 700 pesos.

HOTEL PICK UP
Often, if you've already booked your hotel, that hotel will offer a pick-up service at an extra cost. I have found this service to be a bit more expensive than the options above, but this might be the most convenient option.

BUS
This is the cheapest option and the most adventurous option - but I recommend only taking the bus if you're traveling light with a backpack. The bus isn't very luggage-friendly.

The bus from Puerto Vallarta to Sayulita will cost around $3 USD or 46 pesos and usually takes about 1.5 hours with frequent stops along the way. Buses run daily from 6am to 10pm and come every 20 minutes. The bus will drop you at Terminal Sayulita at Av Revolución # 3B. Once you arrive in Sayulita, either take a taxi to your hotel (taxis will be outside the bus station) or walk straight along the main street called Revolución and now you're heading into town.

◊ **Where to Catch the Bus to go to Sayulita:** Go to the main highway on the side of the road going North. The bus stops are usually located outside the biggest grocery or convenience stores like Mega or Galleria Mall. If you're in Bucerias or Punta Mita, ask your hotel where the bus stops. You're looking for any bus with the word "Sayulita" written on the windshield, usually these buses are green and white Compostela buses.

HOW TO GET AROUND

WALK

Once you're in Sayulita, you can access pretty much everything by foot. The roads are mostly made of cobblestone and there are quite a few hills so make sure your sandals are comfy.

GOLF CART

You heard that correctly. Sayulita has such narrow roads that it just makes the most sense for Golf Carts as the transportation of choice. The golf carts are just meant to zip around town, nothing more.

◊ **Who Should Rent a Golf Cart:** If your hotel is not located in the center of town and you don't want to walk a shit ton, it makes sense to rent a golf cart for a day or longer.

◊ **The Upside to Renting a Golf Cart:** It's a fun way to explore.

◊ **The Downside to Renting a Golf Cart:** It's hard to find parking and if you want to get drunk, you don't want to attempt to drive this thing.

◊ **Things to Know:**
> ➤ The rental company will ask to see your drivers' license, but that's about it.
> ➤ Even if you think you know how to drive a golf cart, ask the rental company for a tutorial.

✒ **Budget:** I rented from Sayulita Golf Car SGC (@saygolfcar) and paid $80 MXN ($4 USD) per day - however that price can fluctuate depending on whether you're renting in tourist season.

WHERE TO STAY
IN SAYULITA

AZUL PITAYA

The best location in Sayulita! AzulPitaya is steps away from both the beach and the boho market, perfect for exploring the town and then coming home and jumping in the heated pool for a late night swim. Speaking of the pool, it is the biggest pool in Sayulita and it sits under these gorgeous palm trees that instantly transport you into vacation mode. I love that the rooms have a little kitchen and fridge for your pizza leftovers! Best of all, AzulPitaya sits right next to my favorite beach bar, Bar La Isla, to the left on the beach. Before you leave, make sure you take an Instagram-worthy picture on the bright pink swing!

🛎 *Budget:* $$
📍 *Where:* Northside
🏛 *Address:* Av. del Palmar 12

 BOOK HERE

PUNTA SAYULITA

One of the most exclusive properties to stay in Sayulita, Punta Sayulita isn't a hotel, but a residence that you can rent or buy. Punta Sayulita has treehouses, bamboo bungalows and 12-person residences with private pools that are surrounded by nature, offering 180 degree views of the stunning sea. If you're coming with a group, this place is a really cool find.

✎ **Budget:** $$$
♥ **Where:** Pescadores #5
🏛 **Address:** South End of Sayulita Beach

 BOOK HERE

HOTEL YSURI SAYULITA

At night, walk into the ocean right in front of Hotel Ysuri and go for a swim in the dark with the glittering ocean. The water is calm and shallow and the moon is bright. This moment was magical for me and I want you to experience it, too. Hotel Ysuri is located on the very south end of Sayulita Beach so it's quieter during the day and darker at night. Most of the rooms have a hot tub on the balcony which is 100% worth the splurge. But if you go for the simple rooms, you'll still be able to enjoy the big refreshing pool and daily happy hour under a lounge chair umbrella.

✎ **Budget:** $$$
♥ **Where:** Sayulita Beach
🏛 **Address:** Pescadores #5

 BOOK HERE

PLAYA ESCONDIDA

Bachelor in Paradise is filmed here in Sayulita! The allure of this resort is the jungle-meet-beach atmosphere. On one hand you have the most gorgeous swimming beach and on the other, you have a bamboo hotel with jungle paths and thatched roofs that really pull you into nature. There will be no need to wear shoes here as you'll be hopping from pool to hot tub to ocean. You'll eat on the beach, drink at the beach bar and you might forget that the world outside even exists.

Budget: $$$

Where: Playa Escondida

Address: Ave. Playa Escondida 1

 BOOK HERE

DISTRITO 88 HOTEL BOUTIQUE

Adults only!

I love when there are no kids in my pool when I'm on vacation! Tan on the rooftop balconys lounge bed or read a book in the swinging chair and just melt into vacation away from the chaos of home. The intimate setting of this boutique hotel really allows you to slow down and not think about anything besides what cocktail you'll be ordering next (yes, they make amazing cocktails).

Budget: $$$

Where: Playa Escondida

Address: Ave. Playa Escondida 1

 BOOK HERE

PEIX HOTEL

Beachfront! The rooms of Peix Hotel overlook all the action on Sayulita Beach. The umbrellas, the surfers, the vendors, the beach dogs - you get to see it all from here. However, that also means that they can see you.Don't expect privacy. This is a place to stay when you want to be entertained! Extra bonuses of staying here are the free beach chairs in the sand and the rooftop bar which is perfect for sunset.

Budget: $$

Where: Sayulita Beach

Address: Playa Sayulita # 9

 BOOK HERE

AMOR BOUTIQUE HOTEL

Quiet and tucked away from the hustle and bustle of Sayulita center, Amor Boutique Villa sits on the most quiet side of the beach, accessible via a secret little path. Want to get away from the crowd? Amor Boutique Hotel is in walking distance to Playa de Los Muertos. Staying here gives you access to bicycles to explore with and spa treatments including body scrubs and wraps for when you return. Not to mention, their restaurant is one of the best kept secrets in town.

💸 **Budget:** $$

📍 **Where:** South End

🏛 **Address:** Pescadores S/N

 BOOK HERE

MY SISTERS HOUSE

Girls, welcome to the beautiful female-only hotel and hostel that will charm and bedazzle you with sparkling clean rooms and chic interior design. This is a hostel that feels pristine, safe and welcoming because #girls. When you stay here, your activities are easy to plan with organized cultural trips, yoga, surfing, jungle walks and more. They also offer monthly rates so you can unpack and stay awhile. This place is the epitome of "Travel alone, not lonely".

💸 **Budget:** $$

📍 **Where:** Sayulita Town

🏛 **Address:** Av Revolución 83

 BOOK HERE

LA REDONDA SAYULITA

This is a backpacker party hostel with lots of booze. 23 year old me would have absolutely loved this place! The garden common area makes it easy to meet other travelers and the organized activities fling you into adventure with new friends from around the world. And hey, this place is cheap. If you're a backpacker who doesn't need air conditioning, you're gonna love it here for a few nights. If you're not backpacking, try another place.

💵 *Budget:* $

📍 *Where:* Sayulita Town
🏠 *Address:* Manuel N. Navarrete 14

 BOOK HERE

HOSTAL TORTUGA

If the two hostels above had a baby, it would come out at Hostal Tortuga. It's not a party hostel, but it's social. It's not a girls-only hostel, but it's comfortable. When you want something middle-of-the-road that will introduce you to other travelers for a beer but have you in bed by 10pm, this is the place I recommend. Plus, there's a pool! The only downside is that it's a 7-minute walk from the center of town and a 10-minute walk to the beach. Make sure if you're walking home at night that you're with someone, just in case.

💵 *Budget:* $

📍 *Where:* Sayulita Town
🏠 *Address:* Tortuga 10

 BOOK HERE

SELINA SAYULITA

More than a hotel, Selina Sayulita offers you a soul retreat! Yoga, meditation, and singing bowls led by dedicated energy workers is a combination that will pull you into an inner journey full of self reflection and healing. Accessible to all budgets, you can stay in dorms or private rooms - all of which are pristine and encourage total relaxation. There's a pool, massages, a movie room and surf lessons to fully help you discover a new side to yourself.

💸 **Budget:** $-$$

📍 **Where:** Sayulita Town

🏛 **Address:** Calle Gaviotas Sur 12

 BOOK HERE

ALL SETTLED IN?
LET'S EAT.

WHERE TO EAT
IN SAYULITA

Coffee & Coworking

SELINA

Digital nomads staying in Sayulita will want to check out Selina Hotel's Coworking space. Fast WIFI, air conditioning and coffee are waiting to help you have a super successful work day, work week or work month - they offer competitive rates for each starting at 190 pesos per day.

⊙ *Hours:* Monday - Friday 9am -5pm
♀ *Where:* Sayulita Town
🛏 *Address:* 41 Alto, Av Revolución
💸 *Budget:* Starting at 190 pesos per day to use their coworking space
f Selina (Sayulita)

COFFEE ON THE CORNER

Inarguably one of the best places for breakfast in Sayulita that hasn't been ruined by the trendy Instagram kids. Keep it fresh with an espresso, fresh fruit and eggs for breakfast. Or go the opposite direction and fill up on some of the best chilaquiles in town

and/or huevos rancheros served in a fresh tortilla.

⊙ *Hours:* Daily 7am - 3pm
♀ *Where:* Sayulita Town
🛏 *Address:* Calle Pelícanos 150
f Coffee on the Corner Sayulita

ALQUIMISTA

Hello, hangover food! It's all about the breakfast burritos and chilaquiles at this joint. I swear Alquimista does the most over-the-top chilaquiles in town which are absolutely smothered in sauce and topped with a fried egg. They've also got smoothies, fresh juice and coffee that will fix you right up after a wild night out.

⊙ *Hours:* Tuesday-Sunday 8am-4pm
♀ *Where:* Gringo Hill
🛏 *Address:* Av Revolución 89
♥ @wearealquimista

ANCHOR CAFE

A little spot where boho meets urban, Anchor Cafe has amazing coffee, and is great for either breakfast or brunch. With some of the best wifi in Sayulita, almost every table is filled with beautiful people on their laptops. My pro tip is to order the Chia Pudding and get your camera ready cause it's gorgeous...

⊙ *Hours:* Daily 8am - 4pm
♀ *Where:* Gringo Hill (almost at the bottom reaching the main plaza)
🏠 *Address:* Calle Marlín 45
♥ @anchorsayulita

MISCELANEA

Another spot to bring your laptop as you wake up with a fresh cup of coffee. The reason I like Misceleanea is that it is tucked off the main road and so, it doesn't tend to get too crowded with tourists. The portions are big and the ingredients are fresh. Order a smoothie bowl or a fresh banana crepe and ease slowly into the day.

⊙ *Hours:* Daily 8am - 3pm
♀ *Where:* Av Revolución 32a
♥ @miscelaneasayulita

TIERRA VIVA

Did someone say mimosas?! Come satisfy your sweet tooth with a bubbly glass of champagne & OJ alongside fluffy pancakes served with bacon, whipped butter and jam. After breakfast, you are only a few steps to the beach where you can either go into full-on food coma mode or just keep drinking. I vote, keep drinking. Oh and this place is crawling with iguanas. Yes, real life iguanas.

⊙ *Hours:* Daily 8am - 10pm
♀ *Where:* Sayulita Town
🏠 *Address:* Calle Marlín 10
f Tierra Viva Restaurant y Bar

Street Food & Local Restaurants

BICHOS

When you want street food but also want to sit down for a while and savour, come to Bichos! This garden restaurant has a collection of picnic tables where you can sit and continuously order classic street tacos, quesadillas, tostadas - whatever. There is a salsa bar so you can customize every bite! The kitchen is super clean and professional, so if you are worried about eating street food, this place will put you at ease. Oh and another reason to come here is that Bichos is below the Iguana Tree...just a tree filled with Iguanas that meander down around the restaurant looking for snacks.

Hours: Daily 5pm - 11pm

Where: Sayulita Town

Address: Manuel N. Navarrete

f Bichos

POLLOS "YOLANDA"

This isn't just grilled chicken; this is Mexican grilled chicken made by tia and tio (aunty and uncle) who tag team this mouthwatering meal with tio basting and tia grilling. Here's what you want to order: the most popular combo with a quarter chicken, rice, coleslaw, tortillas and salsa. And best of all, It will only cost you 55 pesos.

Hours: Open Tuesday - Sunday 11:30am - 5pm

Where: Sayulita Town

Address: Calle Gaviotas Sur 53

f Pollos Al Carbón Yolanda

TACOS TOÑO

Only open at night! A no-frills taco stand serving up cheap tacos around 20 pesos. That's $1 USD per taco! The tacos are a decent size but you'll want to order two or three to start. Follow the crowd and order the fried rib beef tacos!

Hours: Open Friday - Wednesday 6:30pm - midnight

Where: Sayulita Town

Address: Ave. Pelicanos 12

f Exquisitos Tacos Toño

TACOS EL TAL (AKA TACOS AL PASTOR TAL IVAN)

You can't miss the big orange sign of Tacos al Pastor cooking outfront of Tacos El Tal. Come at night around 8pm and you've got a good chance of watching the street performers right in front of you. This is a great place for Sayulita people watching with a beer in hand. Ps: Want a souvenir? Buy one of their little guacamole or al pastor keychains!

Hours: Open daily 5pm - 2am

Where: Sayulita Town

Address: Calle Marlín 12

f Tacos al pastor Tal Ivan

TACOS GABI

You'd miss this little tacos stand if you were just walking by. You have to keep your eyes peeled for an unassuming table placed just in front of a teeny tiny literal hole in the wall with a menu hanging on the small gate.

This is Gabi's Tacos, most popular with the locals for her scrumptious fish tacos! Take the tacos upstairs to her cozy little dining area or sit on a plastic stool on the sidewalk and enjoy supporting local women who kick ass at what they do.

Hours: Tue - Sun 11:30am - 5pm

Where: Sayulita Town

Address: Ave. Revolucion 29a

f Exquisitos Tacos Toño

LA EMPANADERIA SAYULITA

Just fresh empanadas made from scratch and sold out of a storefront. This is a great place to grab a bite to eat while you're walking around town.

The Lola Empanada is my favorite with cheese and mushroom! They've also got drinks like agua fresca and a full coffee menu - all for prices much cheaper than you'd find at a sit-down restaurant in town.

⊙ **Hours:** Open Daily 8:30am - 6pm
♥ **Where:** Northside
🏛 **Address:** Av Revolución 15
f La Empanaderia Sayulita

Restaurants

SI SENOR

Food with a view! Si Senor is past the south end of the beach, right outside the Amor Boutique Hotel. Grab a table overlooking the ocean and order their famous fish tacos. If the ocean tables are taken, grab a seat at the bar and make friends with the super happy-to-see-you bartenders! The stroll to get here is worth it in itself and after you eat, you can keep walking towards Playa Los Muertos.

⊙ **Hours:** Daily 8am - 10pm
♥ **Where:** Camino a Playa los Muertos
🏛 **Address:** Calle Pescadores s/n
f **Contact:** Si Señor Sayulita

CHILLUM BAR

Sushi lovers, get your butt over here. You'd never guess that this eclectic rooftop bar has some of the best sushi in town. Nigiri, rolls, and edamame to hit the spot and for dirt cheap. Order with a huge (and also dirt cheap) margarita. Stay til late or at least make sure you come back when the sun goes down so you can enjoy their live music!

⊙ **Hours:** Tuesday - Saturday 2pm - 1am / Sunday noon - 9pm
♥ **Where:** Gringo Gill (right at the beginning of the slope)
🏛 **Address:** Av Revolución 40C (look for the set of stairs that lead to the second story)
f Chillum Surf House

LA RUSTICA SAYULITA

Arguably the most popular western restaurant in Sayulita. Rustica absolutely kills it when it comes to Italian food that hits the spot with a creative menu and big saucy portions. You can go all out with appetizers, entrees, desserts and of course cocktails which makes this place a fabulous spot for date night. You'll also find this restaurant in our nightlife & cocktails section...

⊙ **Hours:** Wednesday - Monday 9am

- 11pm / Tuesday 2pm - 11pm
♀ Where: Sayulita Town
🚇 Address: Av Revolución 40C
f La Rustica Sayulita

PIZZA VENEZIA

This place is solo girl approved. I ate at Pizza Venezia solo and ordered Pizza Venezia for delivery more times than I'd like to admit. There is a little stool right at the counter where you can sit and eat solo or have them deliver. Must order: Pizza Moro with artichokes, salami, mushroom and garlic is my go-to!

☉ Hours: Daily 6pm - 10:30pm
♀ Where: Northside
🚇 Address: Av. del Palmar 50
🌐 Check out "Pizza Venezia" on Yelp
📱 Order Delivery Here: 322 192 8402

ACHARA

This upscale Thai restaurant is my #1 pick for a candlelit date night! Just make sure you make a reservation or you might not be able to get in. There are only a few tables which means that each dish that comes to your table has had the time to be prepared and plated with no detail spared. Order the Tom Yum Soup to start and savor every spoonful.

☉ Hours: Tue - Sun 5:30am - 10:30pm
♀ Where: Sayulita Town
🚇 Address: Calle Jose Mariscal 33
🌐 acharasayulita.com

SAYULITA PUBLIC HOUSE

What I would consider "grub". Public house is the spot for juicy burgers, sandwiches and wings - and please try the avocado fries! They've got 4 TVs for watching whatever sports you're into (message them before a big game and see if they'll play it) and all the beer a girl could ask for.

☉ Hours: Daily 11am - midnight
♀ Where: Sayulita Town
🚇 Address: Calle Marlín 26
♥ @sayulitapublichouse

Sweets & Desserts

WAKIKA HELADERIA

Ice cream to cool you off under the hot Mexican sun! They've got ice cream pop (paletas), scoops and drinks in refreshing flavors with big chunks of fruit or creamy chocolate and vanilla. This place is located right next to La Venezia so consider treating yourself to a pizza & ice cream night out. You're on vacation, afterall!

🕓 **Hours:** Tue - Sun 11:30am - 5pm
📍 **Where:** Sayulita Town
🏛 **Address:** Ave. Revolucion 40
f Wakika Heladeria Sayulita

SANTA SAL

Come to Santa Sal for crepes and churros. This place has some serious Bali vibes going on with macrame swinging chairs, hanging ivy and Instagrammable plating. This is the place to make all your friends jealous with awesome photos right before you stuff your face with sweet treats.

🕓 **Hours:** Daily 8am - 11pm
📍 **Where:** Sayulita Town
🏛 **Address:** Calle Jose Mariscal
♥ @santasalsayulita

HOT CHURROS

Just a little churro stand whipping up warm, freshly-fried doughy churros tossed with cinnamon and sugar! Made to order, it's fun and fascinating to watch the whole churro-making process happen so effortlessly and quickly. 25 pesos will get you a hefty bag of churros to share or eat by yourself and no one has to know...

🕓 **Hours:** Come after dinner, usually open around dessert time
📍 **Where:** Northside
🏛 **Address:** Av Revolución 21b

Drinking Day & Night

SAYULITA WINE SHOP

Every Wednesday, this little Sayulita Wine Shop sets up some chairs out in the street in front of their shop and offers wine tastings with live music from 5pm to 8pm. The energy feels almost like Barcelona with smiling vino drinkers of all ages mingling and enjoying the last hours of sunshine before the night begins.

⊙ **Hours:** Wednesdays 5pm to 8pm
♀ **Where:** Gringo Hill
🏛 **Address:** Av Revolución 56
♥ @sayulitawines

ATICO BREAKFAST CAFE & BAR

Swings. Live Music. Day drinking. Cash only. Life is simple at Atico. It was so easy for me to sit my butt down on a bar swing and make friends. I love that there were girls behind the bar and the quirky decor with stickers galore gave my eyes easy entertainment. This place is a must in my book. Ps. Try to spot my "Solo Girl Approved" sticker and take a picture for me!

⊙ **Hours:** All day and late into the night
♀ **Where:** Sayulita Town
🏛 **Address:** Calle Jose Mariscal 33
f Atico Sayulita

EL BARRILITO

Any restaurant that has a bartop table with a view of the foot traffic on the street is always solo-girl-approved! Traveling alone, I always look for bar-top tables that allow me to feel less awkward being alone and also sets me up for perfect people watching situations. Girl, get here! I recommend coming for dinner and watching El Barrilito turn from restaurant to super cool (and sometimes super packed) bar.

⊙ **Hours:** Daily noon - midnight
♀ **Where:** Sayulita Town
🏛 **Address:** Calle Jose Mariscal 9
♥ @barrilito_sayulita

YAMBAK

No exaggeration, I come to Yambak once a day when I visit Sayulita. This open-air tap room pours beers made in Mexico that I recommend you order in a beer flight. Do what I do and let the bar staff choose which beers you're going to try. On the weekends at night, Yambak usually has a DJ and awesome dancey tunes that set a super fun social vibe.

⊙ **Hours:** Daily - don't believe the hours on Google, this place is open usually around lunch
♀ **Where:** Sayulita Town
🏛 **Address:** Calle Marlin 29
f **Contact:** YamBak Sayulita

LA RUSTICA SAYULITA

Check out the bar on the second floor.

My go-to cocktail order here is the Mezcal Mule or the Aperol Spritz. Get your camera ready. The bartenders here are wildly impressive with their presentation.

Each cocktail comes out looking like a work of art. That being said, cocktails here will cost you around 145 pesos or around $7 USD to start which is cheaper than home but on the fancy end here in Sayulita.

⊙ **Hours:** Wednesday - Monday 9am - 11pm / Tuesday 2pm - 11pm
♥ **Where:** Sayulita Town
🚇 **Address:** Av Revolución 40C
f La Rustica Sayulita

CHILLUM BAR

Another second-floor bar that you'd miss if you weren't looking! This little surf house plays live music under hanging neon lights and has a bar where you can post up solo without feeling like a loner. Chillum is intimate and welcoming so please don't hesitate on coming here alone! Odds are that you'll make a friend.

⊙ **Hours:** Tuesday - Saturday 2pm - 1am / Sunday noon - 9pm
♥ **Where:** Sayulita Town
🚇 **Address:** Av Revolución 40C
f Chillum Surf House

DON PATOS

Here's where you come when you want to dance! This 3-story bar has it all: live music, foosball, a flirty bar

and sometimes classic Salsa Dancing if the vibe is right! This place is a solid good time. I love that the stage is open air so that you don't feel too sticky in the Sayulita heat especially when you want to go dancing! If you're coming solo, come have a seat at the bar and the atmosphere will slowly pull you in to join the party.

⊙ **Hours:** Daily 8pm - 3am (closes at 12am on Sundays)
♥ **Where:** Sayulita Town
🚇 **Address:** Primer Piso, Calle Marlín 12
f Bar Don Pato Sayulita

WILD IRIS BAR

Here is where strangers become drinking buddies! This bar sits on the corner of a semi-busy walking street and acts like a fishing net in a stream full of thirsty trout! The "good time" vibes catch all the people walking by looking to get a little buzzed on vacation. Order a Mezcal Margarita or two and chat up the stranger next to you.

⊙ **Hours:** Wednesday - Monday 6pm - midnight
♥ **Where:** Sayulita Town
🚇 **Address:** Calle Gaviota 10
♥ **Contact:** @wildirissayulita

SAYULITA PUBLIC HOUSE

Yes, this place is such a staple that it's in this guide twice. After you've had lunch here, come back when the sun goes down and experience a totally different vibe. The cool expats and travelers hang out here with cold beers and cocktails well into the night. Coming solo? Sit at the bar on the second story balcony and make eyes at a cute boy down below.

⊙ **Hours:** Daily 11am - midnight
♀ **Where:** Sayulita Town
🏬 **Address:** Calle Marlín 26
♥ @sayulitapublichouse

ESCONDIDO BAR

New York Cocktails. Mexico price. Escondido Bar is one of my favorites in Sayulita not only because their cocktails are handcrafted with local ingredients but also because they have games! This place is sexy but unpretentious with couples and groups playing Jenga or card games by candlelight. So when you want to go out for a drink and have a good time - but not a crazy time - this is where you come.

⊙ **Hours:** Thursday - Monday 5pm - midnight
♀ **Where:** Sayulita Town
🏬 **Address:** Calle Marlín 45 A
♥ @escondidobar

EL TIBURON

Come for the live music, stay for the fresh seafood. Happy hour is every day from 3pm to 7pm with 60 peso margaritas and beer + a shot for 100 pesos. This is arguably one of the best happy hours in town. Come take advantage.

⊙ **Hours:** Daily 3pm - midnight
♀ **Where:** Sayulita Town
🏬 **Address:** Av Revolución 37A
♥ @eltiburonsayulita

BAR LE ZOUAVE

Another "secret bar" that you'd never notice. Look for the blue door on the big red wall attached to the Le Petit Hotel Hafa. Order the Grapefruit Margarita or try one of their CBD cocktails for an extra boost of relaxation. Post up at the bar, find a snug corner, or sit out on the street at the little bar top table and people watch.

⊙ **Hours:** Daily 6pm - midnight
♀ **Where:** Sayulita Town
🏬 **Address:** Calle Jose Mariscal 3-5
f Le Zouave de Hafa

AALEYAH'S NACHOS & WINGS

Start with a beer, a shot and some tacos or buffalo wings. That'll get your day going. This spot is super local with super affordable prices to match! The girls working here don't speak much English but the menu is in English and a smile is all you need to help you through orders. Oh, and if you're a sports fan, they've usually got some kind of game on.

⊙ **Hours:** Thursday - Tuesday 1pm - midnight
♀ **Where:** Gringo Hill
🏬 **Address:** Av Revolución 60
f Aaleyah's Nachos and Wings

LUCID

Lucid is known as the party spot for travelers to come listen to live music and dance their faces off. The DJs and drink specials tend to attract a wilder vibe than other spots around. And as the bar opens up to the street, Lucid easily pulls in more party goers who just happen to be passing by. Translation: Things heat up here real quick. Drink water in-between those shots and margaritas!

⊙ **Hours:** Daily noon - midnight
♀ **Where:** Sayulita Town
🚉 **Address:** Calle Marlín 18-A
♥ @Lucid Sayulita

COCOS SPORT BAR

Where the expats hang to eat bar food and watch sports on TV. If you want to integrate into the older social scene in Sayulita, come here a few days in a row and make friends with the regulars. As to be expected, Cocos Sport Bar shows every sport imaginable from golf to UFC so expect any sporting event day to get a little extra rowdy!

⊙ **Hours:** Daily 11am - 2am
♀ **Where:** Gringo Hill
🚉 **Address:** Av Revolución 68,
f Cocos Sport Bar

Sayulita Fun Fact!

Those colorful paper banners you see around everywhere? They're called *"papel picado"* (pecked paper) and are a traditional mexican craft. They're commonly made by grouping up to 50 sheets of paper, folding and cutting them in unique designs. And they're used to decorate and adorn celebrations, from Day of the Dead, to weddings and *quinceañeras*.

THINGS TO DO IN SAYULITA

On the Water...

BOAT ADVENTURES

Stop. You don't need to shop around. You won't find anything better than Chica Loca tours when it comes to exploring the waters! While other boat tour companies are cheesy and impersonal, Chica Loca Tours are just the opposite. Personal. Eco-conscious. And they actually give a damn about how your experience goes. This small business has got some big boats! Expect hammocks to lay, beer to drink, and even slides to cool off in the water below! Yes. Slides.

These are the top 5 Chica Loca Tours that will tick every must-see tropical spot off your list.

◊ Marietas Islands

◊ Yelapa Falls

◊ Los Arcos Islands

◊ Chica Fun (Yelapa Falls & Los Arcos in One Day

◊ Whale Watching

See your boat tour options at:

🌐 chicaloccatours.com/tours

♥ @chicalocca

◇ SNORKELING

There are three places to snorkel in Sayulita:

1. At Sayulita Beach: Rent a snorkel at one of the surf shops or dive shops and head into the waters on the south end of the beach. Snorkeling is just okay here.

2. Los Muertos Beach: Colorful fish await you! Walk over to Los Muertos but bring a snorkel with you.

3. Marietas Island: You'll have to jump in a boat to get here. Either join a Chica Loca tour or head to Mictlan Surf School in Punta Mita and ask when they have panga boats heading out on a snorkel trip.

PHOTO / UNSPLASH.COM

◇ WHALE WATCHING

Between December and April, migrating humpback whales swim off the coast of the Banderas Bay for their own little vacation. They are here to escape the cold waters of the south and to mate in the warmer waters of this bay. You'll see the whales breaching, slapping the water with their tail and if you're lucky, fully jumping out of the water!

To see the whales, you can go with Chica Loca tours above, watch from the shores of Sayulita Beach, hike to Monkey Mountain viewpoint or go on a more private whale watching experience with La Orca de Sayulita, Sayulita's first pure whale watching and research company.

◇ SURFING

Surfing is personal. For this experience, pick the style that speaks most to you with one of these options:

➤ El Punto Surf Shop

When I first walked by El Punto, all I saw was women. Female instructors and female students who looked so badass carrying their surfboards. This place not only has a fabulous reputation but also has a cool deal where you take a 1 hour and 40 minute lesson and then you get to keep your board for 5 hours to keep practicing. The waves are gentle enough that you can totally do this on your own.

⊕ elpuntosurfschool.com

➤ Marea Sayulita

Just a surf tent on the beach in front of Bar La Isla. I recommend this place for a girl that's already had a lesson or two and wants a refresher (or wants to learn with cute surfer dudes). I was quoted at 800 pesos for a 2.5 hour lesson. If you want to practice solo, you can rent a board for 150 pesos for an hour or for 400 pesos for the day.

f Marea Sayulita

➤ Surf n' Roll Surf Shop

If this place can teach little kids how to surf, they sure as hell can teach you babe. These guys are so thorough when it comes to preparing you for the water even before you get in the water. If you're nervous about surfing, go with these guys.

f Surf and Roll Sayulita

➤ Leah Tisdale

Leah is a native Canadian chick that has integrated into Sayulita as an expat and can teach you a thing or two about surfing. She has over 20 years of experience with water-based sports, but as a yoga instructor, you'll see that her classes go beyond surfing as she combines a little bit of all her expertise to offer you a one-of-a-kind surf experience.

⊕ leahnicoletisdale.com

Bonus!

HERE ARE SOME POPULAR SURF SPOTS TO CHECK OUT:

➤ Punta Sayulita to El Faro

➤ San Pacho

➤ La Lancha

Pro Tip!

The waves at Sayulita beach aren't massive. The swells vary from medium-sized to baby waves and the breaks tend to be short which means that Sayulita is a good beach to learn or develop your skills.

On Land...

TAKE A PICTURE ON SLAP STREET

You know that photo that's famous across Instagram? The one with the cobblestone street that's canopied with rows of colorful flags? This is it! Look up "Calle Delfines" on GoogleMaps. It's right in the center of town on the way to the beach.

RENT A BEACH UMBRELLA

Toes in the sand and a drink in your hand - this is what country songs are made of. There are two ways to do this.

➤ **Option 1:** Sit outside a beach club like Bar La Isla. As long as you're ordering food and drink, you can post up in one of their lounge chairs with a beach umbrella. This is the quieter but more expensive option.

➤ **Option 2:** Have a beach picnic like a local under a beach umbrella in the middle of Sayulita Beach. You can rent a beach umbrella with chairs for around 100-300 pesos per day depending on how many people you have and how good you are at haggling. Bring your own cooler of beer and snacks; you can get these coolers and fill them with ice at the convenience stores. Vendors will come by all day long offering you more snacks and food on sticks. This is a rowdy day surrounded by locals playing music on their personal speakers.

Pro Tip! The convenience store I went to is next to Coffee on the Corner. But you can try any convenience store, really.

WALK TO PLAYA LOS MUERTOS

The crystal blue beach that most tourists don't know about, Playa Los Muertos has better snorkeling, more space and less vendors! Plus, this is a fantastic swimming beach!

You can rent beach chairs here but I recommend you bring your own snacks and towels. There are some vendors but the options are limited.

> **How to Get Here:** Walk on the road past Hotel Ysuri. After Amor Hotel, take a right. Follow the road until you see a big arch that says Playa Los Muertos. Stop and read the little sign that tells you about the history of this area. Keep walking about 5 minutes along the dirt road, passing cemeteries and chickens until you pass through palm trees and come out on the sands of Playa Los Muertos.

Now, don't expect a totally deserted beach. The locals know all about Playa Los Muertos so you'll be sharing the shore with some families.

Pro Tip to Get a Bit More Privacy: Looking at the ocean, walk to the very right of the beach where you'll see some rocks. Carefully climb over to access a tiny little cove with a small sandy beach.

LOCAL BASEBALL GAME

Wander halfway through the Hippie Market and you'll come to the entrance of Estadio Manuel Rodríguez Sánchez (the baseball stadium). Here is where Sayulita's minor league team, The Jaibos (The Crabs) play and where the locals come out to watch! Buy your ticket inside the stadium when you arrive. Bring cash for snacks and beer.

The team plays in the Nayarit's Winter League November through January and the Playoff Season February to March. To find when they play next, check them out on Facebook: Jaibos de Sayulita Nay.

SAYULITA DAYS

You don't want to miss the carnivals, parades, and rodeo at the end of February in Sayulita! During this festive time, Sayulita goes all out to celebrate itself! Do a quick google of "Sayulita Day" and you'll find all the happenings, dates and times when festivities start being planned.

TEQUILA TASTING

The Tequila Experience is more than just a tasting; it's a mini class that introduces you to 100% Blue Agave artisan tequila that you sip and savor! You'll leave the experience with a buzz and return home with a deeper knowledge and appreciation of tequila beyond the tequila shot.

f The Tequila Experience

YOGA

You've got tons of yoga options in the zen land of Sayulita but here are a couple of my favs.

01
Morning or
Evening Yoga

02
Paraíso Yoga
*- a yoga studio with
tropical jungle vibes*

03
Surf & Yoga with
Leah Tisdale

HORSEBACK RIDING ON THE BEACH

I never go horseback riding when I travel unless the horses are loved, cared for and treated well. Rancho Manuel place qualifies.

Hikes in Sayulita

There are a couple jungle hikes that will spit you out on the beach or take you to a stunning view point. These hikes are usually difficult to navigate without a guide, especially if you're solo - so I recommend either taking a guide or going with a friend. Bring snacks, sunscreen and let your hotel/hostel know that you're going on a hike just so someone knows where you are. #SafetyFirst

PLAYA CARRICITOS

The walk to this gorgeous, preserved beach just south of Playa de los Muertos is easy enough to do on your own but requires a treasure map.

 Let me do us all a favor and pass you over to the experts for this one:

MONKEY MOUNTAIN

There is actually a pin dropped on GoogleMaps for "Start of Monkey Mountain Hiking Trail". Park your car and walk up the road til it dead ends. Climb through the gate and begin your 2 to 3-hour lonely trek until you reach the most stunning viewpoint at the top. Odds are, to start this hike, you'll need to ask some of the locals to point you in the right direction along the way.

I recommend you do this one with Samuel as your guide:

SAN PANCHO

If you're up for a 2-hour 4-mile hile hike through the beach and jungle, you can access the quaint town of San Pancho (aka San Francisco) just north of Sayulita. It's a hike that requires some climbing and the actual path can be tricky to navigate so please download this map to lead the way.

As you notice on the map, the trail will give you a couple outlets where you can choose to stop at some San Pancho beaches or keep going. Pro Tip: Remember to keep left

Day Trips from Sayulita

MARIETAS ISLAND

One of the most unique beaches in the world with turquoise waters and a sandy beach to rest, this is a must-see when you visit Banderas Bay. However, Marietas is a protected national park so there are only 100 tickets available per day - which means you've got to book your trip in advance.

To do so, either hop on Chica Loca's Marietas Tour or Punta Mita's Mictlan Surf Shop that does really fun trips to Marietas plus paddle boarding and snorkeling.

PHOTO / CHRISTIAN FRAUSTO

PLAYA PLATANITOS

2 Hours north of Sayulita is this huge, slightly windy beach with plenty of space to lay and play. The best part is that the top of the beach is completely lined with little restaurants where you can dig into fresh Mexican seafood and cold beers all day long.

Head to the very south of the beach to hike up a path that will bring you to a little vista that overlooks our next beach, Playa Los Tortuga. Unfortunately, you can't reach this beach from Playa Platanitos unless you're a fantastic swimmer.

PLAYA LOS TORTUGA

This place is a picture! It's a dream! It's unreal! Playa Los Tortuga is a 10-mile stretch of beach along a former coconut plantation (hello, palm trees) and is home to a turtle conservation center. There's also a protected mangrove sanctuary here which is home to crocodiles, an array of bird species and of course, turtles.

To go kayaking, surfing or paddle boarding through the mangroves, head over to Playa Las Tortugas Villas and they'll hook you up. You can visit them here. https://playalastortugas.com/

PLAYA CHANCLA

1.5 hours north of Sayulita is this good hang-out beach which is popular with locals but not too many tourists. That means that you can enjoy restaurants that serve up fresh crab but you won't be pestered by too many vendors. This beach is the perfect balance between catering to your needs and leaving you alone. Plus, it's stunning and has great swimming conditions.

LOS AYALA BEACH

A 45-minute drive from Sayulita will bring you to a local town where not many travelers go. This is Los Ayla Beach or "Pez Vela Los Ayala Nayarit" on GoogleMaps.

This is your chance to get away from the gringo crowd and hang like the local Mexicans do. You'll find a long, sandy beach lined with palm trees, crystal blue water and a charming small-town vibe where you can walk around and explore on foot, stopping into little restaurants and sitting down for nice cold coconuts.

Pools & Beachclubs

BAR LA ISLA

I found myself getting accidentally drunk here often. When you're sitting in a swing with your toes in the sand, looking out at the beach, it's easy to lose track of how many beers you've had. And then suddenly it's 2-for-1 margarita time and you can't say no! Just go. Solo or with friends. Just go.

⊙ **Hours:** Tue - Sun 11:30am - 5pm
♥ **Where:** Northside
🏛 **Address:** Ave. del Palmar 10
f La Isla Beach Club Bar

THE BREAK CAFE

It's time to drink. Order a pitcher of margaritas or Sangria and stay til happy hour on the weekdays from 4-6pm. Life is good under the palm trees! For entertainment you can watch the surfers or play with the sandy beach dogs. The food is hit or miss if I'm honest - but the guacamole always hits the spot. This place gets my vote for appetizers and drinks. Save your appetite for a taco stand!

⊙ **Hours:** Daily 9am - 10pm
♥ **Where:** Sayulita Beach
🏛 **Address:** Malecon 1, between Delfin and Marlin streets
f El Break Cafe & Bar

MAJAHUITAS

If Tulum had a west-coast twin, this trendy beach club would be it. Majahuitas is a jungle-meets-beach club where you can finally bust out that pink leather bikini and dance around like you're at Coachella. Majahuitas hosts talented DJs spinning tunes amongst palm trees, cabanas, hammocks and even fire dancers at night.

Located on a private beach, make a reservation that includes roundtrip speedboat transportation for 600 pesos per person. Heads up, there is a minimum spend around 1000-1500 pesos per person which means that's how much you've got to spend on food and drink. Gatherings only on Saturdays and Sundays. Check out www.majahuitas.mx to make a reservation and check out upcoming DJs and parties.

⊙ **Hours:** Saturday 2:30pm–10:30pm / Sunday 2:30pm–8:00pm
♥ **Where:** Playa Majahuitas
🏛 **Address:** 48449 Quimixto
♥ @majahuitas

ANCLA BEACH BAR

Here is a pro-tip from me. Coco's Beach Bar is one of the most popular beach bars around, but I find that their music is way too loud. So I head next door to Anchla where I can enjoy Coco's music and views but still hear myself think. Grab a seat at the little palapa (bar with straw roof) and make friends with the bartender!

♀ Where: Sayulita Beach
🛏 Address: Manuel N. Navarrete 143
f anclamixologybar

EL PATIO SAYULITA

This is Sayulita Vibes in its truest form! You've got beach views, toes in the sand, cold beers, and fresher than fresh mariscos (seafood) like ceviche tostadas and aguachiles (juicy shrimp). Come back at night when you can sip a frozen margarita under big lantern lights and sit on little pillows in the sand for a dreamy change of scenery.

☉ Hours: Daily 10am - 9pm
♀ Where: Sayulita Beach
🛏 Address: Calle Gaviota 1C
♥ Contact: @elpatiococktailbar

ALOHA SAYULITA

A shack with some tables outside, Aloha is just a super chill little beach bar carving up burritos as big as your face and some of the best margaritas in town. Aloha is set on the way to the beach so it's best if you come barefoot and totally embrace the laid back vibe.

☉ Hours: Daily 10:30am 'til late
♀ Where: Sayulita Beach
🛏 Address: Delfines 12
f Aloha Sayulita

CLUB DE PLAYA CAMARÓN

This place looks like a 10-year-old boy built a little play fort on the beach. It's oddly constructed with random boards nailed together, decorated with a mess of seashells hanging off the shanty roof and surrounded by beat up surf boards... and you'll absolutely love it. Come kick it in this Peter Pan surfer vibe beach bar with a great view and even better service.

☉ Hours: Whenever they feel like it
♀ Where: Northside
🛏 Address: Av. del Palmar 100
♥ @clubdeplayacamaron

SHOPPING IN SAYULITA

MERCADO DEL PUEBLO

The Farmer's Market brings fresh produce, jams, snacks and handicrafts to you! For a sneak peek, check out their Instagram @ mercadodelpueblosayulita

🕐 *Hours:* Fridays from 10am - 2pm.
📍 *Where:* Av Revolución. To get here, cross over the bridge and turn right on Av. Revolucion.

SAYULITA TIANGUIS

Every Sunday, you can peruse this two-block open air market on Calle Gaviotas. The first block has vendors selling mostly snacks, toys, clothing and shoes. The second block is more hand-crafted jewelry, handwoven blankets, pottery and more items that you might want to buy to add a splash of Sayulita to your home.

HIPPIE MARKET

The moment you cross over the bridge in Sayulita, make a sharp left on the dirt path and you're at the entrance of the Hippie Market. You'll find stall after stall selling colorful orange and pink and blue earrings, bracelets, purses and paintings inspired by the Huichol Indian tribes.

Keep walking to the very end of the market and turn right on the main road of Av. del Palmar where the market keeps going.

BOUTIQUE SHOPS

As you walk around Sayulita, you'll pass tons of cute boho shops selling everything from linen dresses to dream catchers. To get you started, here are a few of my favourite boutiques...

◊ *Revolucion del Sueño:* The most unique handbags, clutches, and jackets! ♥ @revoluciondelsueno

◊ *Rosemary:* Bring home some candles and soaps
♥ @rosemarysayulita

◊ *Evoke the Spirit:* Bring home some chic home decor ♥ @evokethespirit

◊ *The Laughing Jaguar:* Mexican spiritual tribal art with a cute twist
♥ @laughingjaguar

Alexa's WELLNESS GUIDE TO SAYULITA

SAYULITA HOLISTIC BODYWORK

Best Holistic Massage Treatments

🕐 **Hours:** Monday-Saturday 9am-5pm

📍 **Where:** Av Revolución 43

f Sayulita Holistic Bodywork

NIRVANA SPA

Best Walk-In Massages and Spa Treatments

🕐 **Hours:** Daily 9am-7pm

📍 **Where:** Manuel N. Navarrete 10

f Nirvanna Spa Sayulita

7 SPA BY JESSICA LUSK

Best Facials and Body Scrubs

📍 **Where:** Manuel N. Navarrete 7

🕐 **Hours:** Monday-Friday 9am-5pm

♥ @7spa_sayulita

SALON SAYULITA

Best Nails

🕐 **Hours:** Monday-Saturday 10am-6pm

📍 **Where:** Calle Jose Mariscal 43

🌐 www.salonsayulita.com

THE JOY OF FLOATING

Float Tank

🕐 **Hours:** Monday - Saturday 10am - 6pm

📍 **Where:** Manuel N. Navarrete 10

f The Joy of Floating Sayulita

WHERE TO NEXT?

———

You are not guaranteed to find an Uber or InDriver in Sayulita. So, I recommend you travel to your next destination by private car or bus.

PRIVATE DRIVER TO SAN PANCHO, PUNTA MITA, BUCERIAS AND PUERTO VALLARTA:

To hire a private car/taxi in Sayulita, contact the Sayulita taxi boss named Josue on WhatsApp, tell him where you need to go and he'll give you a good rate: +52 322 182 3970

Important! There is no bus going from Sayulita to San Pancho at the time of this publication. You'll need to get a private car to head there.

BUS TO PUNTA MITA, BUCERIAS AND PUERTO VALLARTA:

From the main station in Sayulita, hop on a bus headed towards Puerto Vallarta/Bucerias.

If you are going to Punta Mita, you'll get on the bus going to Bucerias/Puerto Vallarta. Simply let the driver know you're going to Punta Mita. He'll make sure you get off in Bucerias and then point you across the street where you'll wait at the bus stop on the road heading to Punta Mita. You will get back onto an ATM bus going north. That bus will say "Punta Mita " on the windshield. It's easy once you get going.

TAXIS:

Yes, you can get a taxi in the city center of Sayulita, but taxi cars tend to be older and the prices require a bit more haggling.

COVID TESTING IN SAYULITA

 Check out my COVID Test video here, where I take you through the whole process at the PVR airport.

PUERTO VALLARTA AIRPORT TESTING
➤ Antigen Test - $450 MXN (results within 40 minutes)
➤ PCR Test - $1,450 MXN (results within 48 hours)

DR. PEÑA
They will come to you:
➤ Antigen Test - $1350 MXN - Same day results
➤ PCR Test - $3500 MXN - Results in 24 hours
☐ +52 322 12 0714

COVID EXPRESS SAYULITA
➤ They will come to you! Results in 24 hours
➤ Antigen Test - $1500 MXN
➤ PCR Test - $3500 MXN
☐ +52 322-170-7493

SAINT LUKE'S HOSPITALS
➤ Antigen - $1000
➤ PCR - $2,950
☐ +52 329-688-2338

CHAPTER SEVEN

San Pancho

—

TIME NEEDED:

1-2 days

KNOWN FOR:

Big waves, chill vibes, arts & culture

BEST FOR:

An offline tropical escapade (but be warned, you might
end up staying longer)

INTRODUCTION TO SAN PANCHO

They say there's nothing not to love about San Pancho. And we agree. This little town is what Sayulita used to be: a small bohemian local surf spot with an international community. And it's the perfect place to have a tropical escapade and go offline (literally, because both wifi and signal are terrible).

At first sight, San Pancho is all about the waves, the food and the sunsets. But spend some time here, and you'll realize it's about way much more. This magical little town is mostly about community. Here locals and foreigners share life and space. They greet each other from sidewalk to sidewalk. They know each other by name. They chat and catch-up and care about their neighbours. And they work together to keep San Pancho the good vibes only place that it is.

SP, as people around here sometimes refer to it, is also a hub for creativity and the arts. This has gained the town the title of "The Cultural Heartbeat of the State of Nayarit." San Pancho is plastered with murals and offers a lot of spaces for music and the scenic arts.

There's also a big holistic and spiritual community here. From yoga to healing food. If you find yourself having an inner or healing journey while staying here, don't be surprised. San Pancho has definitely a special energy that sets it apart from the rest of the beach towns in Banderas Bay and that will make your time here so memorable.

Fun Fact! San Pacho's real name is San Francisco. Named after Saint Francis de Asisi. But in Mexico, Francisco's are nicknamed Pancho!

Areas to Know in San Pancho

AND A SUPER QUICK MAP TO GET A LAY OF THE LAND

1. AVENIDA TERCER MUNDO
2. THE CENTER
3. SAN PANCHO BEACH
4. SAN PANCHITO BEACH
5. COSTA AZUL
6. THE WAREHOUSES

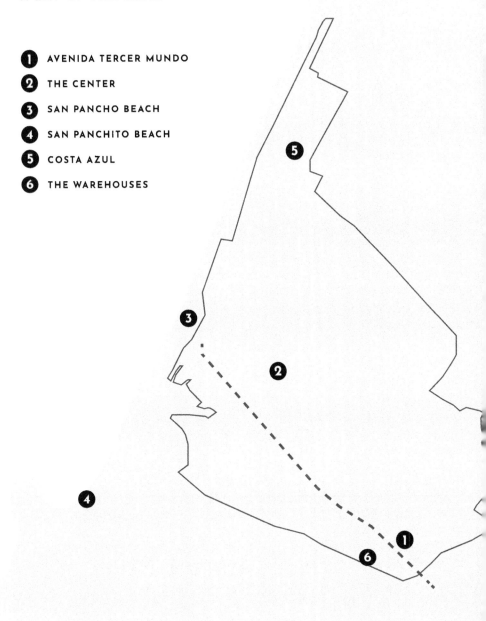

San Pancho is so tiny that it's hard to divide it into areas to explore. But here is an overview of the main sections.

AVENIDA TERCER MUNDO

Aka...the main road. This avenue goes from the highway all the way straight to the beach. And is basically the heartline of San Pancho.

THE CENTER

It can often feel like the whole town is the center, but the actual center are the blocks from the Hermandad Park down towards the beach. You'll find the highest concentration of restaurants, coffee spots and shops in this area

SAN PANCHO BEACH

Go straight on the main road, and you'll arrive at San Pancho beach. This is where people come to enjoy the sun, the surf and the sunsets.

SAN PANCHITO BEACH

Walk to the left (facing the ocean) and you'll arrive at what locals refer to as San Panchito beach. This spot is basically the end of the beach strip and it's a nice little less crowded, but rocky corner.

COSTA AZUL

The northern part of town where most long-time expats reside. It's populated by high-end beachfront properties and the beaches towards this area are basically empty, but friendlier for swimming.

THE WAREHOUSES

Back in the 80's, these warehouses were successful rubber factories. Nowadays they're the heart and home of the cultural and conscious movement in San Pancho. Here you can visit the Entre Amigos Community Center, enjoy theater and dance performances and art exhibits. You can even take part in the various workshops and activities happening around these restored warehouses.

HOW TO GET TO SAN PANCHO

BY CAR

From Sayulita, take a cab. It takes about 15 minutes and costs around 200 pesos. Have the phone number of a private driver to pick you back up, however, because there aren't Ubers in San Pancho. From Puerto Vallarta, an InDriver or Uber will cost around 900 pesos.

BY BUS

From Puerto Vallarta, take a bus by using 1map.com to find the best route depending on where in Vallarta you are. Your best option will most likely be to take the Pacifico Bus line from the Puerto Vallarta bus terminal to San Pancho. Each one-way ticket costs around 50 pesos. It will take from 1.15 to 1.30 hours, depending on the traffic.

For your return trip back to Puerto Vallarta (or any other spot in the Bay) you just need to stand out by the highway next to a large fruit and smoothie stand/restaurant. Buses come by every 10-20 minutes.

HOW TO GET AROUND SAN PANCHO

JUST WALK

Seriously. San Pancho is so small that you can just walk pretty much anywhere. The entrance of the town is a 20 minute walk away from the main beach. And most spots are within the same radius. San Pancho is also super safe to walk around by yourself, even at night.

RENT A BIKE

Riding a bike is also an amazing way to get to know San Pancho. The main road is pretty flat, although most roads are cobblestoned and there are a couple inclines. But nothing you can't handle!

BiCiMAS
🏷 *Budget:* From $4 USD per day

⊙ Hours: Thu - Tue 9:30 PM - 5 PM
♥ Where: Center
🚉 Address: Av. Tercer Mundo 36c
f BiCiMAS

...or you can Rent a Golf Cart

If you're in a more lazy-vacation mood, you can just cruise around town in a golf cart. Probably the easiest and fastest (and fun) way to get around. Just make sure you know how to drive the damn thing before you hit the streets. Ask the rental guys to give you a mini lesson.

San Pancho Golf Cart Rentals

💸 Budget: From $45 USD per day
♥ Where: Center
🚉 Address: Av. Tercer Mundo 35
⊕ www.sanpanchogolfcart.com

TAXIS

If you need to take a trip out of San Pancho and don't want to take the bus, you'll need a Taxi. On La Hermandad Plaza, the park in the middle of the main road, you can find the taxi "station". You'll see the cars parked on the corner of Av. Tercer Mundo and Asia street and all the drivers sitting around waiting for passengers. They're all lovely, chatty people and it's totally safe. A 10 min one-way trip is usually around 70 pesos ($3-4 USD).

PRO TIPS
FOR SAN PANCHO

WELCOME TO THE TWILIGHT ZONE

Because this area is so close to where the time zone changes, the time in your phone can randomly jump from one to the other. To avoid missed flights, plans or hot dates, deactivate the automatic time-zone change in your phone. It can get quite confusing.

BRING CASH

San Pancho is almost cash-only. There's an ATM at the Kiosko and a Multiva ATM on the corner of the Main Road (Tercer Mundo Ave.) and Cuba Street. But don't rely fully on them as they don't work 100% of the time. Bring extra cash from PVR or Sayulita just in case. And don't worry, this place is extra safe.

TOP OFF YOUR DATA

Since Wifi and signal here are so bad, you're gonna be using your data...a lot. However, when I was there, there was also no system for topping it off. So be prepared, and get yourself some more data before you get here.

WATCH OUT FOR THE SURF

Because of the large surf, swimming right on San Pancho beach is not often possible or recommended...unless you're a very experienced swimmer. Walk toward the right side of the beach for friendlier shores (and a less crowded beach!).

WHERE TO STAY
IN SAN PANCHO

HOTEL YSURI BAMBU

A beachfront hotel where you can pick either a garden view room or a room with a balcony looking out onto the ocean for a private sunset session. Ysuri also has an outdoor pool and a beach bar. If you want a bit more of a resort experience in San Pancho, this is it. But in the San Pancho hippie chic kind of way, of course!

💵 *Budget:* $$
📍 *Where:* Center
🏨 *Address:* Calle Cuba 59

 BOOK HERE

HOTEL MARAICA SAN PANCHO

One of the only beachfront hotels in San Pancho that offers views of the ocean right from your bed and sunset views right from the pool. Laying on your big comfy bed while looking up at the palapa-style thatched roof woven together with palm trees catapults you into beach mode. Don't expect luxury, however. Treat this experience like a fancy glamping experience in the jungle...one with a big pool and amazing food.

💵 *Budget:* $$$
📍 *Where:* Costa Azul
🏨 *Address:* Las Palmas 28

 BOOK HERE

PAL.MAR HOTEL TROPICAL

Our favorite little oasis in the heart of San Pancho! This hotelito (little hotel) is a tropical postcard brought to life with lush gardens and sun loungers surrounding the pool, gorgeous rooms filled with furniture made by local designers and staff that will help you arrange everything from boat trips to COVID tests.

The location of PAL.MAR is perfect. Right downtown, a couple blocks away from the beach and half a block away from the main street. You're steps anyway from most things to do and see and eat.

But as much fun as you'll have exploring around, you'll be daydreaming all day about coming back to your little tropical sanctuary. Or you may just not want to leave at all. Thank you for being our casita tropical (tropical little house) in San Pancho.

🏷️ **Budget:** From $
📍 **Where:** Center
🏛️ **Address:** America Latina 777

 BOOK HERE

PHOTO / PAL.MAR HOTEL TROPICAL

GALERÍA SUITES SAN PANCHO

Super affordable private suites surrounded by gardens right in the center of San Pancho, just a few steps away from the beach. This is all you need! If you're going to be out exploring and don't plan to spend a ton of time inside, stay here. While you're here, have a wander around the hotel and soak in the little touches of local art sprinkled all around.

💵 **Budget:** $$
📍 **Where:** Center
🏛 **Address:** Ave. Tercer Mundo #11

 BOOK HERE

AGUA DE LUNA DESIGN HOTEL

An adults-only (16+) boutique hotel inspired by San Pancho's historical culture, this beautiful hotel has 15 unique suites decorated in an earthy, bohemian, minimalistic style that practically begs you to take a photo for the gram. It has a rooftop lounge, a jacuzzi and is only 3 blocks away from the beach.

Pro Tip! Need to work? You can come work at their workstation even when you're not staying here.

💵 **Budget:** $$
📍 **Where:** Center
🏛 **Address:** Asia 8

 BOOK HERE

HOSTAL SAN PANCHO

Cheap private rooms and even cheaper shared rooms! When you're on a budget, save your pennies by staying at Hostal San Pancho. This place is cozy, rustic and offers the perfect amount of socializing where you can make friends but also get a good nights' sleep. Bonus: This hostel is just a 5 minute walk from the beach and they have paddle boards for you to use!

💸 **Budget:** Starting from $9.5 USD dorms / $12.5 USD

📍 **Where:** Near the Town's Entrance

🏠 **Address:** Av. Tercer Mundo 12

 BOOK HERE

PUNTA MONTERREY

Technically not in San Pancho, but close enough if you want to get off the beaten path and do something different. This small eco-friendly hotel is just a 15 minute drive north of San Pancho where you can stay in rustic rooms and cabins surrounded by nature and basically right on a private (and hidden) beach. Come here for a totally quiet, sustainable and isolated experience. PS. Keep in mind that the wifi signal will be weak here. Embrace the time to unplug.

📍 **Where:** Punta Monterrey

🏠 **Address:** Federal Road 200 Tepic - Vallarta km. 113

Book directly on their site https://puntamonterrey.com/

Due to the lack of connectivity in the area, you may not find them in other booking or travel platforms.

PHOTO / PUNTA MONTERREY

WHERE TO EAT
IN SAN PANCHO

Coffee & Coworking

BISTRO ORGANICO

With a clean, local and organic menu, Bistro Organico is easily the best breakfast spot in San Pancho. This place is a little oasis located in an open courtyard at the back of Hotel Cielo Rojo. Both the space and the food are beautiful and you'll probably end up coming here more than once. I sure did. Ps. This place is also great for lunch. Must try the veggie omelette but people also swear by the Huevos Rancheros

⊙ *Hours:* Wed - Mon 8am - 2pm
♀ *Where:* Inside Hotel Cielo Rojo
🛆 *Address:* Asia 6
⊕ www.hotelcielorojo.com/bistro-organico

CAFÉ PARAÍSO

Coffee, smoothies and freshly made pastries every morning. This place was my go-to spot for daily doses of caffeine and a sweet bite to eat. You can order to go or you can hang out for a while and watch San Pancho life go by.

Pro Tip! Cafe Paraíso has, according to locals, one of the best wifi signals around so if you need to get some work done, come here.

⊙ *Hours:* Tue - Sun 7am - 6pm
♀ *Where:* Center
🛆 *Address:* America Latina 1
f *Contact:* Cafe Paraiso

CHIDO GREENS

Need a break from cheese and tortillas? Chido Greens has all the healthy food. Order a fresh-pressed juice or a salad. They also have lots of gluten-free and vegan options available. And keto fans: you can find keto snacks here! Must order: Try their cranberry spicy salsa on anything. It's not too spicy, I promise.

⊙ *Hours:* Mon - Wed 8am - 3pm /

Thu - Sat 9am - 3pm
♀ *Where:* Center
🏛 *Address:* Av. Tercer Mundo 36
f Chido Greens

Street Food & Local Restaurants

SU PANCHA MADRE

There's a little corner in San Pancho that people refer to as "La Esquina" (literally, the corner). And it functions as a mini food truck park where you can find the happy yellow truck of Su Pancha Madre. A gourmet sope stand with both omnivorous and vegetarian options. Try the arrachera sope or if you're a vegetarian, go for the banana "birria". Don't ask. Just try.

Pssst! Can't remember what a sope is? Take a break and head back to our Mexican Food Guide on page 42.

⊙ *Hours:* Daily 4pm - 11pm
♀ *Where:* Center
🏛 *Address:* Corner of America Latina and India
♥ @supanchamadre

THE GRILL DOGS

And in this little corner, you can also find Grill Dogs. A gourmet Hot Dog stand with so many different options. Sit at the bar, have a beer or an "agua el día" (water of the day) and have a chat with the lovely guys that run the place. Don't forget to say hi from us and look for out for the Solo Girls sticker! Emy went here two days in a row because not only was the food great but the guys working there were so friendly and gave her local tips about San Pancho. **Must try:** The chorizo argentino dog

⊙ *Hours:* Daily 4pm - 11pm
♀ *Where:* Center
🏛 *Address:* Corner of America Latina and India
♥ @thegrilldogs

TAQUERÍA LOS ARBOLITOS

Arguably the best tacos in town, this place is unsurprisingly always packed. This place is a hybrid of street food and restaurant food since they have both tables inside and literally on the street. So not only is the food great, but so is the environment. And it's an amazing corner for people watching right after sunset!

⊙ *Hours:* Sun - Fri 7pm - 12am
♀ *Where:* Center
🏛 *Address:* America Latina 7
f TaqueriaLosArbolitos

LA PERLA

When you get to San Pancho beach, you'll see a little restaurant to your left named La Perla. La Perla sits right on the beach where you can sink your toes in the sand, order a cold beer and chow down on the catch of the day! You can order your fish and shrimp in a variety of ways: grilled, fried, breaded with coconut. Just keep in mind that your fish will come still on the bone with the whole head, Mexican style.

⊙ *Hours:* Daily 12pm - 8:30pm
♥ *Where:* Main Beach
🏛 *Address:* Av. Tercer Mundo 48

TACOS LA CUISINELA

Are you ready to hunt for a truly local spot? These street tacos are served out of a street stand on the curb. There's no big sign for La Cuisinela, so look for the red tarp near the EntreAmigos Community Center. If you can't spot it, ask around for La Cuisinela and the locals will happily point you in the right direction. The menu changes, but go with the blue corn tortillas. Don't forget the guacamole salsa.

⊙ *Hours:* Daily early morning until 2pm
♥ *Where:* On the sidewalk, on the corner of Av. Tercer Mundo and Celian street. You'll find the tarp across a clinic called CIU

Restaurants

DOLCE JARDIN EN AMORE

Italian dining in a cozy open courtyard. Emilia tried this place on a date with a lovely guy she met on Tinder, and it was the perfect spot for a casual dinner after a dip in the ocean. The restaurant is filled with plants and a chill ambiance that cocoon you inside and allow you to focus on the experience in front of you. Foodwise, the pastas are big and heart-warming, and the pizzas are fresh and crunchy. Don't want to come on a date? No worries. This place is also perfect for a solo date. #RomanceYourself **Must order:** The Salmon Pasta

⊙ *Hours:* Mon - Sat 5pm - 11pm
♥ *Where:* Center
🏛 *Address:* America Latina 3
f Dolce Jardin En Amore

ITZALANYASAYAN

Healing food by a healer. Founded and run by the amazing Yasmina, this little place is our favorite lunch spot in San Pancho. This place is a mix between comfort and healthy food. Quesadillas, gorditas, sopes and nourishing bowls are all served in this "conscious kitchen". Their mission? To feed both the body and the soul. **Must order:** The Infinito Bowl, a seared tuna salad bowl with a kick of wasabi.

Ps. Yasmina is a very unique healer and she made a huge impact on me. If you're in need of a potent healing session, ask her. She's usually around the restaurant in the mornings, or you can ask her staff how to contact her. But be warned, as it happens with healing sessions, many emotions can be moved. If you feel called to do this, be sure you have the time and space to integrate and process afterwards.

— *Emilia*

🕐 *Hours:* Tue - Sun 11:30am - 10pm

📍 *Where:* Center

🏛 *Address:* Av. Tercer Mundo 28

f Yasmina's Itzalanyasayan Restaurante

PEZETARIAN MX

This place has a slightly fancier feel than most places in San Pancho and gets our vote for the best Bumble Date Spot. From sea to table, Pezetarian MX features a seafood-centric menu with locally sourced ingredients which are plated like little works of art. The food is great to share and the ambiance is beautiful. Get cute, start swiping and tell your new guy, "There's a cute little place in town that I've been dying to try...".

🕐 *Hours:* Wed - Mon 3:30 pm - 11:30pm

📍 *Where:* Center

🏛 *Address:* Av. Tercer Mundo 5

f PezetarianMx

PHOTO / EMILIA IGARTUA

SANTO LOBITO DE MAR OYSTER BAR & GRILL

This is a "go eat and get drunk" kind of place. You'll find Santo Labito on the main where you can order seafood both fresh and from the grill. This place is obviously famous for its oysters but also for their shrimp burger and also their "zarandeado" shrimp (see page 47 for refresher on this regional dish).

For drinks, order a "Cantarito" which is Alexa's favorite traditional mexican drink with tequila and citruses served in a ceramic bowl. Ps. There's live music here every Friday and Saturday. **Must order:** The San Fernando Oysters and / or The Brie Oysters

⊘ *Hours:* Wed - Mon 3pm. - 11 pm
♀ *Where:* Centro
🏠 *Address:* Av. Tercer Mundo #36
♥ @SantoLobitoDeMar

LIMBO

Even for a Mexican girl like Emilia, this place was a delicious surprise. The dishes here are a modern nod to the classics. You've got duck enchiladas, hibiscus tacos, green curry mushrooms alongside a menu of flirty cocktails made with surprising local ingredients. Their handmade blue corn tortillas alone are worth the visit.

⊘ *Hours:* Tue - Sun 11am - 11pm
♀ *Where:* Center, just a block away from the main beach

🏠 *Address:* Av. Tercer Mundo 47
f SFLimbo

BARRACUDA COCINA DEL MAR

I came here for a meet up and a couple beers, with a friend and learned that Barracuda is the go-to spot in San Pancho for fish tacos and happy hour. The tables are right on the street so you can watch the beach goers come and go while you sip a Blonde Ale or a Barracuda Mule. And when it's time to order, make sure to try the octopus and marlin tacos.

⊘ *Hours:* Daily 2pm - 9pm
♀ *Where:* Center
🏠 *Address:* Corner Av. Tercer Mundo and Calle Mexico
♥ @barracocinadelmar

MARIA'S

Owned by three local sisters, María's has been around for years. It's the classic Mexican family-style lunch and dinner spot with handmade flour tortillas and stewed meats wrapped in various ways!

The Burrito Sonorita is a specialty from the north made with machaca (dried beef) and is a tasty opportunity to try something new.

⊘ *Hours:* Mon & Tue 8:30am - 4:30 pm / Thu & Fri 8:30am - 11pm / Sat & Sun 9am - 11pm / Closed on Wednesdays
♀ *Where:* Center
🏠 *Address:* Av. Tercer Mundo 28a

Drinking Day & Night

LA BABA DEL DIABLO

The town's own little mezcalería where you can sample Mexican mezcal spirits from across the country. La Baba del Diablo is a quirky, colorful bar where you come for one mezcal and somehow wind up ordering three. Everyday there's a different promo. On the day that I went, the promo was three-for-one mezcals.

Luckily, I convinced the stranger next to me to take one off my shoulders and drink one with me. What a way to make friends. Ps. I highly recommend you order their mezcal ice cream (yes, you read correctly).

Pro Tip! Want to drink mezcal and skip the hangover? The trick with mezcal is to not mix it with any other alcohol. Stick to mezcal and the morning won't be too hard. You're welcome.

🕐 **Hours:** Tue - Sun 6pm - 12am
📍 **Where:** Costa Azul
🚇 **Address:** Las Palmas 130
♥ @labdeld

PULQUERÍA OCTLI

Or you can ignore my last Pro Tip, and after a mezcal hop right next door to OCTLI to try some pulque which is another mexican spirit made from the fermented sap of agave. Quite a contrast to its neighbor, OCTLI is a subtle and cozy space with moon-inspired decor.

The wall behind the bar is so original that it's what first pulled me in. You'll see. Pro Tip! Be warned, pulque is also quite strong! Mind your quantities and drink lots of water in between drinks.

🕐 **Hours:** Tue - Sun 6pm - 12am
📍 **Where:** Costa Azul
🚇 **Address:** Las Palmas 130
♥ @pulqueria_octli

CERVECERÍA ARTESANAL SAN PANCHO

San Pancho's local brewery serves 100% mexican made artisanal ales and lagers. "La Cerve", as known by the locals, is where both residents and tourists hang out after sunset while enjoying live music, cold beers, burgers and cheese plates. Spend a while here and you'll leave with new friends plus a bit of a buzz.

🕐 **Hours:** Daily 5pm - 12am
📍 **Where:** Center
🚇 **Address:** America Latina 80
♥ @cerveceriaartesanalsanpancho

JUNGLAR

Right on the main road, there's a little entrance that doesn't look like much from the outside. But once you go in, you'll find yourself in one of the coolest spots in San Pancho. Junglar is a cozy courtyard with several restaurants in one space.

You'll find amazing coffee from Casa Linda (see Coffee & Breakfast section), incredible pizza and pasta from Komodo; and succulent steaks from Kaiman. Bonus: There's live music here every weekend.

⊙ **Hours:** Daily 12pm - 12pm
Where: Center
Address: Av. Tercer Mundo 36
Contact: junglarsanpancho.com

EL GALLO

Mexican food with live music almost every night every night! El Gallo has open mic nights, tacos and beers. No frills, no fuss. Come and let loose. And for the weekend hangover, El Gallo has birria on Sundays which is a Mexican go to after a night of drinking.

⊙ **Hours:** Mon 9am - 3pm / Wed, Thu, Sun 9am - 12am / Fri-Satu 9am - 1am
Where: Nearby the Warehouses
Address: Av. Tercer Mundo 17
Contact: @elgallosanpancho

Fun Fact!

Mexicans eat tacos at any time of day. You can find tacos for breakfast, lunch and dinner. Although the kind of tacos you'll find may vary depending on the time of day. Some tacos, like birria, are more common for breakfast. While "asada" (beef) are more of a nighttime thing.

THINGS TO DO IN SAN PANCHO

Top AirBnb Experience

 SAN PANCHO ON A BIKE

Join Samuel in a tour around the town. He's been around San Pancho for over 5 years and he knows all the spots to know and things to see. You can choose a Cultural Tour, a Hidden Beaches Tour or a Custom Private Hour Tour, among others. And the coolest thing about riding with Samuel is that he's a true local and you'll be saying hi everyone along the way. Get your smile ready.

Outdoor Experiences

WATCH THE SUNSET - FREE BADGE -

Every day, San Pancho residents sit on the shore to watch the surfers and the sun go down. Pacific sunsets can be quite the colorful show. And people here even clap every time the tiniest bit of sun disappears into the horizon. Settle in, buy popcorn, or any other goodies, from the walking vendors and enjoy the show.

SURF LESSONS

Learn how to surf with experts in the beautiful beach of La Lancha. Surf lessons with Nativa Surf Shop are open to all levels and include equipment and transport. Or if you're already a pro...you can just hop on the shuttle to surf on your own at La Lancha.

⊙ *Budget:* $$

⊕ www.nativasurfshop.com

Pro Tip! The waves and currents in San Pancho can get gnarly. We strongly suggest not going surfing straight in the surf break if you don't have experience. Or without a teacher. This is why most surf lessons here will be offered in spots outside SP.

EXPLORE THE TOWN

Once you've done your tour and know where everything is, you can just walk around town and explore the nooks and corners. San Pancho is full of murals and urban art that reflect and express the eclectic and artful soul of the town.

VISIT LO DE PERLA JUNGLE GARDEN

Just a 10 min ride from San Pancho, you can find this natural preserve full of stunning orchids, amazing bromeliads, lush tropical plants, fantastic fungi and colorful butterflies. Join a local guide and learn about the biodiversity in the most northern jungle in the world. Or you can bring your own lunch and have your own picnic surrounded by this jungle wonderland.

Pro Tip! Bring comfy shoes, long pants and shirt...and lots of (eco-friendly) bug repellent.

➤ *How To Get There:* You can get a Taxi from La Hermandad Plaza

🎟 *Budget:* $
⊙ *Hours:* Tuesday - Sunday 9am - 3pm
📍 *Where:* 12 min drive away from the center of SP
⊕ lodeperla.org

Hikes in San Pancho

HIKE TO THE BUDDHA STATUE

One of the least known facts about San Pancho, is that there is a sightseeing spot with a human-sized Buddha statue. On this trail you can see Malpaso beach and Sayulita, but most people come for an #InstaMoment with the statue. This is a fairly easy hike.

> ➤ *How To Get There:* Follow the road towards Costa Azul and follow Las Clavelinas road. Once you get to Villas Clavellinas, you'll see a dirt road going uphill known as Buddha Road. Follow that one and you'll reach the Buddha. And who knows, maybe even enlightenment.

TREK TO PLAYA LOS BARROS

This place is both famous and a hidden gem at the same time. Why is it famous? Barro is Spanish for mud. This beach is full of clean mud...making this uncrowded beach a natural outdoors spa.

SAN PANCHO TO SAYULITA

Yes, you can walk from San Pancho to Sayulita. It's a not-to-intense 4 mile trek that involves strolling down the beach, hiking through the jungle and then descending to the beach once again. And a little bit of walking on the highway. It takes around 1.5 hours and the trail is pretty well defined. You get to overlook hidden beaches and see the jungle up close.

While you can do these hikes by yourself, we really recommend you do them with an experienced guide like our friend Samuel from Bicimas (the same smiley guide from the San Pancho on a Bike Tour). He's been around the area for years and you'll be in good and safe hands with him.

Contact him here:

Arts & Culture

VISIT ENTRE AMIGOS COMMUNITY CENTER

This place is one of the engines behind keeping San Pancho a positive, healthy and conscious community. They offer workshops, display local artist's work, and have the biggest library in the area where anyone can come and borrow books. They also have healthy food from Monday to Friday.

📍 **Where:** The Warehouses
🌐 entreamigos.org.mx

CIRCO DE LOS NIÑOS

In 2011, the co-founder of Cirque Du Soleil and his wife founded this children's community center giving low-income kids an opportunity to do something amazing in the world of creative theater. These kids train as performers on stage and/or directors and producers backstage to create non-for-profit mini Cirque Du Soleil-inspired shows. See how you can contribute to this empowering cause at circodelosninosdesanpancho.mx/en/events

📍 **Where:** The Warehouses
🎟 **Budget:** Entrance is on a donation basis of min. 100 pesos
🌐 circodelosninosdesanpancho.mx

PHOTO / EMILIA IGARTUA

Volunteering San Pancho

Pools & Beach Clubs

VOLUNTEER AT THE PROYECTO TORTUGA, AKA THE TURTLE RESCUE CENTER

Did you know that from 100 turtle eggs only 1 grows up to be an adult? San Pancho is a big nesting place for Olive Ridley and Leatherback turtles. Proyecto Tortuga is dedicated to the protection and conservation of these endangered species.

They work with the community to raise awareness on the importance of taking care of "San Pancho's original inhabitants", as they call the turtles. And they protect the turtle eggs from poachers and predators. You can learn and volunteer directly with them and visit their turtle nurseries in their headquarters, just a minute away from the center of San Pancho.

Pro Tip!

Want to Volunteer long term?

You can join their volunteer programs that are open from May through November.

➤ Learn more at :
www.project-tortuga.org/volunteer.html

TIERRA TROPICAL BEACH CLUB BY LA PATRONA POLO CLUB

Tulum trendy vibes in San Pancho. If you're looking for more of a high-end San Pancho experience, this is where you need to spend your day. This bougie beach club sits under an impressive bamboo-palapa and has an infinity beachfront pool surrounded by sun lounges and fancy cabanas.

You can get a Day Pass (400 pesos entrance fee) and have access to the pool, lounges and beach towels. Or you can go straight to the bar or restaurant and order directly from their food and cocktail menu by resident chef Carlos Garcia.

Oh and the best part? This place is only for people ages 13 and older, so your peace and quiet is more-so guaranteed. *Sigh of relief*

🕐 *Hours:* 10am - 10pm
📍 *Where:* Costa Azul
🚻 *Address:* Corner of Amapas and Avenida Las Palmas
♥ @tierratropicalbeachclub

Relaxation & Wellness

EL ESTAR YOGA STUDIO

Take a yoga class in a little palapa surrounded by a lush garden. This place is nothing but healing vibes with a lovely team of teachers and staff.

⊙ *Hours:* 9am - 1pm / 3pm - 6pm
♀ *Where:* Center
🖼 *Address:* America Latina 32
♥ @ElEstarSanPancho

BREATHWORK

Breathwork is a healing technique similar to meditation but aided by conscious breathing techniques to release stuck emotions, dissolve anxiety and even work through trauma. As with any healing experience, make sure you have time and space to process and integrate after.
🌐 www.sanfranciscobreathwork.com/offerings

PILATES SAN PANCHO

If you want something more hardcore, head to Pilates San Pancho. From reformer classes to physical therapy clinics. And of course, they offer yoga as well.

⊙ *Hours:* Mon - Fri 8:30am - 20:30pm / Sat 8:30am - 12:30pm
♀ *Where:* The Warehouses
🖼 *Address:* Av. Tercer Mundo 93
f Pilates San Pancho

ANGELICAL SPA

A local massage parlor known for its massages. With a sacred yet modern approach, this place offers a wide range of holistic treatments.

💵 *Budget:* $$
⊙ *Hours:* Mon - Fri 9am - 6pm / Sat 10am - 1pm
♀ *Where:* Center
🖼 *Address:* America Latina 20
f AngelicalSpa

BLISS STUDIO AND SPA IN LA PATRONA BEACH CLUB

If the bougie life is your thing, then head to Bliss Studio & Spa. This place offers facial, hair and nail services with a beautiful ocean view. Go pamper yourself and spend the rest of the day in bliss at the private beach cabanas downstairs.

💵 *Budget:* $$$
⊙ *Hours:* Mon - Sat 12pm - 6pm
♀ *Where:* Costa Azul
🖼 *Address:* Africa s/n
f La Patrona Polo Club & Tierra Tropical

SHOPPING IN SAN PANCHO

Food Shopping

CASA LINDA MERCADO

If you're staying longer than a few days and you plan on cooking, Casa Linda is your go-to spot. Here you can find snacks, produce and spices in bulk (eco-friendly!). Most products are locally sourced and made by locals and residents of the area. And don't forget about their coffee spot inside Junglar!

☉ *Hours:* Mon - Fri 10am - 20pm / Sat 11am - 20pm / Sun 12pm - 20pm
♥ *Where:* : Center
🏪 *Address:* Asia 44
♥ @casalinda.mercado

Surf Shops

Need some more surf or beach gear after so many adventures? Santa Madre Surf Shop and Nativa Surf Shop got you covered. You can find products from established brands like Billabong, RVCA, Roxy, among others...as well as stuff from local designers.

SANTA MADRE SURF SHOP

☉ *Hours:* Wed - Mon 9am - 9pm
♥ *Where:* Av. Tercer Mundo #100
♥ @SantaMadreAdventures

NATIVA SURF SHOP:

Hours: Daily 9am - 9pm
Where: Av. Tercer Mundo #28
♥ @NativaSurfShop

Markets

Boutiques

FARMERS MARKET (MERCADO DEL SOL)

A mix between artisans selling their creations and local food vendors, here you'll find everything from traditional crafts to vegan snacks. And of course, workshops, activities and live music. Everything you can buy here is straight from the merchants and helps support local families. The market is open seasonally, from Late fall to Late Spring. If you happen to be around during market season, it's definitely a must.

☉ **Hours:** November through June. Every Tuesday 10am to 1:30pm
♥ **Where:** Plaza del Sol

THE MAIN ROAD...

Avenida Tercer Mundo, San Pancho's main road is lined up with shops full of high-end Mexican crafts and products from local designers. Linen garments, hand-made leather sandals, decor objects, artisanal jewellery, colorful bikinis...either for yourself or as a souvenir, you can find so many exquisite pieces around here. So go for a walk up and down the avenue, it's a whole shopping tour!

...and that's it!

YOU HAVE ABSORBED THE MENTAL MAP
OF ALL OF BANDERAS BAY.

NOW, WHAT TO DO WITH ALL THAT KNOWLEDGE? LET'S PLAY
WITH SOME POTENTIAL ITINERARIES...

Banderas Bay

The biggest mistake I see girls making when planning an adventure is trying to see it ALL!

While attempting to cover so many places and visit so many beaches in such short amounts of time, you end up rushing the most beautiful experiences.

In order for you to have the best possible experience, you've got to be realistic with your time.

So, here are some realistic itineraries to help you plan an unforgettable trip with just the right ratio of activity to relaxation.

Want me to plan your trip for you?
TheSoloGirlsTravelGuide.com/Plan-my-trip

One Week Itineraries

UNWIND, UNPLUG, THEN SOUL SEARCH:

DAY 1: SAYULITA

✳ *AM:* Fly into PVR Airport

➤ From the airport, head to Sayulita

➤ Check in to AzulPitaya Hotel

➤ Walk the colorful Boho Market

✦ *PM:* Treat yourself to a sunset Margarita at Bar La Isla

DAY 2: SAYULITA

✳ *AM:* Up early for a sunrise walk

➤ Go horseback riding on the beach

➤ Spend the rest day in the big heated pool with a book

✦ *PM:* Order pizza from La Venezia and chill

DAY 3: SAN PANCHO

✳ *AM:* Have breakfast at Coffee on the Corner

➤ Take a taxi over to San Pancho

➤ Check into Agua de Luna Design Hotel

➤ Aimlessly wander the town on foot, eating whatever looks good

✦ *PM:* Go on an Airbnb Sunset Hike with Fran

DAY 4: SAN PANCHO

✳ *AM:* Wake Up for the AirBnb Bike ➤ Tour of San Pancho

➤ Treat yourself to a massage at Angelical Spa

✦ *PM:* Have a clean, nourishing dinner at Itzalanyasayan

DAY 5: SAN PANCHO

✳ **AM:** Take a morning yoga class at El Estar Yoga Studio

➤ Go for a light lunch at Chido Greens

➤ Join an afternoon breathwork session at San Francisco Breathwork

✦ **PM:** Sit on the beach and watch the sunset

DAY 6: SAN PANCHO

✳ **AM:** Take a surf lesson with Nativa Surf Shop

➤ Lounge on the beach in the afternoon

➤ Go for a late lunch at Bistro Organico

✦ **PM:** In the evening, volunteer at the Proyecto Tortuga

DAY 7: SAN PANCHO

✳ **AM:** Reflect today.

➤ Write, walk and journal. No phones.

✦ **PM:** Head to the airport

BALANCED VACATION:

Absorbing culture and alcohol...

DAY 1: PUERTO VALLARTA

✳ **AM:** Land in PVR

➤ Check in to Casa Maria Malecon

➤ Walk the Malecon

✦ **PM:** Go for sunset dinner and drinks at Sapphire Beach Club

DAY 2: PUERTO VALLARTA

✳ **AM:** Go for brunch at Andale's Restaurant & Bar

> Have a Beauty Day with massages at MedSpa and nails at Una Norma (half the price of back home)

✦ *PM:* Go on a Street Food Tour with @vallartalocalfoodtours

DAY 3: PUERTO VALLARTA

✳ *AM:* Join a boat tour to Yelapa Waterfall with Alley Cat Cruise

✦ *PM:* Go for dinner at El Brujo

DAY 4: PUERTO VALLARTA

✳ *AM:* Zipline with Canpoy River

✦ *PM:* - Attend a drag show at night

DAY 5: PUERTO VALLARTA

✳ *AM:* Check into an all-inclusive resort and wind down

> Do nothing!

✦ *PM:* Get a massage (preferably on the beach at sunset)

Make a reservation at one of the on-site restaurants

DAY 6: PUERTO VALLARTA

✳ *AM:* Wake up for a sunrise walk on the beach

> Live in the pool

> Work on your tan and read a book

✦ *PM:* Get a little drunk on your last night of vacation

DAY 7: PUERTO VALLARTA

✳ *AM:* Sleep-in

> Order room service in your robe

> Check out and head to the airport

BUDGET BACKPACKER:

Do it cheap! Here's how.

DAY 1: PUERTO VALLARTA
✦ **PM:** Check into Hostel Vallarta
➤ Hang out here and get to know the other travelers
➤ Use this book to create a DIY taco tour

DAY 2: PUERTO VALLARTA
✳ **AM:** Take a bus to Boca de Tomatlan
➤ Hike from Boca de Tomatlan to Las Animas
✦ **PM:** In Las Animas, sit in a lounge chair and order just one drink and one appetizer
➤ Walk around Las Animas town to window shop
➤ Bus back to the hostel
➤ Go find a street quesadilla, and take it to watch the Voladores de Papantla

DAY 3: PUERTO VALLARTA
✳ **AM:** Go on the free DIY Art Walk (page 107)
➤ Volunteer at Vallarta Food Bank
✦ **PM:** Buy some beers from Oxxo and take them to the beach
➤ Bring a towel, sit and watch the sunset
➤ On a Tuesday or Thursday, go to La Bodeguita del Medio for a free salsa dancing class

DAY 4: SAYULITA
✳ **AM:** Hop on the bus north to Sayulita
➤ Check into My Sister's House Hostel
➤ Eat at cheap chicken at Pollos "Yolanda" and take some home for leftovers

✦ **PM:** Stroll through the streets of Sayulita, taking photos of the beautiful artwork and architecture

➤ Visit the Hippie Market

➤ Go to Oxxo, buy some beers, and drink them on the beach at sunset

➤ Eat dinner at Tacos Toño

DAY 6: SAYULITA

✳ **AM:** Up early to walk to De Los Muertos Beach

➤ Bring snacks, a book and spend the day relaxing in the sand.

✦ **PM:** Have a beer at Atico Bar while you sit on the swing

➤ Go to Chillum Bar for cheap sushi and enjoy the live music

➤ Swim in the ocean with the glittering plankton when it's super dark

DAY 7: SAYULITA

➤ Get up early to watch the sunrise on the beach

➤ Pack and take a bus back to the airport

Travel is medicine...
**YOU GOING TO MEXICO ISN'T JUST A "VACATION"
AND IT ISN'T SELFISH. IT'S NECESSARY.
IT'S NECESSARY TO CHALLENGE YOURSELF,
HEAL AND GROW INTO A GIRL WHO KNOWS WHO SHE IS.
GO.**

Ten Days Itineraries

TRAVEL LOCAL, SLEEP LUXURY:

That's our motto. Here is how Emilia and Alexa would spend 10 days in the Banderas Bay.

DAY 1: PUERTO VALLARTA
☀ *AM:* Land in PVR
➤ Check into the Marriott All-Inclusive
✦ *PM:* Enjoy the resort and be lazy at the pool

DAY 2: PUERTO VALLARTA
☀ *AM:* Have a Beauty Day with waxing, massages, & nails
✦ *PM:* Back to the resort to enjoy doing nothing (and eating)

DAY 3: PUERTO VALLARTA
☀ *AM:* Tan on the beach with a book
✦ *PM:* Have a frozen daiquiri at Blondies
➤ Go on a Taco Tour with @VallartaLocalFoodTours

DAY 4: SAN PANCHO
☀ *AM:* Hire a driver to take us to San Pancho
➤ Check into Agua de Luna Design Hotel
✦ *PM:* Spend the afternoon + sunset at Tierra Tropikal Beach Club

DAY 5: SAN PANCHO

✳ *AM:* Take a yoga class at El Estar Yoga Studio

➤ Have breakfast at Bistro Organica

✦ *PM:* Take a Breathwork class at San Francisco Breathwork

Eat pizza at Dolce Amore Ristorante

DAY 6: SAN PANCHO

✳ *AM:* Join a catamaran tour with Chica Loca Tours (meet in Sayulita)

✦ *PM:* Explore Sayulita after the boat tour (bring a hair brush and change of clothes)

➤ Dinner at Anchara Restaurant

➤ Drinks at Escondido Bar

➤ Back to San Pancho by 9pm (via Taxi)

DAY 7: SAN PANCHO

✳ *AM:* Free morning, do nothing

➤ Walk around and discover new shops and food

✦ *PM:* Get a massage at Angelica Spa

➤ Eat dinner at Pezitarian MX

DAY 8: PUNTA DE MITA

✳ *AM:* Check into The Four Seasons or The Conrad (they will pick you up)

✦ *PM:* Hop directly in the pool and order a margarita

➤ Eat dinner at one of their on-site restaurants

DAY 9: PUNTA DE MITA

✳ *AM:* Spend the morning on the beach

➤ Have a massage and spa session at the resort

✦ *PM:* Go into Punta Mita town

➤ Go paddle boarding in front of Rocio

- ➤ Have a cocktail and people watch at Rustica Punta Mita
- ➤ Eat dinner at Hector's Kitchen

DAY 10: PUNTA DE MITA

- ✳ **AM:** Have a Bloody Mary and wake up in the pool!
- ➤ Run into the ocean one last time
- ➤ Check-out. They'll drive you to the airport

SOCIAL SOLO GIRL:

Travel alone, not lonely! Make new friends as you explore.

DAY 1: SAYULITA

- ✳ **AM:** From the airport, head straight to Sayulita
- ➤ Check into My Sister's House Hostel or Selina Sayulita (get a private room or a dorm)
- ➤ Hang at the hostel and make friends with the other travel girls
- ✦ **PM:** Invite some girls to go for live music, sushi and cocktails at Chillum Bar

DAY 2: SAYULITA

- ✳ **AM:** Up early for a boozy boat tour with Chica Loca Tours (invite the girls to come with you)
- ✦ **PM:** Back in town (a little drunk, probably)
- ➤ Keep drinking and order a beer flight at YamBak Brewery
- ➤ Dinner at Pizza Venezia or La Rustica

DAY 3: SAYULITA

* **AM:** Sleep in...you might be hungover
- ➤ Go for breakfast at Coffee on the Corner
- ➤ Wander the Hippie Market
* **PM:** Head to Bar La Isla, get a lounge chair on the beach and recoup in the sun
- ➤ Go to Atico bar, sit on a bar swing and easily make some friends
- ➤ See where the night takes you

DAY 4: SAN PANCHO

* **AM:** Check out and head to San Pancho
- ➤ Check in to Hotel Palmar Tropical or Hostal San Pancho
* **PM:** Aimlessly walk around San Pancho looking for taco stands (including Tacos La Cuisinela)

Join an Airbnb sunset hike with Fran

DAY 5: SAN PANCHO

* **AM:** Up early for the Airbnb Bike Tour
- ➤ Afterwards, have lunch at Maria's

Go to La Baba del Diablo for a Mezcal Ice Cream

* **PM:** Enjoy live music and tacos at El Gallo
- ➤...but don't stay out too late - you have an active morning

DAY 6: SAN PANCHO

* **AM:** Take a morning surf lesson with Nativa Surf Shop or with your hotel
* **PM:**- Get a massage at Bliss Studio and Spa in La Patrona Beach Club
- ➤ End your San Pancho Chapter with a sunset walk on the beach

DAY 7: PUERTO VALLARTA

* **AM:** Check out and head to Puerto Vallarta
- ➤ Check into Hilton Hacienda All-Inclusive
* **PM:** Hang at the swim up pool bar and make friends
- ➤ Attend a Drag Show in the evening

Day 8: Puerto Vallarta

➤ Volunteer at Vallarta Food Bank

➤ Ask in my Facebook group, Girls in Puerto Vallarta, who wants to go to dinner with your at Margarita Grill

DAY 9: PUERTO VALLARTA

✳ *AM:* Go on a Taco Tour with @vallartalocalfoodtours

➤ Stop at Blondies for a frozen daiquiri

✦ *PM:* Find a Salsa Dancing lesson in town or go to Incanto Piano Bar for a live show (again ask in Girls in Puerto Vallarta for a friend to visit)

DAY 10: PUERTO VALLARTA

✳ *AM:* Have brunch at the friendly Andale's Restaurant & Bar

➤ Pack up and head to the airport

WANT ME TO PLAN THE
WHOLE DAMN THING FOR YOU?

Yes, I plan trips for my readers all the time.

➤ Check out TheSoloGirlsTravelGuide.com for trip planning services.

Also, subscribe to my YouTube channel and watch my Instagram stories to get all my emerging pro tips and Mexico adventures!

➤ youtube.com/sologirlstravelguide

Things To Know...

BEFORE COMING TO BANDERAS BAY

Festivals & Holidays in Mexico

HOLIDAYS

Mexico is a catholic country, so you'll find that many of the holidays and festivities are religion-based; others are historic milestones. But no matter the occasion, Mexicans love any reason to get together and celebrate. And man, do Mexicans know how to celebrate!

Without further ado, let me introduce you to a few of the most significant holidays in Mexico…

DAY OF THE DEAD - NOVEMBER 2ND

Day of the Dead has become one of Mexico's most iconic celebrations. Every year Instagram is flooded all over the world with ornamented skull-like face paint, flower headbands and opulent jewelry. It's believed that on the Day of the Dead, those who have passed away

PHOTO / UNSPLASH.COM

come back to earth to visit. And rather than mourning death, this is about celebrating life. People visit their deceased ones' tombstones or set up tiered altars displaying symbolic gifts like marigold flowers, candles, and food. And at the very top of the altar, family members will display a photo of whoever that altar is dedicated to.

You'll find that in Mexico, death is not something to be afraid of. It is mourned, of course. But death is celebrated with humor, irreverence and joy. Try it out. See how it feels.

Pro Tip! Watch the movie Coco, by Disney Pixar. It's a very accurate and beautiful representation of this holiday, and culture from Central Mexico.

CINCO DE MAYO - MAY 5TH

Guess what? I'm about to really burst your bubble when I tell you that Cinco the Mayo is not a thing in Mexico. Mexicans don't really celebrate it. And no, it's not Mexican Independence Day. But yes, it is a historical holiday that celebrates the victory of the Mexican Army against a French Invasion back in 1862.

Cinco de Mayo is actually one of the least celebrated holidays in Mexico. If you find yourself in a Cinco de Mayo celebration...you're in a (very) touristic spot. Still, Mexicans will never say no to celebration. So, in local fashion, go ahead and down that tequila anyway.

INDEPENDENCE DAY - SEPTEMBER 16TH

That being said...the real Mexican Independence Day is celebrated on the eve of September 15th to ring in the 16th. Kinda like New Year's, but with tequila instead of champagne. Lots and lots of tequila. If you're around for this day, you will find parties and celebrations pretty much everywhere. From traditional parties to nightclub events.

CHRISTMAS EVE - DECEMBER 24TH

Being such a family-oriented and a catholic culture, Christmas is a big deal in México. The biggest celebration is Christmas Eve (Noche Buena), where people get together, have dinner and exchange presents. And on the 25th, they get together again and have a leftovers feast. However, with such an American influence, Christmas looks a bit like it does in the US. Expect to see sparkling lights, Santas and reindeers all around.

LADY DE GUADALUPE · DECEMBER 12TH

The Lady of Guadalupe is Mexico's representation of the Virgin Mary. And they say that even the most atheists in Mexico are "guadalupanos" (devotees of the Lady of Guadalupe). She's the mother of all Mexicans and she is celebrated in a BIG way. Special masses are held. People pilgrimage for days. Flowers and serenades are delivered to church. And yes, many businesses are closed.

Every year in Puerto Vallarta, massive pilgrimages happen between the 1st to the 12th of December. Groups of locals and residents cross the city in mass to reach the Church dedicated to the Lady of Guadalupe in downtown Puerto Vallarta where the whole plaza turns into an open market of Mexican snacks and a folklore experience.

LABOR DAY - MAY 1ST

Not a holiday that's hugely celebrated but most businesses will be closed on Labor Day. And sometimes, since Cinco de Mayo falls shortly after Labor Day, this weekend will become one big long weekend!

SEMANA SANTA (AKA MEXICAN SPRING BREAK)

Also dependent on the Catholic Church's calendar, the dates of Semana Santa change every year. Semana Santa literally means Holy Week...but it's pretty much the opposite of holy, if you know what I mean. School is out for two weeks and that means party time for the locals. Expect a lot of local tourism during this time.

hey!

ARE WE MISSING ANYTHING? SEND ME AN EMAIL AT HELLO@THESOLOGIRLSTRAVELGUIDE.COM

FESTIVALS IN BANDERAS BAY

VALLARTA FILM FESTIVAL - PUERTO VALLARTA

After the iconic "Noche de la Iguana" with Richard Burton was filmed here, Puerto Vallarta has had a connection with the silver screen. Every year the Vallarta Film Festival gathers the most relevant filmmakers and film projects in the region. And showcases as well both national and international films and creatives from the industry.

➤ For more info, visit http://www.ficpv.cuc.udg.mx/

FIESTAS DE MAYO - PUERTO VALLARTA

This festival is one of the most iconic events around. It's some sort of carnival full of music, art and dance. There's shows and performances all around open to everyone. And even a float parade to kick off the festival. This happens in late May and is a great time to enjoy Puerto Vallarta's local culture.

CLÁSICO EL ANCLOTE - PUNTA MITA

A surf classic competition held yearly in Playa El Anclote focused on single fins only (longboards) and open to locals and mexicans. Dates can change depending on the tides, but it usually happens late spring / early summer. And it's such a show watching people dance on the waves!

SAN PANCHO MUSIC FESTIVAL - SAN PANCHO

A local music festival started by San Pancho residents that has been around for 20 years. It's a three-day event that's one of the largest musical events in the region. This festival is by locals and for locals and foreigners alike. In true San Pancho fashion, it was funded with the premise to celebrate and embrace the talents of musicians from the area, as well as visiting ones. The next edition is projected for late February 2022. Visit sanpanchomusicfestival.com to learn more.

FESTIVAL DEL VIENTO (THE WIND FESTIVAL) - BUCERIAS

Being such a kitesurfing hotspot, Bucerias is home to the biggest freestyle kitesurfing competition in Mexico. It's held every year mid-May. You can watch kite surfers compete in many different modalities, and even race all the way from La Cruz de Huanacaxtle to Bucerias. Plus, watching the sky full of these colorful kites is quite a sight. Learn more about this festival at http://festivaldelviento.mx/

MEXILOG FEST

This surf invitational is a single-fin (longboard) competition with surfers from all around the world (hello, cute surfers!). Once you're over watching all the cute surfers, you can also enjoy the yoga, live music and food happening around the event. This year it was held in Punta Burros, near Punta Mita, but both dates and locations can vary. It's usually held early summer, depending on the swells and the weather. Check out mexilogfest.com to check out their next edition (and all the cool pics from past ones!).

Bonus!

CORONA CAPITAL - MEXICO CITY

Ok, so this one is not in Banderas Bay, but it's worth knowing. Corona Capital is basically Mexico's Coachella. Three days of concerts with an international line-up. It happens every year in the Fall and the line-up is released early summer. There's no fixed dates as of today, because #covid, but visit coronacapital.mx to keep track of any updates.

Crime & Safety Guide

Mexico isn't as scary as the news makes it seem, I promise!

A quick briefing...

◇ Violent crime against tourists is rare.

◇ Crime here typically comes in the form of scams or theft rather than actual violence.

◇ The biggest danger is getting too drunk and having your belongings stolen

◇ Assaults typically happen between two travelers, rather than a traveler and a local.

In general, Banderas Bay is very safe with a very low crime rate! And Puerto Vallarta has been rated the safest destination in Mexico! You're safer here than most cities in the US. But that doesn't mean crime doesn't exist.

So, I'm going to tell you about some of the crimes to watch out for and how to protect yourself, even though odds are that you won't run into these issues during your trip.

CRIMES TO KNOW ABOUT

BAG SNATCHING

The first thing my new friends in Puerto Vallarta told me was that Walmart has been experiencing lots of bag snatching. So don't leave your purse in the cart. If you turn around to grab a bottle of wine, your purse might not be there when you turn back around. The same goes for when you're at a bar

PICKPOCKETS

When you're in a crowded market, watch your pockets and make sure that your purse is either zipped or snapped close. For this reason, I never travel with a non-close beach bag. You need a bag you can close.

DRUGGING DRINKS

This happens here, this happens everywhere. Us women need to be vigilant when we are out drinking, especially in a foreign country. Don't let strangers buy you cocktails. I prefer to order bottled beer. Also, get buzzed but please don't get very drunk unless you're inside your resort or hotel. You never know what kind of creeps are out there looking for drunk girls to take advantage of.

CREATIVE CRIMES

A rare one, but I've heard of a trick where bag snatchers squirt ketchup or mustard on you, and then point the stain out to you. While you look down to investigate the spot, they snatch your bag. Weird, but 5 points for creativity.

BOLD CRIMES

The other day, a woman was at Costco, in her car about to leave. A man banged on her trunk. She got out and he showed her that she had run over his glasses! He picked up his glasses and left. When she got back in the car, her purse from the front seat of her car was gone. It was a tag-team crime. Once you are aware that these things happen, your high-alert state will kick in when needed.

STREET CRIME

If you're in the wrong place at night anywhere in the world, someone may attempt to steal your purse or assault you, just like anywhere else in the world. So always wear a cross shoulder purse while walking at night and walk in lit areas.

Pro Tip! Farmacias Guadalajara (they're everywhere) sells pepper spray! Grab one to make you feel extra safe at night.

WHAT TO DO WHEN YOUR WALLET GETS STOLEN

Thieves act fast to use your credit cards to go shopping immediately after they've stolen your wallet. The first thing you need to do is call your bank right away and cancel your cards. This sucks. I know. If you use one of the reputable banks that I recommend, then you're covered. They will ship you a new card to Mexico ASAP. Check out page 39 to see the card I travel with.

ATM SKIMMING

A rare but real crime in Mexico. Clever thieves can rig the ATM machines to steal your card info and take money out of your account. If you use a reputable bank, don't worry – they will be ready to reimburse you if shit goes down. Seriously, don't stress too much about ATM skimming. Just practice these ATM habits...

1. Use ATMs attached to banks or inside a big glass bank box

2. Cover your hand when typing your PIN. This will block any cameras that might be recording.

3. Jiggle the card reader. Does it move? If it does, so should you. To the next ATM.

Safe Girl Tips for Puerto Vallarta

BEFORE YOU GO...

◊ Leave your travel itinerary and contact information with friends or family.

◊ Make sure you have medical insurance during your adventure

◊ Have emergency numbers and drivers saved in your phone and WhatsApp. Below are some numbers to get you started.

◊ Make sure you've bought the correct purse and bags for going out.

 Shop the bags I like here.

WHEN YOU'RE TRAVELING...

◊ Don't carry all your cards and cash with you. Just take enough out to cover dinner and drinks. Leave the rest at your accommodation.

◊ Don't accept open drinks from strangers and don't leave your drink unattended.

ALWAYS TAKE AN UBER HOME AT NIGHT

Especially if you're alone. Even if it's a 5-minute walk, remember that predators watch for women leaving bars alone.

WEAR A CROSS SHOULDER BAG

Aggressive theft is not an issue over here. No one will run up to you, violently struggle to steal your bag and run away. But if your bag is hanging loosely by your side or on the back of your chair, magic hands will find a way to snatch your stuff without you even realizing.

Wearing a cross-shoulder bag is the best way to keep your belongings secure and is an assurance that you won't take your bag off to place it by your feet, on the table, or the chair beside you...because it will get taken there and you won't even notice until it's too late.

Check my travel store for the best cross-shoulder purses and day bags at TheSoloGirlsTravelGuide.com/travel-shop

USE ATMS INSIDE BANK KIOSKS

As a universal travel rule, ATMs inside bank kiosks (in human-sized glass boxes) or ATMs inside of a bank are your biggest insurance policies against becoming a victim of ATM skimming or having a wad of cash ripped out of your hand - although, I've never heard of the latter happening in Mexico.

AVOID YELLOW TAXIS

They have a reputation for stealing from their riders.

WALKING AT NIGHT

Make smart choices. Stay on lit roads, don't walk down a dark beach late at night, walk with a friend when possible, and don't get super drunk and wander off by yourself. Follow those common-sense rules and you'll be fine.

Biggest Safe Girl Tip!

Don't trust other travelers blindly. Oftentimes, we think we need to protect ourselves from the locals, and so we overlook the possible danger of fully trusting a cute new guy in our hostel or a woman that looks like our sister. The truth is, there are criminals everywhere. More often than not, sexual assault is committed traveler-on-traveler, rather than local-on-traveler. So don't get too drunk with those strangers you just met. When meeting new people, trust your gut always!

LET'S TALK ABOUT SEXUAL ASSAULT

Foreign women (that's us) are statistically more likely to be sexually assaulted by a foreign man (other travelers) on holiday than they are to be sexually assaulted by a local man. Think about it; in hostels, hotels and bars- we are more likely to be hanging around foreign men, quite possibly with alcohol in our systems, and therefore exposed to that risk. Just like you would at home, monitor your sobriety levels and be aware of your surroundings.

MY #1 DATING TIP

That guy you want to sleep with? Before you take him home, ask to take a picture of his ID and send it to your friend. If he has malicious intentions before…he might reconsider his plans now that he can be held accountable. Also, take him to YOUR PLACE the first few nights. Do not go to his place until you feel like you know him.

HOWEVER, that being said.

Puerto Vallarta is filled with some of the kindest people I've ever met, both locals and expats.

If you lose your phone, a nice man might find it, return it to you and invite you for dinner. If you get too drunk at a bar, another girl might spot you and help you get home. Be cautious of the risks but know that you are surrounded by good people.

Remember, Always Prioritize Your Comfort Over Being Polite

PERSONAL STORY TIME...

I decided to try a new massage place in Bangkok. I walked in and was greeted by the nicest old man ever. He changed my shoes and as I began walking towards the back, I realized that all the massage therapists were male – a very strange sight in Thailand.

And then I noticed that all the clients were male.

And then it clicked: this massage shop doubles as a gay massage parlor.

5 years ago, I would have gone along with the massage in order to be polite, all while subjecting my body and my mind to a very uncomfortable situation for an hour...while naked... JUST TO BE POLITE. But not today. Today, I simply stopped, smiled, turned around and gracefully left. No harm done. No one's feelings hurt. No fucks given.

I have a laundry list of uncomfortable and dangerous positions that I have put myself in while traveling in the past... just to avoid embarrassing myself or avoid being rude.

Us women are conditioned to be polite, and it's time we stop.

REMEMBER:

COMFORT FIRST, MANNERS SECOND.

Frequently Asked Questions

IS MEXICO SAFE?

While it's true that Mexico has dangerous areas, Banderas Bay is one of the safest areas in Mexico with Puerto Vallarta being ranked the safest tourist destination in Mexico.

HOW DO I MAKE FRIENDS IN MEXICO?

To make friends fast, stay at a hostel, volunteer, join a gym or a dance class, join a Girls in Puerto Vallarta meet-up, join an Airbnb experience, or just introduce yourself in Girls in Puerto Vallarta (use the hashtag #HeyImAwesome) and ask if anyone wants to grab a drink.

Pro Tip **from a Member of Girls in Puerto Vallarta**: You're "new" for the first few years but you can fast track into the community by supporting your neighborhood. Buy your tomatoes from one person and your lettuce from another. If you're ever in trouble these are the people that will come to your rescue! - Karyn

CAN I BRING MY DOG TO MEXICO?

Requirements for bringing a dog to the US from Mexico by air include a recent health certificate from your vet, current rabies vaccine and heartworm treatment.

DO I NEED A COVID TEST TO ENTER MEXICO?

At this time this book was published, no. You don't need a COVID test to enter Mexico.

DO I NEED A COVID TEST TO LEAVE MEXICO?

Yes, at this time this book was published you need a COVID test to leave Mexico. Americans need only a rapid test, whereas all other countries require a PCR swab test.

> Want to add more FAQs to the list? Reach out to me and let me know at hello@thesologirlstravelguide.com

MINI
Directory
FOR BANDERAS BAY

Important Numbers

Dial 911 in case of an emergency

Local Police +52 322 178 8999

The Green Angels (Free Roadside Assistance) 078

Red Cross Emergencies 065

Red Cross Ambulances 066

Red Cross +52 322 222 1533

Vallarta Tourism Center +52 322 221 2676

NEARBY HOSPITALS

Hospital CMQ Riviera Nayarit (Bucerias) +52 329 298 0717

Hospital Joya Riviera (Nuevo Vallarta) +52 322 226 8181

Hospital Joya Marina Vallarta +52 322 226 1010

CONSULATES

U.S. Consular Agency

+52 333 268 2100

After hours 01 55 50802000

Paseo de los Cocoteros #85, Nuevo Vallarta, Nayarit

Consular Agency of Canada

+52 322 293 0098

After hours 01 800 514 0129

Plaza Peninsula, Blvrd Francisco Medina Ascencio 2485, Puerto Vallarta, Jalisco

Mini Driver Directory

Message these drivers on the app called WhatsApp.

Xavier

Speaks perfect English, drives a 2021 Nissan that's fully insured and provides water!

Based in: Puerto Vallarta

☐ +52 322 118 0127

Miguel Ángel

Will drive you to destinations near and far

Based in: Puerto Vallarta

☐ +52 322 120 1356

Ricardo

Sweet guy who drives safely

Based in: Puerto Vallarta

☐ +52 322 362 2354

 For more drivers, join the 'Girls in Puerto Vallarta" Facebook group > and check under "files" for the official driver list. Or just use this QR Code

If you prefer Facebook to book a driver...

Join this group run by a young guy named Mario and he'll connect you with one of his drivers: Puerto Vallarta & Nayarit - Tours & Transportation Information Zone

How to call...

...MEXICAN NUMBERS FROM A FOREIGN (OUTSIDE MEXICO) NUMBER...

Let's say you're given this number:

03 22 322 1768

If you just type that number in your phone, it might not work.

Solution: drop the 0 and add the country code (+52)

So now the number looks like this:

+52 322 322 1768

Ps. That's the number of my Botox guy, Sergio. Might as well just save that right now.

For more resources, visit TheSoloGirlsTravelGuide.com

Boss Babe Pro Tip!

Need a personal assistant while you're in town to help you move, shop, mail something home or drive you around?

f facebook.com/puertovallartapersonalassistant

Medical, Gynecology Services & Female Stuff

For everything reproductive health including birth control & IUDs, STD testing, pap smears, ultrasounds, and more.

You'll find that OBGYN services in Puerto Vallarta are fantastic, as these doctors have been taking care of foreign women for decades. Plus, these services are so much cheaper than back home. I'm talking PAP smear for $40

If you have medical questions in Puerto Vallarta, message a woman on Facebook named Pam Thompson-Webb or email at pamela@ healthcareresourcespv.com. She is the free liaison between medical practices and you, and she can make appointments on your behalf based on what you need.

QUICK LIST OF RECOMMENDED OBGYNS

DR. LAURA GARCIA

Where: She works out of two offices, one at Sanmare and one at Inova in Old Town.

🏛 *Sanmare address:* Blvrd Francisco Medina Ascencio 2735-9

🏛 *Innova address:* Jacarandas 273 Col. Emiliano Zapata

f facebook.com/InnovaNMD/

DRA. MAGDALENA ROMO BASURTO

🏛 *Address:* Paseo de los Cocoteros 55

⊙ *Hours:* 9 am to 2 pm / 5 pm to 8 pm

🌐 dramagdalenaromo.com

 Scan this code for the full list of OBGYNs, go to the "files" section of Girls in Puerto Vallarta

OVER THE COUNTER
BIRTH CONTROL

CONDOMS

Easy to get everywhere.

PILLS

You can buy birth control pills and contraception over the counter in Mexico at the pharmacies.

Where: All pharmacies but two recommended ones are Ahorro Pharmacy and Guadalajara Farmacia.

Pills to Ask for: Levonorgestrel

Fun Fact! The contraceptive pill was co-invented in Mexico in the 1950's.

Deposhot to Ask for: Cyclofeminia 200 pesos at Farmacia Ahorro, they give you the needle and you can inject yourself at home…not kidding.

MORNING AFTER PILL

Where? Most pharmacies carries it under that name Femelle One, Post Day or Levonelle

 Please, make sure you've come to Mexico with Travel Insurance.
If you don't have it yet, go here.

COVID Testing

You need a COVID Test Before you Fly

Do you need an Antigen Test or a PCR Test? That depends on where you're flying.

✈ USA will take Antigen Tests

✈ Canada and beyond requires PCR Tests

The Antigen Test gives you results within an hour.

The PCR Test gives you results within 48 hours.

Plan accordingly. If you need the PCR Test, you can go 72 hours before you land in your destination.

 To make this easy, I made a YouTube video showing you the whole process.

Note: If you're staying at a nicer hotel or resort, they may pay for and organize your COVID test. Check with your hotel at check-in.

WHERE I WENT:

PVR Airport

Open 24/7. Enter the airport parking lot and drive around to the big white tent. Stand in line, scan a QR code and fill out a form. Give them your passport and flight number. Pay. Take the test. And they'll email you your results.

◊ Antigen Test is 450 pesos.

◊ PCR is 1450 pesos.

Bucket List

Drink each of the following once...

○ Tequila

○ Mezcal

○ An Alcoholic Slushie

Eat each of the following once...

○ Tacos de Cabeza

○ Aguachiles

○ Chilaquiles

Do each of the following once...

○ Get a Massage

○ Swim in the Ocean

○ Use the InDriver App

○ Watch the Sunset on the Beach

○ Have cocktails with a new friend

THE REAL STORY OF HOW THE
Solo Girl's Travel Guide
WAS BORN

I was robbed in Cambodia.

Sure, the robber was a child and yes, I might have drunkenly put my purse down in the sand while flirting with an irresistible Swedish boy...but that doesn't change the fact that I found myself without cash, a debit card and hotel key at 1am in a foreign country.

My mini robbery, however, doesn't even begin to compare to my other travel misadventures. I've also been scammed to tears by taxi drivers, idiotically taken ecstasy in a country with the death penalty for drugs and missed my flight because how was I supposed to know that there are two international airports in Bangkok?

It's not that I'm a total idiot.

It's just that...people aren't born savvy travelers.

I'm not talking about hedonistic vacationers who spend their weekend at a resort sipping Mai Tais. I'm talking about train-taking, market-shopping, street food-eating travelers!

Traveling is not second (or third or fourth) nature; it's a skill that only comes with sweaty on-the-ground experience...especially for women!

In the beginning of my travels (aka the first 5 years), I made oodles of travel mistakes. And thank god I did. These mistakes eventually turned me into the resourceful, respected and established travel guru that I am today.

A travel guru that was spawned through a series of being lost, hospitalized, embarrassed, and broke enough times to finally start learning from (and applying) her lessons.

Year-after-year and country-after-country, I started learning things like...

✓ Always check your hostel mattress for bed bugs.

✓ Local alcohol is usually toxic and will give you a hangover that lasts for days.

✓ The world isn't "touristy" once you stop traveling like a tourist.

✓ And most importantly, the best noodle shops are always hidden in back alleys.

After nearly 11 years of traveling solo around the world (4 continents and 26 countries, but who's counting?) -- I travel like a goddamn pro. I save money, sleep better, haggle harder, fly fancier, and speak foreign languages that help me almost almost blend in with the locals despite my blonde hair.

Yeah yeah yeah. I guess it's cool being a travel icon. But shit...

Do you know how much money, how many panic attacks, and how many life-threatening risks I could have saved and/or avoided if only someone had freakin' queued me into all of this precious information along the way? A lot. A lotta' lot.

So, why didn't I just pick up a travel guide and start educating myself like an adult? I had options...right? I could've bought a copy of Lonely Planet...but how the hell am I supposed to smuggle a 5-pound brick in my carry-on bag? Or DK Eyewitness, perhaps? Hell no. I don't have 8 hours to sift through an encyclopedia and decode details relevant to my solo adventure.

There was no travel guide that would have spared my tears or showed me how to travel safer and smarter.

The book I needed didn't exist. So, I f*cking wrote it myself.

What travel guide do you need me to write next?

Tell me on Instagram ➤ @SoloGirlsTravelGuide

Have any feedback? Love the book? Have a cool story? Want to see something in the book that isn't there? There's always room for love and improvement. Reach out to me and let me know!

DID YOU LEAVE A REVIEW?

As a self-published author – doing this whole publishing thing by myself – reviews are what keeps The Solo Girl's Travel Guide growing.

If you found my guidebook to be helpful, please leave me a review on Amazon.com

Your review helps other girls find this book and experience a truly life-changing trip.

Ps. I read every single review.

JOIN THE

SOLO GIRL'S

REVIEW CLUB

TEST AND REVIEW OUR BOOKS AND MERCH

BE THE FIRST TO GET NEW BOOKS, TOTE BAGS AND MORE TRAVEL GOODIES

SECRET ACCESS STARTS HERE

Acknowledgements

TO EMILIA

I have so much gratitude for Emilia, my co-author, business partner, and best friend. Thank you not only for all your Mexican wisdom that has made this book absolute gold, but for being the fiercest ride-or-die friend I've ever had. Knowing that you would punch someone in the face for me is a true gift.

TO MY TEAM

My editor, Lucy and my design angel, Caro. You girls make The Solo Girl's Travel Guide complete. Before you two came along, I was just one girl writing books alone with no pants on. I still don't wear pants when I write, but now I have a team to support my dreams and bring my visions to life. And to Charlotte, my fact-checker and Girls in Puerto Vallarta Sister, what would I do without you?

TO THE SOLO GIRL'S REVIEW CLUB

The girls who test everything I make and create, you are my inspiration! Your ideas and positive encouragement mean the world to me. Thank you for helping me create only the best resources for girls around the world.

TO MY FACEBOOK COMMUNITY, GIRLS IN PUERTO VALLARTA

Thank you for welcoming me to Puerto Vallarta with open arms and for being such a resource for me and each other. The kindness, support, and friendship you women show each other every day is proof that good exists and that girls have each other's back by nature.

And to everyone that has ever sent me a message or left me a review telling me how these books have impacted you – thank you for reminding me that travel changes people, that these books change people.

I LOVE YOU ALL!
WOMEN SUPPORTING WOMEN IS HOW MAGIC HAPPENS.

WHERE NEXT?

BALI

THAILAND

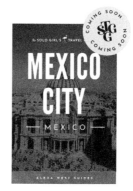

MEXICO CITY

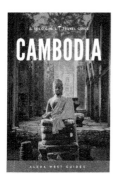

CAMBODIA

JAPAN

VIETNAM

AND MORE...

GET THE WHOLE COLLECTION.

HEY! PASS THIS BOOK ON!

Love the hell out of this book, and when you're done, pass it on to the next travel sister.

Before you hop on a plane back home, find a girl traveling alone and give her the gift of badass, female empowered travel.

But first!

Leave your mark.

On the back cover,
✧ write your name,
✧ where you're from,
✧ when you traveled
✧ and if you have one, a travel tip to add to this book.

Oh, and when you have inherited this book from a travel sister, take a picture! I'm dying to see it. Tag me on Instagram @SoloGirlsTravelGuide

xoxo, alexa

Printed in Great Britain
by Amazon

68847987R40174